9/21/14

Best wishes for a
good new year

שנה טובה ומתוקה לכם

Y. L e

מסורה

ArtScroll® Series

Rabbi Nosson Scherman / Rabbi Meir Zlotowitz
General Editors

RABBI YISSOCHER
FRAND

Published by

ARTSCROLL®
Mesorah Publications, ltd

We're All in This Together

Essays on the challenges that unite us

FIRST EDITION
First Impression … September 2014

Published and Distributed by
MESORAH PUBLICATIONS, LTD.
4401 Second Avenue / Brooklyn, N.Y 11232

Distributed in Europe by
LEHMANNS
Unit E, Viking Business Park
Rolling Mill Road
Jarow, Tyne & Wear, NE32 3DP
England

Distributed in Australia and New Zealand
by **GOLDS WORLDS OF JUDAICA**
3-13 William Street
Balaclava, Melbourne 3183
Victoria, Australia

Distributed in Israel by
SIFRIATI / A. GITLER — BOOKS
Moshav Magshimim
Israel

Distributed in South Africa by
KOLLEL BOOKSHOP
Northfield Centre, 17 Northfield Avenue
Glenhazel 2192, Johannesburg, South Africa

ARTSCROLL® SERIES
WE'RE ALL IN THIS TOGETHER
© *Copyright 2014, by* MESORAH PUBLICATIONS, Ltd.
4401 Second Avenue / Brooklyn, N.Y. 11232 / (718) 921-9000 / www.artscroll.com

---

ISBN 10: 1-4226-1520-0 / ISBN 13: 978-1-4226-1520-1

Typography by CompuScribe at ArtScroll Studios, Ltd.

Printed in the United States of America by Noble Book Press Corp.
Bound by Sefercraft, Quality Bookbinders, Ltd., Brooklyn N.Y. 11232

*I*n memory of one of the pillars of Kiruv of our generation who toiled with all his strength to better the relationship between his fellow Jews and the Ribbono Shel Olam

Rab Moshe Filler זצ"ל
מו"ר ר' משה פילער זצ"ל
נפטר ט"ז אדר ב' תשס"ח

He was educated in Yeshiva Ner Israel of Baltimore, where he established Ohr Haner Institute through which he inspired thousands of young men from Central and South America to dedicate themselves and their families to live lives of Torah.

Dedicated by admiring friends
David M. Hanono
Eli N. Hanono
Panama

ברכה לראש משביר

הנדיב היקר והנעלה שתמך בעין יפה

לטובת הספר, לזכות בלימוד בו

כבוד שם תהלתו

מר' אליעזר ירמיהו שרעבי

ובני ביתו הי"ו

המקום ברוך הוא ימלא כל משאלות ליבם

לטובה ולברכה ברוחניות ובגשמיות, ומכל

צרה ונזק יצילם, ויהיו כל צאצאיהם עובדי ה'

באמת ובלבב שלם ועוסקים בתורה לשמה,

ויזכו להמשיך להגדיל תורה ולהאדירה, אכי"ר.

In memory of

ז״ל *Maurice M. Rothman*

and

ע״ה *Golde N. Rothman*

לחמו מלחמות ה׳
"who lived and fought for Torah-true Judaism"

Published through the courtesy of the
HENRY, BERTHA AND EDWARD ROTHMAN FOUNDATION
Rochester, N.Y. ∗ Circleville, Ohio ∗ Cleveland

Dedicated in loving memory of

Shlomo and Zelda Pazornick

Mordechai and Shaindel Gelber

Yosef and Gittel Akselrud

Baruch and Zlata Kogan

by

Their Grandchildren

Table of Contents

Acknowledgments

As we get older the balance between what we do for our children and what they do for us begins to shift. *Chazal* tell us that one's *talmidim* are like one's own children, and the publication of this present volume marks such a generational shift.

This book was made possible in part by the devoted help of several *talmidim*. Let me therefore begin by thanking those *talmidim* who helped make this book a reality.

Chazal also tell us that *"gadol ha'me'aseh yoseir min ha'oseh,"* and I must therefore begin with mentioning two such *me'asim*.

First and foremost is my dear *talmid* (no pun intended) Rabbi Moshe Dear, headmaster of Yavneh Hebrew Academy in Los Angeles. Besides being a masterful principal who cares deeply about each of his students, he is a very devoted *talmid* and did not rest until he was confident that the necessary funds would be available.

Rabbi Ariel Shoshan, the rabbi of Khal Ahavas Torah in Scottsdale, Arizona, is responsible for nothing less than a religious revolution in the desert southwest. Yet, despite his many responsibilities he did not hesitate when I asked for his help.

Rabbi Aaron Dov Friedman is really more of a *chaver* than a *talmid*. What he and his wife Devora have accomplished in their "spare time" with the *baalei teshuvah* community in Los Angeles is nothing short of breathtaking. They were extremely helpful in the publication of this volume.

I would be remiss if I did not take this opportunity to wish their parents, Rabbi and Mrs. Yaakov Friedman, long life and continued good health and much *nachas* from their children, grandchildren, and great-grandchildren for many more years to come.

Rabbi Bernard Rothman, a pioneer in American *rabbanus*, and rabbi emeritus of Congregation Sons of Israel of Cherry Hill, New Jersey, was instrumental in securing a grant from the Rothman family foundation, of which he serves as president.

Every year Yeshivas Ner Yisroel hosts boys from Central America during their winter and summer vacations. Many of these boys come with very little background and when they arrive here they certainly don't look like yeshivah *bachurim*. But some decide to come back and enroll as students in the yeshivah and leave here as *bnei Torah*.

Mr. Eli Hanono is such an individual; he has become part of a new generation of *askanim* and *oskim be'tzorchei tzibbur* in his native Panama and remains a devoted *talmid*.

Over the last twenty years the average age of my *talmidim* in the *shiur* that I give in the yeshivah has increased dramatically. That is not because the *bachurim* in the yeshivah have gotten older; rather it's because several retirees and *baalebatim* take out time from their schedules to come to listen to *shiur*. Two such individuals are Mr. Elliot Sharabi and Mr. Jason Gelber, *asher nafsham chashkah ba'Torah. Ashrei chelkam.* Their contributions are very much appreciated and may they be blessed with *hatzlachah* in all their endeavors.

Brian, I know who you are and you know who you are, but most importantly, the One above knows who you are. Thank you very much.

I want to wish each of these *talmidim* and friends good health, and much *nachas* from their wonderful families for many years to come.

When I first started working with Rabbi Yehuda Heimowitz as my editor he was a relative unknown in the world of Jewish publication. That is no longer the case. With such credits to his name as the biographies of Rav Nosson Tzvi Finkel and Rav Ovadia Yosef, he is now a superstar in Jewish publications. His contributions to this book are invaluable.

Actually there is a co-author to this book. Her name is Nechama Frand, my wife. Her editorial comments and literary talents have made this a better read. But more importantly, her comments and insights in preparing these essays were, as always, spot on. To thank her for being the *ezer ke'negdo* and *akeres habayis* that she is, and the role that she has played in my life, would require an entire volume.

Rabbi Meir Zlotowitz is not just my publisher; he is a dear, dear friend, who goes out of his way to help me in so many different ways. I cherish our relationship. May he, together with Rabbi Nosson Scherman and the entire ArtScroll staff — including Mendy Herzberg, Eli Kroen, Mrs. Estie Dicker, Mrs. Esther Feierstein, and Mrs. Mindy Stern — who worked so diligently to make this book a reality, continue their trailblazing *avodas hakodesh* in Jewish publication for many years to come.

Last year marked my 50th year in Yeshivas Ner Yisroel, first as a *talmid*, and now, for almost forty years, as a rebbi. In our very mobile society, and in a world that is constantly changing, to be in the same place for half a century is rare. But to be in a *makom Torah* with the opportunity to teach Torah to *talmidim* is a privilege afforded to very few people. I'm convinced that it is in the *z'chus* of my parents and ancestors that the Ribbono Shel Olam has given me this gift, for it is certainly not in my *z'chus*.

Grateful is such an overused word. But what other word can my wife Nechama and I use to express our deepest emotion for the *berachos* that the Ribbono Shel Olam has showered on us, *bli ayin hara*. We have been *zocheh* to see each of our children given the opportunity, together with their spouses, to also be involved in the teaching of Torah to Klal Yisrael. May they be *zocheh* to *schep* as much *nachas* from their children, as we have from ours.

When we started this book, my editor and I didn't know what the title would be. We chose the name *We're All in This Together,* which is the title of one of the essays in the book. As I sit here writing, we are in the midst of a terrible battle for survival with the Arab terrorists who occupy Gaza and send rockets into Israel on a daily basis. We also read of demonstrations in France, Germany, and other European cities in which crowds chant words like "Death to the Jews" and "Hitler was right." I never thought I would ever witness this happening again in my lifetime. I was confident that the guilt that the world felt after the Holocaust would prevent them from doing this again so soon. I was wrong!

We as a Jewish people once again feel isolated and threatened. In retrospect, how fitting is the title, *We're All in This Together.*

Chazal tell us: נוֹתֵן הוֹדָאָה עַל שֶׁעָבַר וְצוֹעֵק **עַל הֶעָתִיד**. My wife and I beseech the Ribbono Shel Olam that He should grant us good health in the years to come, give us continued *nachas* from our children, grandchildren, and *talmidim*, and may we merit to see the day of the only *yeshuah* for Klal Yisrael — בִּיאַת מְשִׁיחַ צִדְקֵנוּ בִּמְהֵרָה בְיָמֵינוּ.

Yissocher Frand

Erev Rosh Chodesh Menachem Av, 5774
July 27, 2014
Baltimore, Md.

SECTION I:

Together
We Stand

Our Mission Statement

In today's corporate world, every company must have a mission statement. Even the smallest firm will find a few words — the fewer the better, in fact — to describe what it's trying to accomplish.

Sometimes, as financial and technological conditions change, a company's mission — and therefore, its mission statement — will have to change as well.

Take the brands Kodak and AT&T as examples.

Readers with a fair amount of mileage on their odometers might recall that Kodak used to be the world's largest producer of camera film. The company was on the Dow Jones industrial index for 74 years, from 1930-2004, and was a Fortune 500 company.

Mention the words "roll of film" to a teenager today, however, and the most likely response will be a blank stare. Had Kodak continued with the mission of creating quality camera film, they could have closed their doors forever at the turn of the millennium. And although Rochester, NY, once teeming with Kodak employees, is unlikely to return to that former glory, by altering their mission — and their mission statement — Kodak was at least able to remain in business.

Even AT&T, another Dow Jones entity that is perpetually ranked high on the Fortune 500 list, has retained that status only because it has altered its mission statement. Had it remained in the home telephone market alone and not branched out into cellular phones and other telecommunications markets, it, too, might have fallen into bankruptcy. The market changed, and it had to change its mission — and its mission statement.

The Jewish people, too, have a mission statement.

As a whole, our mission has remained the same throughout our history, but after the sin of the Meraglim (Spies), there was a shift from the original plan that required a reframing of our mission statement.

> *As a whole, our mission has remained the same throughout our history, but after the sin of the Meraglim (Spies), there was a shift that required a reframing of our mission statement.*

◦§ From Near or Far?

When the Meraglim returned from their espionage mission to Canaan and delivered a negative report about Eretz Yisrael, Klal Yisrael accepted their report and cried bitterly over their perceived fate, The Ribbono Shel Olam was so disappointed with the Jewish people that He wanted to destroy them on the spot. Moshe Rabbeinu employed two strategies in beseeching Hashem to spare the Jewish people: First, he predicted that if Hashem were to follow through and destroy the Jewish people, the Egyptians would say that He did so because He wasn't powerful enough to fulfill His promise to take them to Eretz Yisrael (see *Bamidbar* 14:1-16). This would obviously cause a *chillul*

Hashem, terrible desecration of Hashem's Name, and Moshe therefore concludes this line of reasoning with the words: וְעַתָּה יִגְדַּל נָא כֹּחַ אֲדֹנָי כַּאֲשֶׁר דִּבַּרְתָּ לֵאמֹר, *And now — may the strength of my Lord be magnified as You have spoken* (v. 17).

Moshe's first approach, then, was a logical argument; he asked Hashem not to destroy the Jewish people because it would cause a *chillul Hashem*.

Moshe's second approach would seem to be the more reliable one: drawing on what Hashem had taught him after Klal Yisrael had worshiped the Eigel (Golden Calf), Moshe invoked the *Middos HaRachamim*, the Thirteen Attributes of Divine Mercy: ה' אֶרֶךְ אַפַּיִם וְרַב חֶסֶד נֹשֵׂא עָוֹן וָפֶשַׁע וְנַקֵּה לֹא יְנַקֶּה פֹּקֵד עֲוֹן אָבוֹת עַל בָּנִים עַל שִׁלֵּשִׁים וְעַל רִבֵּעִים, *Hashem, Slow to anger, Abundant in Kindness, Forgiver of Iniquity and Willful Sin, and Who cleanses — but does not cleanse completely, recalling the transgression of parents upon children to the third and fourth generations* (v. 18).

Which one did Hashem accept? The logical argument, or the invocation of the *Middos HaRachamim*?

The Torah states: וַיֹּאמֶר ה' סָלַחְתִּי כִּדְבָרֶךָ, *And Hashem said, "I am forgiving them as per your words"* (v. 20). Rashi explains that Hashem told Moshe that He was going to forgive the Jewish people because of Moshe's logical argument, *not* because of the *Middos HaRachamim*.

Hashem then adds a somewhat cryptic verse: וְאוּלָם חַי אָנִי וְיִמָּלֵא כְבוֹד ה' אֶת כָּל הָאָרֶץ, *But as I live — and the glory of Hashem shall fill the entire world* (v. 21). This passage does not seem to flow with the rest of the narrative.

What message is this *pasuk* conveying?

In his *Ha'amek Davar*, the Netziv, Rav Naftali Tzvi Yehuda Berlin, unveils the message of this *pasuk* by first posing another question.

Dovid HaMelech devotes *Tehillim* 106 to the story of Yetzias Mitzrayim (the Exodus) and the subsequent sojourn in the Wilderness. As part of the narrative, he writes: וַיִּשָּׂא יָדוֹ לָהֶם לְהַפִּיל אוֹתָם בַּמִּדְבָּר. וּלְהַפִּיל זַרְעָם בַּגּוֹיִם וּלְזָרוֹתָם בָּאֲרָצוֹת, *Then He lifted up His hand [in an oath] against them, to cast them down in the*

Wilderness, and to cast down their descendants among the nations, and to scatter them among the lands (vv. 26-27).

We can understand the first verse: Hashem originally raised His Hand to strike the Jewish people dead in the Wilderness. But what does the second verse mean? At that point, Hashem didn't scatter the Jewish people among the lands; they continued on to Eretz Yisrael. Where did Dovid HaMelech find an allusion to an event that doesn't seem to be part of the narrative in the Torah?

The Netziv answers that although Hashem forgave Klal Yisrael for the sin of the Meraglim, there was a dramatic change in the way events would play out from then on.

The Jewish people have a mission in this world: to spread Hashem's Name in the world until every being recognizes Hashem as the one and only God. In the words we pray on Rosh Hashanah: וְיֵדַע כָּל פָּעוּל כִּי אַתָּה פְעַלְתּוֹ, וְיָבִין כָּל יְצוּר כִּי אַתָּה יְצַרְתּוֹ, וְיֹאמַר כֹּל אֲשֶׁר נְשָׁמָה בְּאַפּוֹ ה׳אֱלֹקֵי יִשְׂרָאֵל מֶלֶךְ, וּמַלְכוּתוֹ בַּכֹּל מָשָׁלָה, *Let everything that has been made know that You are its Maker, let everything that has been molded understand that You are its Molder, and let everything with a life's breath in its nostrils proclaim: "Hashem, the God of Israel, is King, and His Kingship rules over everything."*

Hashem's original plan was for Bnei Yisrael to proceed directly to Eretz Yisrael, led by Moshe Rabbeinu, after a short time in the Wilderness. Had this transpired, the Beis HaMikdash Moshe would have built would never have been destroyed, and the *kiddush Hashem* that is our mission in this world would have emanated from Eretz Yisrael to the entire world.

When the Meraglim came back with their report, however, conditions changed fundamentally, and the mission statement had to change.

Hashem declared that the *kiddush Hashem* would no longer emanate only from Eretz Yisrael. There would be a period in Jewish history called *galus*, exile, and Jews would be dispersed throughout the world — and create a *kiddush Hashem* there, among the non-Jewish nations. And this wouldn't be a matter of a few years; *galus* has now lasted for the majority of Jewish history. Even if we count the years preceding the first Beis HaMikdash, when we had a Mishkan, the total reaches about 1,200 years — far less than the over 2,000 years in *galus*.

That's what the seemingly misplaced *pasuk* means, explains the Netziv. וְאוּלָם חַי אָנִי וְיִמָּלֵא כְבוֹד ה' אֶת כָּל הָאָרֶץ, *But as I live — and the glory of Hashem shall fill the entire world.*

From that first-ever Tishah B'Av, when the Jews cried upon hearing the report from the Meraglim, the *kiddush Hashem* would no longer be created only in Eretz Yisrael: It would *fill the entire world.* The Jewish people would be scattered throughout the world — וּלְזָרוֹתָם בָּאֲרָצוֹת, in Dovid HaMelech's words — and they would have to find a way to spread Hashem's Glory

From that first-ever Tishah B'Av, when the Jews cried upon hearing the report from the Meraglim, the kiddush Hashem would no longer be created only in Eretz Yisrael: It would fill the entire world.

in Bavel and in Spain, in Morocco and in France, in Germany, Russia, Hungary, and America, and in all the other nations among which we have been scattered.

Our mission statement changed from a *geulah* mission — in which we would spread the Light of Hashem from Eretz Yisrael, from a distance — to a *galus* mission. We now have to be among the nations and reflect Hashem in this world to the extent that Hashem will say: עַבְדִּי אָתָּה יִשְׂרָאֵל אֲשֶׁר בְּךָ אֶתְפָּאָר, *You are My servant, Israel, in whom I take glory (Yeshayah 49:3).*

◦§ Our Report Card

Time for a report card. How well is the Jewish nation doing in our current mission of making Hashem proud?

Though the Bernie Madoff saga dates back a few years, I don't think any Jew in the United States will be

Time for a report card. How well is the Jewish nation doing in our current mission of making Hashem proud?

able to hear that name without cringing for many years to come.

But in more recent years, as well, we've been subjected to equally cringe-inducing images on the front pages of newspapers, with frum Jews being led in a "perp walk" by police or the FBI, having been arrested for financial scandals of some magnitude or another.

One particularly memorable image appeared during the Nine Days of mourning for the loss of the Beis HaMikdash a few years back. The front page of *The New York Times* carried a picture of what in the old days of mafia lore might have been members of an organized crime syndicate being led by the FBI, chained to one another. But these weren't mobsters, these were Orthodox Jews, in full regalia, arrested for a bribery scandal in New Jersey.

Contrast that picture with what the Smag (*Sefer Mitzvos HaGadol, Asin* 74) writes in the mitzvah of *hashavas aveidah* (returning lost objects):

> Now that the *galus* has extended for so long, [we] must distance ourselves from the frivolities of this world, and grasp hold of the insignia of Hakadosh Baruch Hu, which is *emes*, truth. We should not lie — not to Jews and not to non-Jews — nor should we defraud them in any way...
>
> If we are not deceitful, when Hakadosh Baruch Hu brings us salvation, the non-Jews will say, "He is just for doing so, because they are people of truth..."
>
> If we are deceitful with the non-Jews, however, they will say, "Hakadosh Baruch Hu chose thieves and swindlers for His lot."

When we juxtapose these words with that image on *The New York Times* of the frum Jews arrested for the bribery scandal, it should shake us to our core.

Now, one could argue that a correction is in order. I used the term "frum Jews" to describe these felons, but in reality this is reminiscent of a conversation Rav Mottel Katz, the Rosh Yeshivah of Telshe in Cleveland, had with an irreligious Jew.

This Jew asked Rav Mottel, "How do you explain all those religious Jews who lie about their income and cheat on their taxes?"

"How do you explain all those religious Jews who drive on Shabbos and eat on Yom Kippur?" asked Rav Mottel.

"Those are not religious Jews," the irreligious man exclaimed.

"Neither are those who cheat on their taxes," replied Rav Mottel.

So perhaps we could argue that these are not frum Jews. In truth, however, we can't escape the fact that those pictured on the front page of *The New York Times* are perceived and identified as frum Jews, and they live the rest of their lives as frum Jews — and the resulting *chillul Hashem* is inevitable.

I heard a story that would be humorous if it weren't true. A rav who serves as a chaplain in U.S. prisons related that he brought a *lulav* and *esrog* to a frum inmate before Succos. This fellow took one look at the *esrog* and said, "I'm *makpid* on a *pittam*."

How did we get to this level of disconnect? How can we have a person who is *makpid* on a *pittam*, but not on *chillul Hashem*? How is it that the same people who will eat only the best *hechsherim*, and won't eat *gebrokts* on Pesach, don't seem to have the concept of *emes* — and especially in business — in their vocabularies?

◆§ Two Millennia of Conditioning

Before I try to explain the disconnect, I feel the need to issue a disclaimer: I am not trying to justify the behavior of Jews caught in financial scandals, because there is no justification for it.

Having said that, I think that it behooves us to try to uncover the roots of this behavior, which might lead to some sort of solution.

I believe that this lack of integrity is the result of thousands of years of conditioning. For 2,000 years, Klal Yisrael wandered among non-Jewish nations that persecuted them in every way possible, including forbidding them from taking part in regular commerce. For two millennia, Jewish people had no rights, and they had to look for loopholes, for black market deals, and resort to bribery and other illicit activities in order to survive.

> *For two millennia, Jewish people had no rights, and they had to look for loopholes, for black market deals, and resort to illicit activities in order to survive.*

The United States of America is not like that. Jews have equal rights. We can enroll in any educational program and work in the occupational field of our choice. And the mentality that has been part of the Jewish people for so many years — the feeling that if we don't "pull *shtick*" we won't survive — has to change.

⊷§ We Need Too Much

Another factor that leads people to cut corners when it comes to integrity is that we live in a country in which the worst thing is to be poor.

For centuries, poverty was part of the Jewish ethos. Not that there weren't some wealthy Jews in the various stations in the Diaspora; most often, there were some wealthier community members. But for the most part, people were poor. They just barely got by. That was part of *shtetl* life.

Not so in the United States. Most Americans can't really fathom the concept of being poor.

And frum life in the U.S. is a very, very expensive proposition. A family can easily spend upwards of $40,000 on elementary school tuition alone — and that's before you count high school or seminary. Add to that the astronomical living costs of the average Jewish family.

Take housing as an example. I can offer you a four-bedroom house, with a two-car garage, for about $100,000.

In Omaha, Nebraska.

But you can't get that in Flatbush or Monsey, nor in any other established frum community.

A frum family has to cover tuitions that are above the median household income in the United States, housing costs that are above average for the country, higher prices for kosher food, the costs of Shabbos, Yom Tov, bar mitzvahs, *chasunahs*, summer camps... You're talking about a LOT of money.

What are the options to bankroll a frum lifestyle? There are three general tracks: Have a very well-paying job, be poor, or... try to make "a fast buck" to supplement your income. Nobody wants to be poor, and not everyone can be a successful attorney with an income bordering on seven figures, which leaves number three as the sole option for a lot of people. And again, this is not a justification, but an explanation of why people who wouldn't cut corners in any other area of halachah might try to do so when it comes to business.

So we understand some of the roots of the problem. What's the solution?

Take housing as an example. I can offer you a four-bedroom house, with a two-car garage, for about $100,000. In Omaha, Nebraska. But you can't get that in Flatbush or Monsey, nor in any other established frum community.

✌ A Change in Attitude

My first suggestion is based on something I've observed in action over the past few decades: it *is* possible to change societal attitudes.

An example: When I first began to learn in Ner Yisrael, by the middle of the afternoon *seder*, there was a cloud of smoke hovering under the ceiling in the *beis midrash*. Smoking was totally acceptable in those days. So acceptable, in fact, that at my wedding, we gave out matchbooks with our monogram.

Need I remind you that thirty years ago, there was a smoking section on an airplane? Try smoking on a plane today and you'll find yourself in a federal penitentiary.

Today, smokers are pariahs. They stand outside their office buildings, shivering in the cold, to snatch a cigarette. People shudder in disgust just *thinking* about smoking.

And this attitudinal shift finds its way into every area of life. For decades, I've been getting calls about *shidduchim*. These days I get approximately half a dozen calls a week about boys who are in my *shiur* in yeshivah. A frequent question is, "Does he smoke?" That's not a question I got thirty years ago, because it was an accepted norm for people to smoke.

How did this change come about?

It came about because the government spent billions of dollars educating the country that smoking is bad for you. And voila — society changed!

Don't think that this works only when the government spends billions, either. Within our tiny subset of Orthodox Jewry we have seen a manifestation of how society can change. Thirty years ago, the concept of not speaking *lashon hara* existed, but what can I say — it wasn't nearly the big deal it is today. Yes, some people learned *Shemiras HaLashon* — especially those who needed something to do during *mussar seder* in yeshivah — but it just wasn't a big deal.

> Today? We might still speak lashon hara, but at least we preface it with: "This may be lashon hara, but..." At least we now feel guilty enough to issue that disclaimer!

Today? We might still speak *lashon hara*, but at least we preface it with: "This may be *lashon hara*, **but...**" At least we now feel guilty enough to issue that disclaimer!

How did that change? It changed through education. It changed because wonderful organizations undertook to make the public aware of how damaging *lashon hara* is — whether with children in schools, or adults through programs such as the annual Tishah B'Av events.

Slowly, people's attitudes toward *lashon hara* changed.

We need a similar campaign in regard to integrity. If card-carrying members of our communities are being caught in financial scandals, it's because there's a tacit acceptance of it in frum society. We have to create a public sentiment in which cheating and deceiving is considered absolutely disgusting.

⌁ Shining the Spotlight Inward

Before we cast a disapproving glance at others who have cheated on a grand scale and have come under the public eye for it, we should turn the spotlight on ourselves — uncomfortable as that may be. Are our tax returns 100 percent honest? When we fill out tuition forms, do we report every cent of our income? Do we spend time shopping online when we should be working? When you go to an amusement park and it's cheaper for children under 12, do you tell your 13-year-old who happens to be on the short side to say that he's 11? You might save a couple of dollars, but what kind of lesson does that send to our children?

A little "white lie" leads to much bigger, blacker lies.

If there's one *gadol* who personified honesty and integrity — who, in fact, named his *sefer* "Emes LeYaakov" because of his insistence on *emes* in all matters — it was Rav Yaakov Kamenetsky.

Someone once asked Rav Yaakov the following *sh'eilah*: Each year, he would take a personal leave day on Purim, so that he could observe the day properly. His office was particularly busy that year, however, and his employer had announced that no one was allowed to take personal vacation days during a certain period, which included Purim. "No one is feeling particularly well the day after the fast of Taanis Esther," this man reasoned with Reb Yaakov, "and certainly by the end of Purim everybody's a little sick to the stomach.

"Can I call in sick that morning so that I can daven and hear the Megillah without rushing off to work, and then deliver

Mishloach Manos and eat the *seudah* with my family?"

Reb Yaakov wouldn't hear of it. "Purim is a *d'rabbanan*," he replied, "and *midvar sheker tirchak* (distancing oneself from lies; see *Vayikra* 23:7) is a *d'Oraisa*. You don't observe a rabbinic level mitzvah by transgressing a Torah prohibition.

> *Reb Yaakov wouldn't hear of it. "Purim is a d'rabbanan," he replied, "and midvar sheker tirchak (distancing oneself from lies) is a d'Oraisa. You don't observe a rabbinic level mitzvah by transgressing a Torah prohibition."*

"Go to work."

Had this man posed this *sh'eilah* to us, we may have felt that he was truly altruistic. How many people are willing to forfeit a sick day to be able to daven properly? But to Rav Yaakov it was so simple, so straightforward: you don't tell a "white lie" in order to observe the mitzvos of Purim.

ᘿ The Antidote

Fully inculcating Rav Yaakov's attitude toward integrity will take decades or generations. With so many scandals being uncovered by the authorities and causing communal black eyes every few months, what can we do in the short term to turn the tides?

Rabbeinu Bachya points out that the very same *pasuk* in which the Torah cautions us not to make a *chillul Hashem* also includes the mitzvah of *kiddush Hashem*: וְלֹא תְחַלְּלוּ אֶת שֵׁם קָדְשִׁי וְנִקְדַּשְׁתִּי בְּתוֹךְ בְּנֵי יִשְׂרָאֵל, *You shall not desecrate My holy Name, rather I should be sanctified among the Children of Israel* (*Vayikra* 22:32). The reason why they're listed together, he explains, is because the antidote to *chillul Hashem* is *kiddush Hashem*. If there are people desecrating Hashem's Name, we must find ways to sanctify His Name as an atonement.

This seems easier said than done. What are we supposed to do — look around for money left behind by non-Jews and return it, hoping that the media will pick up the story and reverse the public view of Orthodox Jews? If it happens — as it did to Rabbi Noach Muroff in 2013 — that's wonderful. But it's hardly something we can orchestrate.

So how do we reverse the trend of *chillul Hashem*?

The answer is that a *kiddush Hashem* is easier to create than we tend to think. Opportunities are available at every turn.

If you're obviously Jewish looking — a yarmulke, a beard, a long skirt — you can do little things that will change the public perception of all Orthodox Jews.

When I'm in the supermarket lane and my cellphone rings, I ask the checkout clerk, "Do you mind if I take this phone call?"

> *If you're obviously Jewish looking — a yarmulke, a beard, a long skirt — you can do little things that will change the public perception of all Orthodox Jews.*

Not once has a clerk told me, "No, you can't." I end up taking the call, but I've managed to make a positive impression on her — and I've been told as much.

The alternative to that was a story I heard about a fellow who was on his cellphone when he reached the checkout lane, and never bothered to acknowledge the clerk's existence. He stayed on the call while she calculated his bill and bagged his groceries; he flipped her his credit card, retrieved it, and walked out without a hello, goodbye, or thank you.

The next man on line was another frum Jew. "I hope you don't mind me asking," the clerk said, as the man started to load his purchases onto the belt, "but why is it that so many of *you people* don't seem to even acknowledge my presence?"

That's a *chillul Hashem*, and it can only be rectified by a corresponding *kiddush Hashem*.

When you're leaving an airplane, the pilot and flight crew stand at the door to the cockpit. Unless I'm on the verge of losing the contents of my meal due to turbulence, I make a point of telling them, "Nice flight, thank you." I look like a rabbi, and those few words may make a *kiddush Hashem*.

Rav Elchonon Wasserman once visited the United States, and he stayed at the Broadway Central Hotel — and you've *really* dated yourself if you remember the Broadway Central. He asked Reb Moshe Sherer, "*Vi azei zogt men gut morgin oif Einglish?*" He wanted to acknowledge the elevator operator — another anachronism — so he learned how to say *good morning* in the native tongue. Reb Elchonon refused to cross the street against the light, because it was against the law. He felt that as an obviously Orthodox Jew, it was incumbent upon him not to make a negative impression on anyone.

ᴥᢌ Workplace Rules

What if you don't have the bearded rabbi look. Does the *kiddush Hashem* imperative still apply?

Absolutely. As long as your coworkers know that you're Jewish, you are equally capable of making a *kiddush Hashem* — and therefore equally culpable if you don't.

Rav Pam had three rules for the workplace: (1) be the hardest worker in the office; (2) be the most pleasant person in the office; and (3) be the most honest person in the office.

That's how you make a *kiddush Hashem*. You don't have to go out and have a beer with your coworkers after work. You don't have to engage in their often inappropriate chatter at the water cooler. Be *professionally* friendly. Don't be *socially* friendly — and especially with members of the opposite gender — but if you're professionally friendly, they'll respect you for who you are. Ask them about their families. Speak to them about politics. There are plenty of subjects you can talk about and maintain a professional, friendly relationship without crossing any boundaries.

Above all, remember at all times that you're an ambassador of the Ribbono Shel Olam. You're on display, whether you like it or not. We represent the Ribbono Shel Olam, and that can have far-reaching implications — much broader implications than we can fathom. Maybe one day your coworker will find his way to the Supreme Court, or to the Federal Reserve, and the impression you made on him will affect the way he views and rules on issues pertaining to Orthodox Jews.

Rabbi Berel Wein tells a story about the editor of the *Detroit Free Press*, who, at a time when Detroit was a major American city, and at a time when newspapers still had an effect on people, invariably wrote pro-Israel editorials. Why?

This editor explained that when his mother immigrated to the United States from Ireland, she worked as a housekeeper for a Jewish family. The family went on vacation during Chanukah, and they returned around December 23 or 24. When she noticed that they weren't going to be back in time to buy and decorate a tree, she felt really bad for them, so she went out and purchased one.

Maybe one day your coworker will find his way to the Supreme Court, or to the Federal Reserve, and the impression you made on him will affect the way he views and rules on issues pertaining to Orthodox Jews.

These people lived in a frum neighborhood. You can only imagine the scene: as they drive up to their home upon returning from vacation, what do they find winking at them from their dining room window? An Xmas tree, decorated with tinsel and lights, with all the *hiddurim*.

Did we make a wrong turn? The owner of the home must have thought to himself. He checks, and it's the right house!

He walks inside, turns to the housekeeper and says, "What's that?"

"I knew you were coming home right before the holiday, and I felt bad that your house would be bare," she replied, "so I went and bought you one."

The homeowner sat down at the table with this fresh immigrant. "This is one of the nicest things anyone has ever done for me," he said calmly, "but we don't celebrate this holiday. Could you just take the tree down and put it away."

He then pulled out $50 — a tidy sum in those days — and handed it to her as a holiday bonus.

For years afterward, this woman would tell this story to her son, who went on to become the editor of a major U.S. newspaper — and Jewish people living in Israel benefited from his positive editorials decades later.

There was a brokerage company with a motto of, "Changing the world, one client at a time."

This has to become our statement: Make a *kiddush Hashem*, one person at a time.

There are people who have a beautiful *kabbalah* (resolution) to do one *chessed* each day. Imagine if we could resolve to make one *kiddush Hashem* each day! It can be as easy as holding the door for a coworker, saying a nice "good morning" to your neighbor, or even complimenting his dog. That's all it takes to make a *kiddush Hashem*!

≈§ Impressing the IRS

Once we learn to make a *kiddush Hashem* we'll start to see results.

Rav Manis Mandel, the longtime Rosh Yeshivah of Yeshiva of Brooklyn, was once audited by the IRS (Internal Revenue Service) because they flagged certain charitable deductions on his tax return. He came to the audit with all of his cancelled checks, but they did not equal the amount that he claimed as deductions. When the IRS agent questioned him about the discrepancy, he explained that the rest of his deductions were for cash donations.

"How do we know that you're telling us the truth?" the agent asked. "You need to prove this to us."

Rav Mandel reached into his pocket and pulled out a wad of checks made out to charitable institutions for which he had not claimed deductions, and had the agent add them up. The tally *far exceeded* the number he had claimed as a deduction.

"If you have all these checks to prove your donations," the IRS agent asked in astonishment, "then why didn't you claim a bigger deduction?"

Rav Mandel pointed to the memo line, where he had written one word in Hebrew: חליפין, *exchange*. He explained to the agent that money children collected for charitable institutions would often be a variegated assortment of coins and small bills. Rather than have them hand over the small change, he would write out a check to cover the full amount, and use the cash for himself. To ensure that he wouldn't erroneously claim these checks as deductions, he would write the word חליפין on the memo line.

Rav Mandel could easily have claimed those checks as deductions without anyone raising an eyebrow. But when this agent saw how honest the Rav was, he immediately ended the audit.

Now, did the IRS agent have a fighting chance of knowing what that word meant? Certainly not. Rav Mandel could easily have claimed those checks as deductions without anyone raising an eyebrow. But when this agent saw how honest the Rav was, he immediately ended the audit.

✎§ The Sum Total of a Life

Generally speaking, when the Torah commands us to do a mitzvah, it does so in direct first person: בָּעֶרֶב תֹּאכְלוּ מַצֹּת, *at night you shall eat matzos (Shemos* 12:18); בַּסֻּכֹּת תֵּשְׁבוּ שִׁבְעַת יָמִים, *you shall sit in tabernacles for seven days (Vayikra* 23:42).

The verse in which we are taught about the mitzvah of *kiddush Hashem* is an anomaly. Rather than issue it as a commandment, the Torah states: וְנִקְדַּשְׁתִּי בְּתוֹךְ בְּנֵי יִשְׂרָאֵל, *And I should be sanctified among the Children of Israel* (ibid. 22:32). Why not state directly, "תקדשו שם ה'*,You should sanctify Hashem's Name*"?

Rav Nissan Alpert offered a beautiful explanation for this unusual verbiage.

There are times when Jews are called on to offer the ultimate sacrifice — to die על קידוש ה', to give up their lives to sanctify Hashem's Name. Our parents and grandparents were often put to that test.

In America, we don't have that challenge. We don't have to die *al kiddush Hashem*. But we, too, can bring about a *kiddush Hashem* when we pass on to the next world. How? By living a life that is one long *kiddush Hashem*. This mitzvah is not merely about performing a *kiddush Hashem* every so often, as we do when we eat matzah or sit in a *succah*; it's about living a life — morning, afternoon, and evening — that will ultimately lead to Hashem's Name *being sanctified* by the sum total of a person's life.

A fellow who worked for the foreign service of the United States government told me that their training stressed one message: "You may be the only American that people in the country you are placed in will ever meet. You represent the United States government, and you must act accordingly."

As frum Jews, we are the ambassadors of the Ribbono Shel Olam, representing Him in this world.

Kiddush Hashem is about living a life upon which He will proudly proclaim: עַבְדִּי אָתָּה יִשְׂרָאֵל אֲשֶׁר בְּךָ אֶתְפָּאָר, *You are My servant, Israel, in whom I take glory.*

Nowadays, It's All About Me

I hope that "narcissism" is not a word that you find yourself using on a regular basis, so before discussing the concept, a definition is in order.

Dictionaries define narcissism as an excessive interest in one's self — egocentrism on steroids, if you will. Traditionally, the DSM (Diagnostic and Statistical Manual of Mental Disorders) had a listing for a disease called *narcissistic personality disorder*, described as a person who focuses excessively on himself.

The word actually stems from Greek mythology. I generally refrain from quoting from such sources, but there's a purpose to it in this case.

The myth goes that there was a fellow named Narcissus who was absolutely enamored with himself. He was searching for a perfect mate for his wonderful self, when he passed by a pool of water. When he saw his own image reflected in the water, he was so taken by his beauty that he just sat there and stared, unable to move. He eventually shriveled up and died at that spot, and a flower grew there. That flower, which is called a *narcissus*, is part of the daffodil family.

The reason I felt that it was important to quote this myth is because it contrasts so sharply with a story in the Gemara (*Nedarim* 9b).

The Gemara relates that Shimon HaTzaddik, who was a Kohen Gadol, never ate from an *asham* (atonement offering) brought by a *nazir* who became *tamei*, ritually impure. [Briefly, a *nazir* is a person who accepted upon himself not to partake of any grape derivative, become impure through contact with a corpse, and cut his hair. If a *nazir* becomes *tamei*, he must bring an *asham* offering in the Beis HaMikdash and shave his head, and he then restarts his *nazir* vow.]

Shimon HaTzaddik wouldn't eat from the *asham* of a *nazir* who became *tamei* — even mistakenly — because he felt that a person generally shouldn't accept vows that are so difficult to keep until the end. He related, however, that there was one instance in which he departed from this practice:

> Once, a *nazir* from the South [of Eretz Yisrael] came [to the Beis HaMikdash], and I saw that he had beautiful eyes and was handsome, with his locks curled neatly. "My son," I asked, "why are you destroying your beautiful hair?"
>
> "I work as a shepherd for my father in my village," he replied, "and one day, when I went to draw water from the spring, I saw my reflection. My *yetzer hara* accosted me and sought to remove me from the world. 'Evil one,' I said to my *yetzer hara*, 'why are you becoming haughty in a world that is not yours, with one who is destined to be infested with worms! I swear that I will shave my head for the sake of Heaven.' "
>
> I kissed him on the head and said, "My son, may there be more *nezirim* like you in Israel."

The contrast between these stories is startling. One young man sees his own beauty and dies from pining for himself, and the other sees his beauty as something the *yetzer hara* will use to destroy him, and he chooses to eradicate that challenge from his life.

Unfortunately, the approach of the Greek myth seems far more popular nowadays.

I was walking through an airport recently and I saw someone wearing a t-shirt — and I am *not* making this up — with three words emblazoned on it: "I love me."

In fact, the reason why I said that

> *One young man sees his own beauty and dies from pining for himself, and the other sees his beauty as something the yetzer hara will use to destroy him, and he chooses to eradicate that challenge from his life.*

narcissism was *traditionally* diagnosed as a disease in the DSM is not because narcissism has faded from society and we no longer have people struggling with the disease of excessive self-interest. On the contrary, a recent book, *The Narcissism Epidemic*, written by two secular sociologists, uses statistical evidence to prove that narcissism has become so widespread as to be on the level of an epidemic. The DSM decided to delist it because far too many people in the United States were being branded with this mental illness. Though they later returned "narcissistic personality disorder" to the list, they redefined it to ensure that it would include less people.

⋙ When "Michael" Becomes Outdated

The Narcissism Epidemic cites some interesting examples that may seem almost trivial, but actually speak of much deeper problems in society.

In the past, most people were named simple names like Bob, Sue, Mary, or Alex. Today, you can't just give a child a simple name. Each child is so breathtakingly special that you have to give them a unique name — or at least a unique spelling of their otherwise common name. So Michael can no longer be spelled

M-i-c-h-a-e-l. Now it's Mychal.

So the kid can grow up thinking, *Ich bin nisht kein pashuteh Michael.*

He's a MYchal.

Names have become so obfuscated that when I read the newspaper, I often have a hard time figuring out whether the protagonist in a news item is male or female.

> *So the kid can grow up thinking, "Ich bin nisht kein pashuteh Michael." He's a MYchal.*

In the 1940s, 33 percent of children were named with the ten most popular names in those days, with the most common names, if you're wondering, being James and Mary. It was fine for a child to carry the same name as many of his peers.

No longer.

And then there's a mind-boggling statistic: In the 1950s, 12 percent of high school seniors felt that they were, "a very important person." By the 1990s, that figure had reached over 90 percent.

Over *ninety percent* of high school seniors think they're very important. Why? Because they got through high school?

So the DSM decided at some point that if you can't beat 'em, join 'em, and they redefined narcissism so that most people can be narcissists and still be classified as normal.

Widespread narcissism has led to a sense of entitlement that brought along with it many of the ills plaguing society today. In fact, the subtitle of *The Narcissism Epidemic* is "Living in the Age of Entitlement."

> *Why do they deserve an A? Because they got 90 or above on the final? No. Because their parents have been telling them from their first day on earth that they're so special, they must deserve that A.*

After all, if I'm so very important that my name has to be Mychal, then I deserve _____ (fill in the blank).

According to the book, college professors complain that students have no compunctions about barging into their offices and declaring, "I *deserve* an A."

Why do they deserve an A? Because they got 90 or above on the final? No.

Because their parents have been telling them from their first day on earth that they're so special, they must deserve that A.

It's frightening to comprehend that so many young people seem to suffer from a subcategory of Narcissistic Personality Disorder called "Elitist Narcissist," the symptoms of which are defined by psychologists as follows:

> Feels privileged and empowered by virtue of special childhood status and pseudo achievements; entitled façade bears little relation to reality; seeks favored and good life; is upwardly mobile; cultivates special status and advantages by association.

And the disease doesn't strike only in college halls. One cause of the housing bubble that eventually deflated and sent the entire world economy into recession in 2008 was the fact that people felt entitled to a big house, and they felt justified taking mortgages to buy houses they couldn't afford.

My parents — and I'm sure many of your parents were the same — never bought anything on credit. They saved, they scrimped, and they bought what they could afford.

But if everyone deserves to live in a mansion, then the economy can't sustain them.

⫘ What Happened to Civility?

Another manifestation of narcissism is the lack of civility in society.

Narcissists feel no need to display basic common courtesy when driving, because the general attitude is, "I own the road."

The New York Times reported that the New York Philharmonic Orchestra was performing Gustav Mahler's ninth symphony, and someone's cellphone rang — once, twice, and then a third time.

Finally, the conductor put down his baton, turned around to this fellow in the audience and said, "Are you finished?"

But no, since he's convinced that he's the only person who matters in this world, all the other concert-goers should just suffer through his phone call.

The same lack of etiquette explains why some people seem to think that it's perfectly fine for them to whip out their smartphones and start clicking on the keys while they're talking to you.

The same lack of etiquette explains why some people seem to think that it's perfectly fine for them to whip out their smartphones and start clicking on the keys while they're talking to you. And if you stop talking, they'll say, "You can continue, I hear every word you're saying."

Lehavdil, Rav Moshe Feinstein was a prolific writer and spent much of his waking time with pen in hand, which is the only way he was able to produce such a large number of extremely complex *sefarim*. Someone told me that he once saw Rav Moshe writing a *teshuvah*, when a young boy came over to ask him a *sh'eilah* — probably something as basic as, "What *berachah* do you make on pretzels?"

Rav Moshe put down his pen, looked this boy in the eye, and answered his *sh'eilah*. Rav Moshe had all the time in the world for this young boy, but we're too busy writing that text message to focus on the person with whom we're having a conversation.

◆§ Marriage Disappears

Narcissism has a direct effect on our community as well, because narcissists make terrible spouses. It is extremely difficult to be married to a person who is only able to love and care about themselves.

When Rav Dessler would attend a *chuppah*, he would address the *chassan* and *kallah* as they stood at the cusp of their marriage. "Right now," he would say, "your greatest desire is to give to each other. Keep it that way, because the moment the desire to give turns into a desire to take, the happiness and bliss will desert your marriage."

But narcissists tend to be oblivious to other people's needs, which makes it impossible for them to give.

Nowadays, approximately one-third of all households are led by single parents. In 2010, over 40 percent of births in the United States were to unwed mothers, and that figure climbed to over 50 percent among mothers in their twenties.

The basic unit in society, however, is the family, and America is facing a disaster — as is nearly every other Western country in the world — as the concept of family collapses.

Now, secular society may just roll over and capitulate to these trends, but how do we, as Torah Jews, fight the underlying plague of narcissism that is the root of all these ills?

◦§ How Big Is Your "I"?

Simply stated, narcissism is the antithesis of what Torah is all about.

I could cite endless sources for this principle, but I'll suffice with two:

The Mishnah (*Avos* 1:14) states: אִם אֵין אֲנִי לִי, מִי לִי. וּכְשֶׁאֲנִי לְעַצְמִי, מָה אֲנִי, *If I am not for myself, who will be for me? And if I am for myself, what am I?*

In his classic introduction to *Shaarei Yosher*, Rav Shimon Shkop expounds on this Mishnah, explaining that Judaism recognizes a person's need to care for himself: אִם אֵין אֲנִי לִי, מִי לִי. If, however, a person constricts his concept of *"ani,"* his sense of self, to where his own skin ends, he reduces it to a lump of matter: וּכְשֶׁאֲנִי לְעַצְמִי, מָה אֲנִי. Because a person's sense of self can reach far beyond himself.

Based on this concept, Rav Shimon offers a clear delineation of what makes a person an *adam gadol*.

Have you ever thought about what makes a person into a *gadol*? Do we define someone as great if he knows *Shas*?

Shulchan Aruch? There are people out there who know both, but Kl̀al Yisrael has not accepted them as *gedolim*.

Rav Shimon Shkop writes that there is one common denominator among all the people whom we consider *gedolim*, and it bridges all societal divides. The same principle that makes an Ashkenazi into a *gadol* will hold true for a Sephardi, and what makes a Lithuanian Rosh Yeshivah great will also define whether a Chassidishe Rebbe is considered a *gadol*: the size of their *ani*, their sense of "I."

The same principle that makes an Ashkenazi into a gadol will hold true for a Sephardi, and what makes a Lithuanian Rosh Yeshivah great will also define whether a Chassidishe Rebbe is considered a gadol: the size of their ani, their sense of "I."

When simple people think of the word "I," they think of themselves and only themselves. Nobody else is included in their "I." Someone who is a little greater will include his family in his "I." Those who graduate from including their family in their "I" might move onto including their neighbors and their community in that delineation.

A really great person, says Rav Shimon, includes every member of Klal Yisrael in his *ani*, in his sense of self. When a person becomes as concerned for all of Klal Yisrael as he is for himself, he is considered a true *adam gadol*.

✍ A Gadol's Way

Let me share a few stories of how an *adam gadol* includes others in his sense of self.

Rav Yaakov Kamenetsky's wife had to undergo major surgery, and he asked a fellow who was traveling to Eretz Yisrael to ask the Steipler Gaon, Rav Yaakov Yisrael Kanievsky, to daven for his wife. The person succeeded in securing an audience with the Steipler, and when he emerged, he was so excited to share the news with Rav Yaakov that he immediately picked up the phone and called his house, forgetting one detail: it was 9 a.m. in Eretz Yisrael, which meant that it was 2 a.m. on the East Coast.

Picture the scene: His wife is facing surgery, and the phone rings at 2 a.m.

Now I ask you honestly: how would you react? Would you say, "Are you *nuts*? Do you know what time it is? Do you realize that you scared me half to death?"

What did Reb Yaakov say?

"How are you? How was the trip?"

He knew that the person would realize after a few moments that it was the middle of the night in New York, and he didn't want to make him feel like a fool.

On that same occasion, Rav Yaakov took down the telephone numbers of all his wife's friends so he could call them immediately after surgery to update them without having to find the numbers. Generally speaking, when a person has a loved one in the hospital, they think only about themselves and their loved one.

But to Rav Yaakov, his wife's friends weren't outsiders, they were part of the "self."

In the preface to Rav Chaim of Volozhin's classic *Nefesh HaChaim*, his son Rav Yitzchak of Volozhin relates that his father — the star pupil of the Vilna Gaon — would admonish him if he did not empathize with other people's pain, saying:

שזה כל האדם, לא לעצמו נברא, רק להועיל לאחריני בכל אשר ימצא בכחו לעשות, *For this is the essence of man — he was not created for himself, but to help others in whatever way he can.*

This is the *essence of man*! You weren't created to serve yourself your entire life, but to help others.

This concept is the prevailing factor upon which *gedolei Yisrael* predicate their decisions.

A man once approached Rav Shlomo Zalman Auerbach with a *sh'eilah*. He and his wife had been blessed with a baby boy, and they wanted to name him Yonatan. Shortly before his *bris*, however, a little boy in their apartment building who had the same name passed away. This man wanted to know whether that was a bad omen, and he should avoid giving the name Yonatan.

If you are at all familiar with Rav Shlomo Zalman's approach to *psak* you might realize that bad *mazel* was not among the factors he generally took into account in formulating a ruling. Those standing nearby were therefore shocked to hear him say, "Don't name the baby Yonatan."

One person couldn't help but vocalize his surprise. "Is bad *mazel* really a factor in this decision?" he asked.

"That's not why I told him not to name the baby Yonatan," Rav Shlomo Zalman replied. "The reason I told him not to use the name Yonatan is because one day, when that baby gets a bit older and goes to play outside, his mother will call out to him, 'Yonatan, come in,' 'Yonatan, where are you...' Each time the woman who lost her son Yonatan will hear that name being called, it'll be another dagger in her heart, reminding her of the loss."

> *"Each time the woman who lost her son Yonatan will hear that name being called, it'll be another dagger in her heart, reminding her of the loss."*

That's a big *ani*, a big "I." That bereft mother's feelings were all part of Rav Shlomo Zalman's sense of self.

But this concept is not only for *gedolei Yisrael*. Before I was bar mitzvah, Rabbi Sholom Rivkin told me that chassidim would say that a person must keep two pieces of paper in his two pockets. On one paper he should record Avraham Avinu's declaration: וְאָנֹכִי עָפָר וָאֵפֶר, *I am but earth and ash* (Bereishis 18:27). On the other he should write *Chazal's* teaching: כל אחד חייב לומר בשבילי נברא העולם, *Every person is obligated to say, "The world was created for me."*

Every person must strike the balance between realizing that Hashem has created a world just for him, while keeping his ego in check at the same time.

Or in Rav Shimon Shkop's version, אִם אֵין אֲנִי לִי, מִי לִי, a person must feel that he has value, that what he does in this world is important. But if it gets to the point of אֲנִי לְעַצְמִי, if everything is about himself — that's a problem.

The Rosh Yeshivah Draws a Heart

After Rav Nosson Tzvi Finkel, the Rosh Yeshivah of Mir Yerushalayim, was *niftar*, hundreds of stories were told about how he cared about every individual. One of the most moving stories was told by Rabbi Mordechai Grunwald, a fundraiser for the Mir.

At a *hesped* he delivered in Teaneck, Rabbi Grunwald related that when a *talmid* of Rav Nosson Tzvi's passed away at a young age, leaving a widow and orphans, Rav Nosson Tzvi forged a connection with the young *yesomim*. He told them to write to him and he would write back, and he would make a point of meeting with them when he came to America and helping them get into appropriate yeshivos as they grew of age.

After he finished delivering his *hesped*, a young man approached Rabbi Grunwald and said, "Let me tell you the rest of that story.

"That man didn't only have four sons, he also had a young daughter. The daughter felt left out; her brothers received letters from the Mirrer Rosh Yeshivah, and she didn't. When Rav Nosson Tzvi heard about this, he wrote her a note and drew a picture of a heart on it to indicate that his heart was with her."

Most people would find this shocking. A rosh yeshivah sending a heart to a little girl?

But the young man who told this story also knew the results. "You know how I know this story?" he said to Rabbi Grunwald. "That little girl is now my wife, and she says that that letter helped her through the pain of her orphanhood."

> *Most people would find this shocking. A rosh yeshivah sending a heart to a little girl?*

This is the essence of man — to help others in whatever way he can.

ᵈᵍ To Give Is to Live

The Gemara (*Nedarim* 64b) lists several types of people who are considered to be akin to a dead person: a poor person, a leper, and a blind person, for instance. Superficially, these types of people seem to differ sharply from one another. But in *Sichos Mussar* (5732, Essay 31), Rav Chaim Shmulevitz, a previous Mirrer Rosh Yeshivah, found a common denominator: all are limited in their ability to do things for others. A pauper has no money to distribute, a leper is sent outside of the encampment where he is all alone, a blind person cannot perceive other people's needs as well as those who see.

A person who can't give, concludes Rav Chaim Shmulevitz, is akin to being dead. Because to give is to live.

I heard a radio interview with a woman who was laid off. Initially she thought that she would weather the storm by living on savings until she found a new job. But she used up all her savings and still hadn't been hired. One thing led to another, and she found herself on the street, homeless. She had no choice but to stand on a sidewalk with a sign reading: "Will work for food." One day, a man passed by and gave her a $10 bill. In her financial state, $10 was real money; if she would spend it carefully, she might be able to use it for a few decent meals. But listen to what she did with some of the money.

"I used some of it to buy my daughter a birthday card," she related in a tear-choked voice. She had no food, she had no shelter, but she realized that in order to live, she had to give.

"I used some of it to buy my daughter a birthday card," she related in a tear-choked voice.

She had no food, she had no shelter, but she realized that in order to live, she had to give.

~§ One Line Replaces a Bookshelf

If you go to a Barnes and Nobles bookstore, you'll find a huge section of self-help books, many of which are meant to teach people how to be happy. I have one line that can eliminate the need for entire shelves of books:

For this is the essence of man — he was not created for himself, but to help others.

What seems to fly over the heads of most Americans today is that the more you give, the less you focus on yourself. And the less you focus on yourself, the happier you are. People who are constantly busy with whether they have their needs met are miserable people. Those who focus outward and try to help others are happy people.

I had a friend, David Hyman, who was diagnosed with lung cancer at the age of 52, never having smoked a single cigarette in his life. He waged a 2½-year battle with the disease, and ultimately passed away. When I visited him two weeks before he died, he shared an incredible insight. "When a person is battling cancer, he has to be on the receiving end of most interpersonal relationships. During treatment, he has no choice but to accept favors from others.

"One day, my son-in-law came to visit me, and I had a shoe-shine kit on hand. Nowadays, nobody polishes shoes anymore, but I felt strong that day, and I asked my son-in-law, 'Can I polish your shoes?'"

David Hyman took out the polish and buffer, and he polished his son-in-law's shoes.

"Rabbi Frand," he said, "it felt so good to help someone — even a little. It felt so good to give."

Several years ago, Gallup and Healthways released a study in which they polled 372,000 people to gauge how happy they were. The last question the pollsters asked was whether the person answering the poll was religious.

One of the 372,000 people polled was a religious Jew, and

when they reached that last question, he replied in fine Jewish fashion: "You tell me, what do you think? Based on my previous answers, am I religious?"

He replied in fine Jewish fashion: "You tell me, what do you think? Based on my previous answers, am I religious?"

"Yes," the pollster replied, "based on your answers, I think you are religiously observant. Because we have found that religiously observant people — no matter which religion they adhere to — are happier people."

You know why? Because in any religion, it's not about you. You're part of something bigger than yourself. And that makes you happier.

◆§ Learning to Give...by Giving

Living for others is a lofty goal. Becoming a giver is difficult. People always want to know how to translate a good speech into practice. I thought long and hard about how to become a bigger giver, and I have only one piece of advice: You become a bigger giver by giving. There is no other way than to practice it in real life.

Now, I don't mean that everyone has to join the *chevrah kaddisha* tonight. That's a great thing to do, but you don't have to go so far. You can start with really small things, however.

When you walk out of a door, turn around to see whether there's someone behind you, and hold the door for him.

Find a way to compliment someone around you.

Before you leave a bank, thank the teller.

These are little things, but they expand your *ani*, they make you more aware of other people. The closest people to practice with are your spouse and your kids, but you should also try this with total strangers.

I often travel by train, and there are luggage compartments overhead for people to store their baggage. Do you know how often I see people leave the doors open, so that the next person who walks by bumps his head? The prevailing attitude is, "I get my luggage, and goodbye." How much of an effort is it to close that compartment?

You don't have to be an *adam gadol* to do these things. You might become an *adam gadol*, but you don't have to be one to start.

ᴥᔐ The Bride in the Emergency Room

Reb Aryeh Rodin of Dallas, Texas told me that he has a congregant who made *aliyah* and was working in the pediatric emergency room in a hospital in Eretz Yisrael. One evening, a woman walked into the emergency room dressed in a wedding gown. What was she doing there on the way to her *chuppah*?

"A *kallah* has a special *koach* to give *berachos* on the day of her *chuppah*," she explained, "and I want to give a *berachah* to every child in this hospital so they will merit a *refuah sheleimah*."

This was on the day of her wedding!

Do you remember the day of your wedding, or the day of your daughter's wedding? There's something about brides on their wedding day. The expression "bridezilla" didn't come from nowhere. That a *kallah* could think about sick children on the day of her wedding is truly remarkable, but that is what humans were created for.

> *"A kallah has a special koach to give berachos on the day of her chuppah," she explained, "and I want to give a berachah to every child in this hospital so they will merit a refuah sheleimah."*

✥ A Seven-Hour Check Delivery

One final story.

I knew a man in Baltimore who is no longer alive. If you would have asked someone to name the 100 biggest *tzaddikim* in Baltimore while this man was still alive, he would not have made the list. As a businessman, he was tough as nails. A hard guy to deal with. But he was a *baal chessed*.

One day, he calls his son-in-law and says, "I want to drive to New York, you want to come along?"

"Why are you going to New York?" his son-in-law asked.

"My friend is making a *l'chaim*," he replied, "and I want to be there."

"You're going to drive 3½ hours each way to stay for 15 minutes?" the son-in-law asked in surprise.

"I want to give him a check toward the wedding costs," he explained.

The son-in-law agreed to accompany him. They get into the car, and the son-in-law asks, "Why can't you put the check in the mail?"

"I know," the man replied, "that my friend will not enjoy his daughter's l'chaim because he will spend the entire time worrying about how he will pay for the wedding. I want to hand-deliver the check so that he can enjoy the simchah."

"I know," the man replied, "that my friend will not enjoy his daughter's *l'chaim* because he will spend the entire time worrying about how he will pay for the wedding. I want to hand-deliver the check so that he can enjoy the *simchah*."

You want the icing on the cake? He made sure to have someone else write the check — though the money was his — so his friend in New York wouldn't know who it came from and wouldn't feel indebted to him.

For this is the essence of man — he was not created for himself.

You Are Not Alone

In an irony of the Jewish calendar, Tishah B'Av, the saddest day of the year, is followed very closely by Tu B'Av, a day that *Chazal* described as one of the most joyous on the Jewish calendar.

The Gemara (*Taanis* 30b-31a) offers a variety of reasons why this was considered such a joyous occasion. I'd like to focus on one that holds a practical lesson for every one of us, throughout the generations.

The Gemara states that the 15th of Av was the day when the Romans allowed those slaughtered in Beitar to be buried. Now superficially, this seems like a dubious reason to celebrate. The genocide at Beitar was so awful that it is listed as one of the five terrible things that happened to the Jewish people on Tishah B'Av, ranking up there with the destruction of the two Batei Mikdash (Mishnah, *Taanis* 4:6). There are varying reports of just how many Jews were killed by the Romans in Beitar, but it was a minimum of a few hundred thousand, and some say that it was over a million.

Beitar had been the last Jewish stronghold in Eretz Yisrael after the Beis HaMikdash had been destroyed, and when the Romans finally captured it, they wanted to leave a lasting reminder for the Jews remaining in Eretz Yisrael not to revolt again, as Bar Kochva and his comrades in arms had done in Beitar. After killing all the Jews in Beitar, therefore, they forbade them from being buried.

Only on the 15th of Av many years later did they finally permit the Jews to bury the dead. To the shock of those who went to tend to the burial, not one of those bodies had decomposed. The *chachamim*, who were stationed in Yavneh at the time, immediately coined a new *berachah: HaTov VeHaMeitiv*. This *berachah* speaks about Hashem's Goodness (*HaTov*) in that He prevented the bodies from decomposing, and of His Benevolence (*VeHaMeitiv*) that burial was allowed.

In truth, it is difficult to understand why *Chazal* would formulate such a beautiful *berachah* to commemorate so tragic an occasion. Aside from reciting it as the fourth *berachah* in *Bircas HaMazon*, we also recite a concise form of *HaTov VeHaMeitiv* on certain joyous occasions, especially those involving another person. If you buy a car that will benefit more than just yourself — for instance, your family, or friends to whom you will offer rides — you recite *HaTov VeHaMeitiv*. If you drink from a second bottle of wine at a meal and it is finer than the first wine, under certain criteria you recite *HaTov VeHaMeitiv*. Now imagine, *lo aleinu*, being called to the grisly scene of hundreds of thousands of Jewish bodies waiting for burial. Would your reaction be to thank Hashem for His Goodness and Benevolence?

Why did *Chazal* institute a *berachah* that is normally recited under joyous occasions after so tragic an event?

> *It is difficult to understand why Chazal would formulate such a beautiful berachah to commemorate so tragic an occasion.*

❧ I'm With You

I once heard the following explanation for this Gemara: Until this point, the relatively small number of Jews remaining in Eretz Yisrael felt as though Hashem had abandoned them. Aside from those killed, millions of their brethren had been exiled to the four corners of the earth. They had lost their Beis HaMikdash. They felt like a wife whose husband, whom she still loves, throws her out of the house. Depressed, forlorn, and disconsolate, they thought that Hashem no longer had any interest in them.

The miracle of the bodies remaining intact proved that even when a situation looks extremely bleak, Hashem does not abandon us. He is there with us through the most trying circumstances. *Hashem hasn't divorced us*, they suddenly realized. *We are not alone.*

> *Even when a situation looks extremely bleak, Hashem does not abandon us. He is there with us through the most trying circumstances.*

In Beitar, Hashem proved once again that one of His key *middos* (Attributes) is that of being *nosei be'ol*, to share the burden of Klal Yisrael. He feels our pain.

I say "once again" because this *middah* was actually the "Shalom Aleichem" Hashem gave to the Jewish people.

Hashem appeared to Moshe for the first time in a *sneh*, a burning thornbush (*Shemos* 3:2). Rashi explains that Hashem chose a thornbush to show that He felt the pain of the Jewish people in Mitzrayim.

When Bnei Yisrael finally escaped the torture of Mitzrayim and stood at Har Sinai, Hashem gave them a glimpse of His Heavenly Throne. The *pasuk* states: וַיִּרְאוּ אֵת אֱלֹקֵי יִשְׂרָאֵל וְתַחַת רַגְלָיו כְּמַעֲשֵׂה לִבְנַת הַסַּפִּיר וּכְעֶצֶם הַשָּׁמַיִם לָטֹהַר, *They saw the God of Israel, and under His feet was the likeness of sapphire brickwork, and it was like the essence of the heaven in purity* (*Shemos* 24:10).

Rashi explains that this "brickwork" had been under Hashem's Heavenly Throne from when the Jews had been exiled in Mitzrayim and had been forced to create bricks with which to build cities for Pharaoh. He wanted every Jew to know that He had been with them through thick and thin, because He is *nosei be'ol*. If they had to suffer from creating and building with bricks, then Hashem would keep bricks under His "feet" to commiserate with them.

The message Hashem wants to send Klal Yisrael — at the *sneh*, during that most intimate encounter at Har Sinai, and once again at Beitar — is that He feels our pain and empathizes with us.

The Alter of Kelm adds a vital point: Does Hashem need brickwork under His feet in order to remember Klal Yisrael's pain and commiserate with them? He's Omniscient and Omnipresent; he can certainly share our burden even without that sapphire brickwork!

In truth, says the Alter, Hashem didn't need the bricks there for Himself, they were there for *us*! He knew that one day He would appear to us at Har Sinai and allow us to catch a glimpse of those bricks, and we would learn from Him that we, too, must share the burden of those around us.

In the words of the Alter, who may have been one of the humans least prone to hyperbole, the bricks were there "to inform us of the great obligation to share the burden of one's friend, to feel his pain and to share in his joy, and this is הַפְלֵא וָפֶלֶא, *exceedingly wondrous*."

⮂ The Gift of Imagination

For most of us, feeling other people's pain does not come naturally. How can we train ourselves to be *nosei be'ol*?

I think that Hashem has granted each human a gift that can be channeled to help in this effort: the gift of imagination.

If you're like most Americans, when the Powerball lottery

jackpot reaches a few hundred million dollars, you probably imagine what you might do with that money.

I certainly do.

When the jackpot reached $600 million one time, I started to think about how I would spend the money. I wouldn't want much. Perhaps a *dirah* in Eretz Yisrael and maybe a Lear jet to travel to it…

Mind you, I didn't bother to purchase a ticket, but it didn't stop me from imagining what I would do with the money if I won.

Even without the Powerball, we tend to imagine things. Have you ever imagined expanding your kitchen, daydreaming about what it would be like to have those new gleaming granite countertops and state-of-the-art appliances, so that you could cook for your ever-expanding family? How you could make Pesach with ease — and then go to a hotel for Yom Tov?

We all imagine.

But it's a gift Hashem granted to us not to imagine Powerball windfalls and new kitchens and Lear jets, but to imagine what it would be like to be in someone else's shoes.

> *It's a gift Hashem granted to us not to imagine Powerball windfalls and new kitchens and Lear jets, but to imagine what it would be like to be in someone else's shoes.*

Commenting on the *pasuk*: אִם כֶּסֶף תַּלְוֶה אֶת עַמִּי אֶת הֶעָנִי עִמָּךְ, *When you lend money to My people, to the poor person who is with you (Shemos 22:24)*, Rashi writes, הֱוֵי מִסְתַּכֵּל בְּעַצְמְךָ כְּאִלּוּ אַתָּה הֶעָנִי, *View yourself as though you are that pauper.*

If someone visits your home or approaches you in shul and says, "I can't make my mortgage payment this month, and the bank is threatening foreclosure, can you please lend me some money?" it's not enough to take the money out and give it to him; you actually have to envision what it must be like to be afraid of being thrown out of your home.

You have to imagine what it must be like for a family when

the school calls and says, "We're sorry, but if you don't send in your tuition check, your children cannot come to school." When that father comes to you for some help, it's not enough to write a check. You have to envision what it would be like to be in his shoes. How would you want someone to treat you if you were the one asking for money?

The Torah is telling us that the obligation to be *nosei be'ol* is an integral part of the mitzvah of lending money.

✑ No Spending While Losers Weep

Let me tell you a story about how a very wise father taught his children about *nosei be'ol*.

Many years ago, one of Rav Avraham Pam's children, all of whom now have many grandchildren of their own, found a $5 bill on the street — this in the days when $5 could actually buy something of value. In *hilchos hashavas aveidah*, there was no obligation to return the money; there was no *siman* (identifying mark). It was a classic case of "finders keepers losers weepers."

And that was exactly the lesson Rav Pam wanted to teach his child. He took the money, put it on a shelf, and said, "Right now, there's someone who is very sad because he lost his $5. We'll wait a few days before you spend it, because it's not right for you to rejoice when someone else is feeling pain."

> "Right now, there's someone who is very sad because he lost his $5. We'll wait a few days before you spend it, because it's not right for you to rejoice when someone else is feeling pain."

This is what *nosei be'ol* is all about — feeling someone's pain enough to delay one's own joy.

There are hundreds of stories about how *gedolei Yisrael* displayed this trait; I'll share just a sampling.

Rav Isser Zalman Meltzer, the father-in-law of Rav Aharon Kotler, moved to Eretz Yisrael after escaping Europe. Rav Aharon's son, Rav

Shneur, was learning in Eretz Yisrael when he was a *chassan*. When it came time to return to America to get married, he went to part with his grandfather. Rav Isser Zalman escorted Rav Shneur partway down the stairs, but he suddenly stopped in his tracks, kissed him goodbye on the steps, wished him mazel tov, and Rav Shneur walked the rest of the way to the waiting car on his own.

One of Rav Isser Zalman's *talmidim* asked why he hadn't escorted his grandson all the way.

"Do you know how many of our neighbors are not *zocheh* to see their grandchildren get married, because their children didn't make it out of the Holocaust?" Rav Isser Zalman replied. "They will never get to celebrate the wedding of a grandchild and they will never get to see the *nachas* that I'm seeing. Yes, I'm happy, but I'm going to keep my joy private so as not to hurt the feelings of those who are not as fortunate."

> *"Yes, I'm happy, but I'm going to keep my joy private so as not to hurt the feelings of those who are not as fortunate."*

In 1970, terrorists hijacked a plane carrying Rav Yitzchak Hutner, the Rosh Yeshivah of Chaim Berlin, among other Jews. They landed the plane in Amman, Jordan, and held the passengers hostage, demanding that Israel release Palestinian terrorists imprisoned in Israeli jails.

Rav Hutner was one of the first captives to be released, and upon his arrival in New York, the Torah community held a welcoming celebration at a hangar in JFK Airport. Rav Moshe Feinstein walked into that hangar and noticed that there was a band playing music. He immediately instructed that the band stop playing. "We are here to show our *kavod haTorah* for Rav Hutner, and we are rejoicing upon his release," he explained, "but as long as there are people whose relatives are still being held hostage on that plane, we don't celebrate with music."

That's being sensitive to someone else's plight.

The Delayed Flower Purchase

While the *middah* of *nosei be'ol* may be a common denominator among *gedolei Yisrael*, it's not one that is limited to them.

Rav Yaakov Bender, the Rosh Yeshivah of Darchei Torah in Far Rockaway, N.Y., related that there's a fellow who comes to sell flowers in his yeshivah every Thursday night, enabling the boys to purchase flowers for their mothers.

Once, a high-school boy who would buy flowers every week for his mother walked up to the vendor for his weekly purchase, but then suddenly turned and walked away.

Five minutes later he was back, but once again, as he was about to buy the flowers, he mysteriously walked away.

Finally he returned a third time, and this time he bought flowers.

"What happened the first two times?" the vendor asked. "Why did you come and leave?"

"There's a boy in the yeshivah whose mother just passed away," explained the boy. "The first two times I came, I noticed him wandering nearby just as I was about to buy flowers. I didn't want to remind him that he no longer has a mother for whom to purchase flowers."

That's not Rav Avraham Pam, it's not Rav Isser Zalman Meltzer, and it's not Rav Moshe Feinstein. It's a yeshivah *bachur* from our own times, from one of our regular families. But he had the sensitivity to feel someone else's pain.

The Girl Who Went the Extra Mile

Rav Yoel Bursztyn, the principal of the Beis Yaakov of Los Angeles, told the story of a couple who did not have children for a number of years, until they were finally blessed with twin girls.

When the girls were toddlers, the mother was feeling the burden of handling her two lively little girls, and the couple decided to go up to a hotel in the mountains for a weekend to rest up. After Shabbos, the mother felt that she could use some more rest and relaxation, so she asked her husband if she could stay for another week while he returned to work, and then he would join her for the following Shabbos.

He readily agreed.

One day during that week, she sat her twins down at a table in the dining room, and went to wash for bread. When she returned, she was dismayed to find that one of her twins was gone. She lifted the one who remained and shouted, "Did you see a little girl who looks just like this? I'm missing my other baby!"

She lifted the one who remained and shouted, "Did you see a little girl who looks just like this? I'm missing my other baby!"

Everyone in the dining room gave a perfunctory look around, but gave up when they didn't see the girl. The mother ran out into the hallway, looking high and low, but she still couldn't locate her baby. Finally she saw a group of Beis Yaakov girls. "Can you help me find my baby?" she pleaded.

One girl took charge. "Let's organize this," she said briskly, pointing to each of her compatriots in rapid succession and issuing instructions. "You go to the dining room, you go to the playground, and you go to the meeting rooms…"

The mother of the twins stood there, anxiously waiting for them to return with her baby. One by one, the girls returned empty-handed, until the girl who had taken charge suddenly burst in with the baby.

"Where did you find her?" her friends asked.

"I found her in that meeting room," she answered, pointing to a room.

"But I checked in that room," her friend said, "and I didn't see the baby."

"Did you check under each desk?" the organizer asked. "She was sitting under one of the desks."

She handed the baby over to the mother, who could not find

the words to thank her enough. But then she asked this teenager a question. "Everyone else just gave a perfunctory glance around the room, and even your friends went about searching methodically, but without much energy. You were the most devoted to finding my child. Why did you go the extra mile to find her?"

At first, the girl was hesitant. But finally, she broke her uneasy silence. "Because I'm Leiby Kletzky's sister," she said.

Sometimes it's life that teaches us how to be *nosei be'ol im chaveiro*.

A Practical Primer

Now that we have seen how others are *nosei be'ol,* how do we train ourselves to share the burden of others?

I think it's actually important to start with what we should *not* do — the *don'ts* of *nosei be'ol.*

Example number one: If you are speaking to someone who hasn't been blessed with children yet, don't talk about your children.

Of course, you must be thinking to yourself, *that's pashut (simple)!*

You would be shocked to know how often people will talk about children in front of those who are suffering from infertility. Not maliciously, but inadvertently.

A former member of the *kollel* in Ner Yisrael was *zocheh* to two children only after many years of childlessness. He told me that he once walked into *seder* in the morning during those frustrating years, and he heard the *chavrusa* partnership sitting next to him discussing their respective nights. "Boy, did my kids give me a rough one last night," one said.

"So did mine," the other replied. "I was up half the night with one of them..."

They must have noticed this childless fellow giving them the "do-you-want-to-trade-places" stare, because they suddenly guiltily looked down at their Gemaros and started learning.

They weren't being cruel; they just weren't being sensitive. They were not looking at their tablemate and thinking about his circumstances.

Rabbi Ron Yitzchok Eisenman, Rav of Ahavas Yisrael in Passaic, N.J., tells the flipside of this story. When he was a youngster, he once spent a Shabbos in Monsey. It was a bitterly cold Shabbos, and most members of the community cut their trek to shul

> *They must have noticed this childless fellow giving them the "do-you-want-to-trade-places" stare, because they suddenly guiltily looked down at their Gemaros and started learning.*

drastically by taking a shortcut — with permission, of course — through someone's yard. Rabbi Eisenman's host, however, did not take the shortcut; he went around the block, adding quite a few minutes to their walk. When the young Rabbi Eisenman asked why he had taken the longer route, the man replied, "The person whose yard everyone cuts through does not have children. I didn't want to walk through his property with my children in tow and remind him of his fate."

Example number two: If you are making a wedding, and the details are weighing you down, don't call your neighbor whose daughter is still waiting for her *shidduch* to complain about how difficult it is to make the wedding.

And if you see an older single, don't say, "*Nuuuuuu?*"

If you think that this doesn't happen, you're mistaken. An older woman, a *meyucheses*, wrote me a letter beseeching me to speak about the insensitivity people have toward those who are single through no fault of their own.

While we're on that topic, there comes a stage at which the older singles would prefer that you *not* come over to them at a *simchah* and say "*Im

> *There comes a stage at which the older singles would prefer that you not come over to them at a simchah and say "Im yirtzeh Hashem bei dir."*

yirtzeh Hashem bei dir (with God's will, by you)," because it's no longer perceived as a *berachah*. It's a punch in the gut.

If you're speaking to a widow, try not to mention that your husband is out doing errands. The last thing she needs is a reminder that she no longer has a husband to do that.

Another point: Reb Yerucham Levovitz said that if we truly felt the pain of another person, we wouldn't be tempted to speak *lashon hara*.

There are many people out there whom we might classify as "nudniks," whose behavior or conversation we find annoying. Why do you think they are that way? Usually, the difficult cards they've been dealt in life made them be that way. If you would go into their shoes for a moment, you would certainly treat them with more compassion.

ᴥ§ The Dos

So much for the "don'ts." What are the "dos" of *nosei be'ol*?

Rav Pam once performed the most difficult form of *nichum aveilim*, visiting parents who were mourning a child who had passed away. This family later reported that his visit brought them the most consolation. What were the magic words Rav Pam said to bring them such comfort?

It wasn't the words. Rav Pam walked in, sat down, and began to cry. After a few minutes, he stood up, and said the standard "*HaMakom yenachem eschem...*"

> It wasn't the words. Rav Pam walked in, sat down, and began to cry. After a few minutes, he stood up, and said the standard "HaMakom yenachem eschem..."

Without uttering another word, he turned and left.

And this, in fact, is the best form of *nichum aveilim*. Rashi (*Shabbos* 12a) explains that the reason we are not *menachem avel* on Shabbos is because this causes us to commiserate with those who are in pain, and one is not allowed to cause themselves pain on Shabbos. Rav Pam's *nichum aveilim* brought consolation because the family felt that their pain was his.

On that note, if you are ever at a *shivah* of a family who lost a child, do not — I stress: *do not* — try to explain why they lost their child. Unless you happen to be a *navi*, you do not know why it happened. Although it sounds ridiculous that anyone would try to explain such a thing, you have no idea how frequently people try to explain Hashem's actions at a *nichum aveilim*.

Most of us are not on the level of Rav Pam, however. We aren't capable of sitting and crying with a grieving family at a *nichum aveilim*. How can we be *nosei be'ol* with mourners on our level?

I can answer that question from personal experience. Both my wife and I lost older siblings in recent years. On both occasions, our neighbors brought in food, from soup to nuts, including a full *seudah hamafsekes* for us to eat as my wife got up from *shivah* on Erev Yom Kippur. We both found this extremely comforting. Why? Can a potato kugel really mitigate one's loss?

The answer is yes, because that kugel says, "You are not alone." It says, "I can't replace your loss. I may not be able to find the words to console you. I can't even sit and cry along with you. But I want you to know that I'm with you."

Just as the Ribbono Shel Olam brought joy to Klal Yisrael in Beitar even as they suffered the horror of burying the myriads of dead bodies by showing them that they were not alone, so can we bring comfort to those who suffered a loss just by being there for them.

Finally, the last thing — though certainly not the least — a *nosei be'ol* can do for people in pain is to daven for them. Daven for those who are ill. Daven for those who need a *shidduch*. Daven for those who are out of jobs.

⇜§ Double Bounty

If you need an added incentive to feel the pain of others, realize that there is tremendous bounty of reward awaiting those who are *nosei be'ol*, both *b'ruchniyus ub'gashmiyus* — in the spiritual realm and in the material realm.

In *Parashas Beha'aloscha*, we read how Moshe Rabbeinu empanels the first Sanhedrin of 70 *dayanim* (judges). Who were the 70 people chosen? *Chazal* (cited in Rashi) reveal that these were the Jewish policemen whose job it was to enforce the daily brick quota the Egyptians set for the Jewish slaves. If the Jews did not reach the quota, do you know who took the beatings for it? Not the slaves, but the policemen. They allowed themselves to be whipped to protect their brethren who were toiling so hard to reach their quota. As a reward for their selflessness, they became the first Sanhedrin.

Let me ask you a question: Were these former policemen nice people? Yes. Were they *tzaddikim*, yes. But were they *talmidei chachamim*? To join the Sanhedrin, one had to be an expert in every area of Torah, as well as mastering all seventy languages. *Lehavdil*, you can't become a supreme court justice simply because you are a "nice guy." How did these former policemen become members of the Sanhedrin overnight if they were not *talmidei chachamim*?

> *How did these former policemen become members of the Sanhedrin overnight if they were not talmidei chachamim?*

Said R' Moshe Shmuel Shapiro, the Rosh Yeshivah of Be'er Yaakov, that we see an astounding reward here: when a person puts himself on the line for the Jewish people, he is gifted overnight with greatness in Torah! They weren't awarded positions on the Sanhedrin despite being ignoramuses; rather, they were gifted with all the Torah and general knowledge they needed to become worthy of sitting on the first Sanhedrin as a reward for their selflessness.

That's on the *ruchniyus* end. If it's material success you

seek, listen to a Baal HaTurim, with an addendum from Rav Mattisyahu Salomon.

When Pharaoh appointed Yosef as viceroy in Mitzrayim, he also gave him a wife, Osnas bas Poti-phera. The Torah makes a point of telling us that their two children, Menashe and Ephraim, were born during the seven years of plenty that commenced immediately upon Yosef's rise to power, and before the beginning of the years of hunger: וּלְיוֹסֵף יֻלַּד שְׁנֵי בָנִים בְּטֶרֶם תָּבוֹא שְׁנַת הָרָעָב אֲשֶׁר יָלְדָה לוֹ אָסְנַת בַּת פּוֹטִי פֶרַע כֹּהֵן אוֹן, *Now to Yosef were born two sons — when the year of famine had not yet set in — whom Osnas daughter of Poti-phera, Chief of On, bore to him* (*Bereishis* 41:50). Rashi comments that we learn from here that one may not engage with his wife during a hunger.

The Baal HaTurim often points out when a specific verbiage is used only a few times in the Torah. In his comment on this *pasuk*, he notes that the word וּלְיוֹסֵף appears in just one other place in the Torah, in the *berachah* Moshe Rabbeinu gives to the *shevatim* right before he passed away: וּלְיוֹסֵף אָמַר מְבֹרֶכֶת ה' אַרְצוֹ מִמֶּגֶד שָׁמַיִם מִטָּל וּמִתְּהוֹם רֹבֶצֶת תָּחַת, *Of Yosef he said: Blessed by Hashem is his land — with the heavenly bounty of dew, and with the deep waters crouching below* (*Devarim* 33:13).

Rashi explains that there was no land in Eretz Yisrael that was more lush than the portion of Yosef.

Do you know why Yosef merited such material bounty? Because he cared about others. As the viceroy who saved Egypt and the entire region from starving to death, you can be sure that Yosef and his family had the food they needed. Yet he felt the pain of those who were affected by the hunger and did not take pleasure while others were suffering.

By using the word וּלְיוֹסֵף in only these two verses, the Torah is hinting to us that Yosef received the greatest portion in Eretz Yisrael for being a *nosei be'ol*, says the Baal HaTurim.

But that's not all.

Take a look toward the end of Yosef's *berachah*, says Rav Mattisyahu Salomon. The *pasuk* says: וּמִמֶּגֶד אֶרֶץ וּמְלֹאָהּ **וּרְצוֹן שֹׁכְנִי סְנֶה**, *With the bounty of the land and its fullness, and **by the favor*** *of He Who rested upon the thornbush* (ibid. v. 16).

The Torah is telling us, "Do you know Who is giving this bounty? The One Who dwells in the *sneh*." The Ribbono Shel Olam's introduction to us was at the *sneh*, where He showed Moshe that He feels the pain of Klal Yisrael, and He granted Yosef this great material success because He rewards those who feel the pain of others.

> *The Ribbono Shel Olam's introduction to us was at the sneh, where He showed Moshe that He feels the pain of Klal Yisrael, and He granted Yosef this great material success because He rewards those who feel the pain of others.*

This is the *shelo lishmah*. We're not all *tzaddikim*, and we can't always do things altruistically. The Torah promises us a tremendous payout here, both *b'ruchniyus ub'gashmiyus*.

You want to be *zocheh* to Torah? You want to become a *talmid chacham*?

Nosei be'ol.

You want material success? You want to be able to support your family with ease and to be able to help others?

Nosei be'ol.

It comes with all the *berachos* in the world, because Hashem rewards those who emulate Him and commiserate with those who are suffering.

SECTION II:

Together
We Return

We're All in This Together

Rav Yisrael Salanter, the father of the *mussar* movement, is reported to have said that a true *baal teshuvah* is a person who starts to think about *teshuvah* immediately after Yom Kippur.

While I can't claim to have reached anywhere near that level, I will admit that there is something related to *teshuvah* that I do each year after Yom Kippur: I keep my eyes and ears primed for a topic for the following year's *teshuvah derashah*. As I've told people who ask me how I prepare my *derashos*, the hardest part of preparing is choosing a topic. Half my work is done when I have decided on a topic.

There are years when that effort turns out to be entirely unnecessary. In 2001, no matter what a *darshan* had planned to speak about prior to the catastrophic terrorist attacks on September 11, which occurred just a few days before Rosh Hashanah, his *derashah* was invariably replaced with some message dealing with the fallout from those events.

Similarly, in 2008, the year that the world financial markets collapsed, every rav had a built-in topic for a *teshuvah derashah*.

The year 2011 was another such year in a certain way, because within a short time frame, two tragedies occurred that left frum communities throughout the world reeling: the killings of Leiby Kletzky and Baba Elazar Abuchatzeira, *yehi zichram baruch*.

Now, far be it from me to determine what the message of these killings was. *Lo navi ani, velo ben navi ani* — I'm not a prophet in any way. Nevertheless, these events raised some questions that I think we have to consider.

⋙ Kol Nidrei Conundrum

Before we get to those events, however, have you ever wondered why we begin Yom Kippur with Kol Nidrei, which seems to be a technical *tefillah*?

> *Have you ever wondered why we begin Yom Kippur with Kol Nidrei, which seems to be a technical tefillah?*

Kol Nidrei is simply a statement that we annul any vows we've made during the last year. Not much emotional pull to this introductory *tefillah* — at least if you're paying attention to the meaning of the words, and not just being swept up by the haunting melody.

This question is particularly perplexing because men have already annulled their vows on Erev Rosh Hashanah, just ten days earlier, and the average man doesn't spend much time on that *heter nedarim*. They say the words as quickly as possible, and rush off to do the Yom Tov shopping.

Somehow, however, when the *chazzan* begins to intone those words with that haunting *niggun* used by Yidden worldwide, we all feel a shiver up our spine. Yom Kippur is beginning.

Why would we start with so technical a *tefillah*?

Furthermore, we follow Kol Nidrei by reciting the *pasuk*: וְנִסְלַח לְכָל עֲדַת בְּנֵי יִשְׂרָאֵל וְלַגֵּר הַגָּר בְּתוֹכָם כִּי לְכָל הָעָם בִּשְׁגָגָה, *And it shall be forgiven to the entire assembly of Israel and to the convert who sojourns among them, for it happened to the entire people unintentionally (Bamidbar 15:26).*

Taken out of context, we can understand why this *pasuk* is recited at the beginning of Yom Kippur. We obviously want Hakadosh Baruch Hu to forgive us as we head into Yom Kippur. Once we look at the context in which this *pasuk* appears in the Torah, however, it becomes extremely difficult to understand why we recite it immediately after Kol Nidrei.

The *parashah* in which this appears discusses an unusual occurrence: a case in which all of Klal Yisrael has worshiped idols because *beis din* mistakenly ruled that a certain action was permissible, when, in fact, it constituted idolatry. The Torah states that Klal Yisrael must bring a *korban* called a *par he'eleim davar*, and they will be forgiven for their sin.

This circumstance is so uncommon, in fact, that the Gemara in *Horayos* says that it happened all of… never. *Not once* did Klal Yisrael worship idols with the imprimatur of *beis din*.

Why, then, would the *Chachamim* pluck this *pasuk* out of context and place it into the Yom Kippur davening immediately after Kol Nidrei?

❧ Finding Common Ground

The Tolna Rebbe of Yerushalayim, R' Yitzchak Menachem Weinberg, has a beautiful insight to answer these questions.

He suggests that in order for us to merit complete forgiveness from Hashem, we must accomplish something as Yom Kippur descends upon us: we must become one *eidah*, one community. If we meld into one cohesive unit, then we have the power of community, and the Ribbono Shel Olam relates differently to a community than He does to an individual.

> *We must accomplish something as Yom Kippur descends upon us: we must become one eidah, one community.*

We have to set aside our differences, the issues that set us apart, and become one *tzibbur*, one unit. If there's one day of the year when we can accomplish that, it's Yom Kippur. Because Yom Kippur is a day when we focus on the internals, not the externals. On Yom Kippur, what you wear on your head is not the focus, it's what's inside of you that counts.

Gashmiyus, physicality, takes a break on Yom Kippur. We're all in the same boat — we're all hungry, tired, and our feet are hurting. Yet we are the closest we can get to being angels because we're focused on the spiritual, not the physical. We focus on what we all have in common: the *neshamah*, the soul. Every soul comes from under the *Kisei HaKavod*, the Heavenly Throne, and that makes us more similar than we can imagine.

Returning to the Leiby Kletzky story, if you'll recall, during the 36 hours when this 9-year-old boy was missing, something rare happened: We all came together as one unit: Chassidim and misnagdim; Ashkenazim and Sephardim; Jews of German, Hungarian, and Polish descent; right-wingers and left-wingers — even frum and secular. People all over the world joined in *tefillah* for a child, taking no heed of what Chassidus he was part of or whether he was a chassid at all.

A *talmid* told me that he drove to Boro Park to take part in the search. He had to wait in line to get a street assignment and a map; so many people volunteered to search that there was a long queue. Once he got his assignment, as he drove around searching, he noticed older Jews sitting on their porches, saying *Tehillim* for this little boy.

Why were we able to put aside all our issues and come together to conduct this search? Because for those 36 hours, we didn't see ourselves with our usual labels, we saw ourselves as parents. Each of us imagined how horrifying it would be if that was our child missing, and that united us. All differences melted away, and our shared mission as parents glued us together into one cohesive unit.

For those 36 hours, we didn't see ourselves with our usual labels, we saw ourselves as parents.

Sadly, we were able to see this cohesiveness more recently as well. During the summer of 2014, during the weeks that three Israeli teenagers, Naftali, Gil-ad, and Eyal, were missing after being kidnaped by terrorists. In the weeks before they were found murdered, all of Klal Yisrael came together to daven for them, regardless of their perspective or politics. And that unity in *tefillah* continued in the weeks afterward, when Israeli troops had to enter Gaza to destroy tunnels dug out by Hamas to infiltrate Israel and massacre Jews.

This is what's supposed to happen on Yom Kippur as well.

That's why we annul all vows as we walk into shul on Yom Kippur, says the Tolna Rebbe.

Vows have a curious way of separating people. A person who takes a vow — no matter how pure his intention may be — can easily come to think of himself as being holier than thou, of operating on a higher spiritual plain than all others. *I have this chumra, I have that chumra,* the person might think to himself, *and therefore I'm better than the others in this shul.*

Kol Nidrei is an equalizer. You have a *chumra* that you won't eat a meal before hearing a *dvar Torah*? Leave that *neder* at the doorstep of Yom Kippur. You want to keep it after Yom Kippur, by all means, keep it. But Yom Kippur is not the day to think you're on a higher level than others.

This explains why we begin Kol Nidrei with the words עַל דַּעַת הַמָּקוֹם וְעַל דַּעַת הַקָּהָל...אָנוּ מַתִּירִין לְהִתְפַּלֵּל עִם הָעֲבַרְיָנִים. We pronounce our intentions that on this one day of the year,

> *Yom Kippur is not the day to think you're on a higher level than others.*

we can daven with people whom we generally wouldn't associate with, because on Yom Kippur we must meld into a *tzibbur*, not seek out our differences.

And that's why we invoke the *pasuk,* וְנִסְלַח לְכָל עֲדַת בְּנֵי יִשְׂרָאֵל. As long as it's כָּל עֲדַת בְּנֵי יִשְׂרָאֵל, as long as we're one community, then we can merit forgiveness.

✧ City of Unity

This idea also explains a Midrash on a *pasuk* that discusses the *avodah* of Aharon HaKohen on Yom Kippur: בְּזֹאת יָבֹא אַהֲרֹן אֶל הַקֹּדֶשׁ, **With this,** *Aharon shall come into the Holy* (*Vayikra* 16:3).

The Midrash wonders what the word בְּזֹאת, *with this,* refers to, and answers that it refers to four merits with which Aharon enters the *Kodesh HaKodashim* on Yom Kippur, citing biblical sources that each of the four is described as "זאת": (1) Torah, (2) Bris Milah, (3) Shabbos, (4) Yerushalayim.

Now, the first three are easily understood as obvious merits that would enable the Kohen Gadol to succeed in his *avodah*. But what's the *zechus* of Yerushalayim? How does a city provide merit?

You know what's special about Yerushalayim? It unifies.

Talmud Yerushalmi (*Chagigah* 3:6) points out that the *pasuk,* יְרוּשָׁלַם הַבְּנוּיָה כְּעִיר שֶׁחֻבְּרָה לָּה יַחְדָּו, *The built-up Jerusalem is like a city that is united together* (*Tehillim* 122:3), teaches us that Yerushalayim brought people together.

How?

During the times of the Beis HaMikdash, *chaveirim* and *amei ha'aretz* — those who kept the laws of *tumah* (ritual impurity) and those who did not — were not allowed to eat together, or even borrow vessels from one another.

Three times a year, that all changed. During the Yomim Tovim, when all of Klal Yisrael made the pilgrimage to Yerushalayim, everyone was allowed to eat together, out of the same *keilim*. That ability to get together created a sense of unity, and that unity was the merit with which the Kohen Gadol would enter the *Kodesh HaKodashim*.

✧ Mastering the Art

Unfortunately, however, nowadays we often find unity only in tragedy. Whether it's Leiby in Boro Park, or Naftali, Gil-ad, and Eyal in Eretz Yisrael, Klal Yisrael tends to unite only under dire threat.

And that is a sad commentary on our state of affairs. After 2,000 years of *galus*, we still haven't mastered a very basic art that we need in order to survive as a nation: the art of disagreeing agreeably.

After 2,000 years of galus, we still haven't mastered a very basic art that we need in order to survive as a nation: the art of disagreeing agreeably.

We have to learn how to disagree, to have differences of opinion — but do so with respect, not with contempt. Because I am not suggesting that we all put our differences aside, and, in the great tradition of liberal Americans, follow the moral relativistic slogan of, "I'm right, you're right, we're all right." I don't believe that we should all be sitting around a campfire singing "Kumbaya" together. Sometimes people are wrong.

Just. Plain. Wrong.

And when someone is wrong, we have the right — nay, the obligation — to disagree. But that doesn't mean that we have to lose respect for someone else in the process.

Hashem *wants* us to disagree with others on occasion, but to do so respectfully.

We know that there were *Keruvim* (Cherubs) on top of the *Aron HaBris* in the *Kodesh HaKodashim*. There is a contradiction in a *pasuk*, which describes the *Keruvim*, as follows: וְהָיוּ הַכְּרֻבִים פֹּרְשֵׂי כְנָפַיִם לְמַעְלָה סֹכְכִים בְּכַנְפֵיהֶם עַל הַכַּפֹּרֶת וּפְנֵיהֶם אִישׁ אֶל אָחִיו אֶל הַכַּפֹּרֶת יִהְיוּ פְּנֵי הַכְּרֻבִים, *The Cherubim shall be with wings spread upward, sheltering the Cover with their wings with their faces toward one another; toward the Cover shall be the faces of the Cherubim* (*Shemos* 25:20).

The Gemara (*Bava Basra* 99a) wonders which is correct: were the *Keruvim* facing each other, or were they looking toward the *Kapores*, the covering of the Aron?

Rav Nosson Adler, the rebbi of the Chasam Sofer, offers his own explanation. On one hand, the *Keruvim* faced the *Kapores*, which covered the *Aron* that held the *Luchos* and a Sefer Torah, because they wanted to know what the Torah teaches. Yet despite the inevitable disagreements between Jews who are trying to ascertain what the Torah says about any given topic, they were still וּפְנֵיהֶם אִישׁ אֶל אָחִיו, they faced each other, never turning their backs on each other.

If you've ever been in a *beis midrash* in a yeshivah, you've heard the cacophony of people learning, and you've probably heard exclamations that, in any other setting, would be "fightin' words." Statements such as, "You have no idea what on earth you're talking about!," are among the milder things one *chavrusa* will shout to another.

Rav Noach Weinberg told a story about a woman who became religious, and the first time she observed the goings-on in a *beis midrash* she said, "Why do they hate each other?"

"They don't hate each other," Rav Noach replied, "they are merely trying to ascertain the truth together."

> *In the law libraries she had previously visited, there was no yelling, no animated gesturing, no exaggerated statements doubting another's ability to understand the text.*

But this woman's question was not out of place. In the law libraries she had previously visited, there was no yelling, no animated gesturing, no exaggerated statements doubting another's ability to understand the text. Nevertheless, what seemed to her like hatred was actually two *talmidei chachamim* who actually love each other.

Because we can disagree profoundly, but still be agreeable with one another.

✑ Respectful Opposition

Perhaps the paradigm of two people who disagreed with each other vigorously yet respected one another was the relationship between Rav Yosef Chaim Sonnenfeld and Rav Avraham

Yitzchak HaKohen Kook. The former was the leader of the Eidah Chareidis, and led the battle against the secularists who settled in Eretz Yisrael and planned to establish a state. The latter was the first rav to hold the title of Chief Ashkenazic Rabbi of Palestine, and his writings would define the philosophical underpinnings of the Mizrachi movement, which supported the establishment of a self-governing state.

These two Torah giants disagreed on practically every issue: whether children should receive secular education, how the religious should interrelate with the irreligious, among a host of other issues. Each one held that the other was wrong — absolutely, fundamentally *wrong*.

But when reports circulated that the new secular kibbutzim in the north of Eretz Yisrael were serving children *treife* food and feeding them on Yom Kippur, Rav Sonnenfeld and Rav Kook went hand-in-hand to bring those children back to Yiddishkeit.

Why?

Because I may disagree with you about whether there should be a state or not, but that doesn't affect the way I interact with you — and certainly when Jewish souls are on the line.

For close to a month in 1913, Rav Sonnenfeld and Rav Kook put aside their ideological differences and journeyed throughout the north of Eretz Yisrael, visiting dozens of kibbutzim in the hopes of eventually bringing the youth closer to Yiddishkeit.

A particularly telling story occurred when the two were scheduled to be at a *bris* together, with Rav Sonnenfeld serving as the *mohel* and Rav Kook as the *sandak*. When they arrived at the same time at the shul where the *bris* was to take place, they reached an impasse. Rav Sonnenfeld felt that Rav Kook, who was a Kohen, deserved to enter first, while Rav Kook wanted Rav Sonnenfeld to enter first.

Neither of the two would budge. Each one stood there insisting that the other enter first. Finally, Rav Kook noticed that they were actually standing in front of a set of double doors. He reached inside, unlatched the second door, and they entered together.

We can disagree, but we can do so agreeably.

ᵉᵍ Who's More Intolerant?

So you may be wondering at this point: which side am I addressing — the left, or the right? Who is less tolerant of the other side? Are the right-wingers less tolerant of the left, or vice-versa?

I think that I am uniquely suited to answer this question, because I'm actually both a leftist and rightist, depending on which community I'm visiting. When I go to a modern community, they say, "Ooh, he's affiliated with Ner Yisrael, he must be a right-winger." In right-wing communities they say, "*Ach*, he's from Baltimore; he's a left-winger."

> *When I go to a modern community, they say, "Ooh, he's affiliated with Ner Yisrael, he must be a right-winger." In right-wing communities they say, "Ach, he's from Baltimore; he's a left-winger."*

From my standpoint as the "other side" no matter which community I visit, I'll be honest: I feel that both sides are equally guilty.

Right-wingers are occasionally so sure of their way that they see the other side as completely flawed. They don't just attack the opinions they consider to be wrong; the arguments become personal, and they treat individuals from other camps with utter contempt and disdain.

If you're on the right, don't be so quick to condemn, because you don't know where the person you're condemning is coming from.

There was a *bachur* in Ponevezh who was caught smoking in the dormitory on Shabbos. A group of *kana'im* (zealots) came to the Rosh Yeshivah, Rav Shach, and demanded that the boy be expelled from the yeshivah. Smoking on Shabbos? It was beyond the pale!

"Do you know what's going on in his life?" Rav Shach asked. "Do you know what's happening in his family?"

The zealots just stood there, unsure of what to answer.

"Do you even know who his *chavrusos* are?" Rav Shach pressed.

Silence.

"A *bachur* does not smoke in the dorm in Ponevezh in a vacuum," Rav Shach said strongly. "If you know nothing about him, how can you demand that he be expelled?"

With those words, he promptly threw these self-proclaimed zealots out of his office, and then helped the boy overcome the challenges that prompted the *chillul Shabbos*.

✑ Overstepping the Boundaries

On the other hand, I hear the left describing the right as "fanatical, benighted, narrow-minded, parasitic" and several other adjectives that I'll leave to your imagination.

After a speech in an extremely modern community, a couple gave me a ride to the train station, and I asked them who they thought was the more intolerant side, left or right.

The woman did not hesitate for a moment. "The left," she responded instantaneously.

Bear in mind that this woman is married for close to thirty years, living in what you have to describe as an extremely left-wing community. Why was she so sure that the left was more intolerant?

She had two stories to support her opinion.

One happened ten years before my conversation with her. It seems that after twenty years of marriage, this woman decided to start covering her hair. When she met one of her neighbors for the first time after putting on a *sheitel*, the latter said, "Your *sheitel* is beautiful, but I would never wear one."

"What right does she have to offer her opinion?" my host demanded. "Imagine me walking over to her and saying, 'Your hair is beautiful, but you should really be wearing a *sheitel*.'"

Her second example occurred when they enrolled their 15-year-old son in a yeshivah high school in which the secular studies department left something to be desired. A member of their community walks up to her son, out of the blue, and says, "I really think you should go to such-and-such yeshivah, because it has a better English department, and you can become a Harvard-trained physician like your father."

What gives this person the right to say that? It bothered him that someone might come out a little frummer?

What gives this person the right to say that? It bothered him that someone might come out a little *frummer*? It made him feel so guilty about his own observance that he couldn't tolerate it?

The left-wingers like to think of right-wingers as intolerant, but they might be surprised to realize that they aren't necessarily more tolerant themselves.

⋙ The Chessed Fix

So what can we — and by "we" I refer to both ends of the Orthodox spectrum — do to unite, even if we retain our individual identities?

I have two ideas that could work: *chessed* and Torah.

Let's start with *chessed*.

As is the case in many Jewish communities, Baltimore has a *chessed* organization that delivers Shabbos packages to needy families. They package groceries and other necessities and deliver them to the doors of these families.

If you are involved in a *chessed* effort and you need a partner, do you choose someone who dresses, thinks, and acts exactly like you? Or can you bridge the divide by partnering with someone who is different?

United as you are by the agenda — your joint *chessed* project — you can come to appreciate people from the "other side."

The same is true for Hatzolah, *shomrim* patrols, or any other communal effort. These initiatives present opportunities to reach out to members of different communities.

A classic example of *chessed* bridging gaps between Jews is the work of Satmar Bikur Cholim in New York.

Women from the Satmar community visit the huge New York hospitals: Columbia Presbyterian, Cornell, NYU, Mount Sinai — not to mention, *lo aleinu*, Sloan-Kettering Cancer Center — and distribute food and spread goodwill to all the Jewish patients.

So do you think these Satmarer women will ever ask a patient, "What do you hold about *Medinas Yisrael*?" Do they ask you what you wear on your head?

They don't care.

Because you're a Jew, and you need help, and *chessed* is a great unifier.

> *Do you think these Satmarer women will ever ask a patient, "What do you hold about Medinas Yisrael?" Do they ask you what you wear on your head? They don't care.*

Rabbi Refoel Mendlowitz of Silver Spring, Maryland told me that he was in Alaska one summer, and that week, seven backpackers went into a national forest, and were mauled by a grizzly bear. They escaped, but with terrible injuries. Rabbi Mendlowitz, who was staying with the Chabad *shaliach* in Anchorage, told me that his host related that he got a call that week from the Satmar Bikur Cholim, inquiring whether these seven men were receiving the care they needed.

Let me just expand that for clarity:

The *Satmar* Bikur Cholim calls the *Lubavitcher shaliach*. For whom? For four of those backpackers who were Jewish. And trust me, they were not Satmar chassidim.

These were people they didn't even know, but they needed help. And when they're trying to help another Yid, they don't care what that person thinks of their opinions on world events.

Rabbi Mordechai Kamenetsky of Long Island was once asked to hold an appeal for Satmar Bikur Cholim in a shul on Long Island. Here he was in a modern Orthodox congregation, making an appeal for Satmar Bikur Cholim — with an Israeli flag standing in the background.

Satmar and an Israeli flag? What's wrong with this picture?

The answer is that there is absolutely *nothing* wrong with

this picture. Because if you've ever been on the receiving end of Satmar Bikur Cholim, you forget about what they think of the flag or the State it represents. They don't care, and you don't care.

◄§ Project Inspire: Take Two

As for the power of Torah to unite us, first let's begin with the concept of Project Inspire. The brainchild of Rav Noach Weinberg *zt"l*, Project Inspire seeks to turn every Torah observant Jew into a *kiruv* worker — no experience necessary.

You meet someone at your office, in the gym, the store, or on the subway, invite them to spend a Shabbos in your home. You don't have to know proofs of God's existence or the Rambam's approach to *yediah* and *bechirah* or how to refute a Christian missionary. All you have to know is how to eat *cholent* with them.

I have an idea to piggyback on the Project Inspire mold: Project Inspire that looks inward, toward frum Jews. If you wear a white shirt, sit down once a week to learn with someone with a blue shirt. Or if you wear a suede yarmulka, sit down to learn with someone who wears a *shtreimel* on Shabbos.

> *If you wear a white shirt, sit down once a week to learn with someone with a blue shirt. Or if you wear a suede yarmulka, sit down to learn with someone who wears a shtreimel on Shabbos.*

Bava Metzia is the same. The *perek* of *Shnayim Ochazin* is the same. And *Chazal* taught us that when people learn together, *naasim ohavim zeh lazeh*, they come to love one another.

There was a *kollel* that was established in an out-of-town community, and the *kollel* members wanted to make inroads into a modern Orthodox shul, but the members of the latter would have nothing to do with the "black hatters."

You know what they did? The *kollel* members started an *Avos U'Banim* program, in which fathers come to learn with their young children on the long Motza'ei Shabbosos of the winter. Almost against their will, on the first week 20 members of the modern-Orthodox shul came to the program, and it quickly doubled to 40 members.

Today, they have come to love the *kollel*. They realized that even a person who wears a black hat can be normal.

Chessed and Torah are great unifiers. And it's our choice: Will it be tragedy that will bind us together, or can we come together through *chessed* and Torah?

⋖§ True to Yourself

The other shocking incident that made the 2011 *derashah* a no-brainer was the murder of Baba Elazar Abuchatzeira.

What was your reaction when you heard that story? If you are like most frum Jews, you were absolutely shocked.

How could a so-called frum Jew pick up a knife and kill — kill! — another Yid?

We see it as a total contradiction to the term frum Jew.

Which leads us to a second point we need to consider: Do we always live up to our own convictions, or are there contradictions in our lives as well? Certainly, our contradictions are not as blatant as those that will bring one Jew to murder another, but do we live a life of consistency?

> *Certainly, our contradictions are not as blatant as those that will bring one Jew to murder another, but do we live a life of consistency?*

Let me offer an example that might hit hard.

The *pasuk* in *Eichah* (1:3) states: גָּלְתָה יְהוּדָה מֵעֹנִי וּמֵרֹב עֲבֹדָה, *Judah has gone into exile because of suffering and great servitude.*

One of the early commentators on *Tanach* offers an alternative translation. We find wealth described in the Torah as עֲבֻדָּה רַבָּה (*Bereishis* 26:14). Accordingly, the words גָּלְתָה יְהוּדָה מֵעֹנִי וּמֵרֹב עֲבֹדָה means that Klal Yisrael was chased into exile because of poverty — amid great wealth. Isn't that a contradiction? Were they poverty stricken or wealthy?

You know what it means? It means that when someone approached them for a donation, they would *claim* poverty. "I would love to give you, but I just don't have." And yet these same people would spend lavishly on themselves.

The *churban* came about because people lived contradictory lives.

As I said, it might hit hard, but doesn't that idea bear a striking resemblance to stories we hear in our times of people who tell the tuition committees of their children's schools that they need reductions, and shortly thereafter, they put a massive addition onto their houses?

Living with contradictions is so contemptible because it's hypocritical. This does not mean to say that each time we slip on something we profess to keep, we are hypocrites. We are all human, and we have our foibles and missteps. But to live a life that is an obvious contradiction to our own values is indeed contemptible.

The Midrash teaches that Shaul HaMelech, the first Jewish king, lost his kingship because of a contradiction. When Hashem commanded the Jewish people to wipe out Amalek, he took pity on Agag, the king of Amalek, as well as on the animals. "If the people have sinned," he reasoned, "what have the animals done wrong?"

Somehow, however, when David was reported to have been sheltered by Nov, the city of Kohanim, Shaul ordered them all killed.

The Torah viewed this as a terrible contradiction: if he was so concerned about the wellbeing of Amalek, how could he then wipe out a city of Kohanim? Are you the compassionate Shaul, or the cruel Shaul?

⇜§ Make Up Your Mind!

An inconsistent life is so dangerous because it leaves little hope for repentance.

One of the most dramatic *perakim* in *Tanach* contains words that we will recite as Yom Kippur reaches a crescendo at the end of Ne'ilah.

Eliyahu HaNavi famously challenged the prophets of Baal to a showdown on Har HaCarmel. They would each prepare a *korban*, and the side who succeeded to bring down fire from the Heavens would prove that it represented the true God.

Of course, Baal didn't come through — and neither did the prophets who had hidden under their altar to light a fire to make it seem as though it had descended from the Heaven, because Hashem struck them dead — and Hashem sent a fire from Heaven to devour the *korban* Eliyahu HaNavi had prepared. When Bnei Yisrael saw this miracle, they called out: הי הוא הָאֱלֹקִים, הי הוא הָאֱלֹקִים, *Hashem is the God, Hashem is the God* (*I Melachim* 18:39).

In the lead-up to this cataclysmic moment, Eliyahu says something that seems shocking. וַיִּגַּשׁ אֵלִיָּהוּ אֶל כָּל הָעָם וַיֹּאמֶר עַד מָתַי אַתֶּם פֹּסְחִים עַל שְׁתֵּי הַסְּעִפִּים אִם ה' הָאֱלֹקִים לְכוּ אַחֲרָיו וְאִם הַבַּעַל לְכוּ אַחֲרָיו, *Elijah approached all the people and said, "How long will you dance between two opinions? If Hashem is the God, go after Him! And if the Baal, go after it!"* (ibid. v. 21).

How could Eliyahu say, "If the Baal, then go after it?" Was he sanctioning Bnei Yisrael's idolatry?

Eliyahu was saying: "Make up your minds." If you're an observant Jew, then worship the Ribbono Shel Olam all the way. If you want to worship *avodah zarah*, I can work with you. I can be *mekarev* you. As long as you're consistent, I can show you the fallacy of your ways and hopefully bring you to *teshuvah*.

> How could Eliyahu say, "If the Baal, then go after it?" Was he sanctioning Bnei Yisrael's idolatry?

What I can't deal with, says Eliyahu, is a hypocrite. If someone worships Hashem one day and Baal the next, he's a faker. And he's beyond redemption.

"Make up your minds," he said. "Stand up and be counted. Who are you for? Hashem, or the Baal?"

Ultimately, Bnei Yisrael made their choice: ה' הוּא הָאֱלֹקִים, ה' הוּא הָאֱלֹקִים, *Hashem is the God, Hashem is the God.*

This message has to resonate with us until today.

My barber is an Italian by the name of Joe Cimino. We don't have all that much in common. As I sit there in his chair for my monthly snip, Joe tells me about his passion in life: gambling. Every few days, Joe drives up to Atlantic City to win or lose some money.

Now, Joe knows a little bit about Jews — and especially about *peyos*. He knows to cut around them. Every so often, he'll say, "You know, I see those hassids in Atlantic City."

Now, he obviously doesn't mean true chassidim, because he wouldn't be able to tell one frum Jew from another. But he does know that *peyos* mean a frum Jew.

That's a contradiction. Shabbos in Brooklyn, and Motza'ei Shabbos in Atlantic City? Make up your mind: אִם ה' הָאֱלֹקִים לְכוּ אַחֲרָיו וְאִם הַבַּעַל לְכוּ אַחֲרָיו.

That's a contradiction. Shabbos in Brooklyn, and Motza'ei Shabbos in Atlantic City?

Perhaps this is the reason why the final moments of Ne'ilah, after 25 hours of fasting, 10 Days of *teshuvah* that was preceded by 30 days of Elul, all come to a climax with those very same words: ה' הוּא הָאֱלֹקִים, ה' הוּא הָאֱלֹקִים.

We are saying to Hashem: I want to be consistent. I vote for You, and only You!

✍ Resolving Our Inconsistencies

In the *Shemoneh Esrei* that we recite five times on Yom Kippur, we say, אַתָּה יוֹדֵעַ רָזֵי עוֹלָם וְתַעֲלוּמוֹת סִתְרֵי כָל חָי, *You know the secrets of the world and the hidden secrets of all who live.*

סִתְרֵי generally means secrets, but perhaps it can also mean the סְתִירוֹת, the contradictions that we live in our lives. As we search within ourselves on Yom Kippur, we realize that Hashem sees our סְתִירוֹת, our inconsistencies, and we are aware that we have to resolve them.

While I was preparing this *derashah*, I received a phone call from Rabbi Aryeh Rodin of Dallas, Texas, whom I've never met but who calls me on occasion to share stories.

"You want to hear a story?" he asked, beginning with the sweetest words a public speaker can hear.

Dallas usually has some really hot weeks during the summer. And when I say "really hot," I mean REALLY hot — it can be over 100 degrees for days at a time. During one such heat wave, Rebbetzin Rodin was walking to shul with her little daughter, who suddenly piped up and said, "I can't walk anymore, Mommy. It's too hot."

What was Rebbetzin Rodin to do? She was still far from the shul. She realized that she knew one non-religious Jewish family on the block, and she knocked on the door and explained her predicament.

"You can leave her here," the woman of the house offered graciously. Rebbetzin Rodin forged onward, pledging to be back within the hour to retrieve her daughter.

The woman gave the young girl some toys to play with. A few minutes later, the phone rang, and the woman answered. This 5-year-old girl goes over to her and asks, "Are you Jewish?"

"Of course I'm Jewish," she answers.

A few minutes later, this woman's daughter comes downstairs and asks, "Mom, can I go swimming?"

"Sure," the mother answers, "but please be careful."

Young Miss Rodin's ears perk up once again, and she wanders over to this woman and says, "Are you *sure* you're Jewish?"

To a 5-year-old's mind, if you answer the phone on Shabbos, you're not Jewish. It's a contradiction. She doesn't understand the nuances we adults master.

But even to those of us who are able to understand that there can be Jews who don't keep Shabbos, we have to ask ourselves: is there something in our own repertoire that is not appropriate for a frum Jew?

> *She had been forced to ask herself, "How am I different from my neighbor who is not Jewish?" and she became shomeres Shabbos because of a question from a 5-year-old.*

Incidentally, this 5-year-old's questions hit home. A few months after what turned out to be a fateful Shabbos, this woman called Rabbi Rodin and asked him to *kasher* her home. She had been forced to ask herself, "How am I different from my neighbor who is not Jewish?" and she became *shomeres Shabbos* because of a question from a 5-year-old.

During the Aseres Yemei Teshuvah, we have to ask ourselves: Are we Jewish? Are we *ehrlich*? Are we consistent?

✑ The Reward for Unity

On a final note: if we would retain our awareness of just how much we gain from uniting with all Jews — not only in times of tragedy, but at all times — we would have a much easier time overlooking the differences and retaining our respect even as we disagree. And the reward can be nothing short of miraculous.

On the tenth anniversary of the 9/11 attacks, *Mishpacha* Magazine ran an interview with some of the Hatzolah members who rushed to the World Trade Center to try to save the lives of people escaping the inferno.

Heshy Jacobs, one of the heads of Hatzolah, related:

"At the end of the day, when the head of the Emergency Medical Service [EMS] system, Chief Robert McCracken, asked Itzy Stern, 'How many guys did you lose?' Itzy didn't want to tell him how many we lost, because we hadn't lost any, and they had lost hundreds. So he began describing a broken leg here, a broken arm there. Chief McCracken interrupted him: 'No, I mean how many died?' So Itzy sheepishly said, 'None.'

"The chief thought for a moment and said, 'Tomorrow I'm staying with you. It's evident G-d was with you today.'"

"For ten years I've walked around wondering, '*Why?*'" continued Heshy Jacobs. "We were in the Towers, we were close on all sides, so why did the Master of the Universe do that miracle for us openly? And I believe the answer is because we all came *b'achdus* [unity of purpose]...

The chief thought for a moment and said, "Tomorrow I'm staying with you. It's evident G-d was with you today."

"You heard where they came from: Boro Park, Flatbush, Williamsburg, Crown Heights, Upper East Side, West Side, Lower East Side, Riverdale, Canarsie, Queens ... Every single neighborhood came for one reason: because Jews and other people needed them."

For those of you who are unfamiliar with the New York landscape, these neighborhoods represent Jews of every stripe: Chassidim and *misnagdim*, Lubavitchers and Satmarers, Ashkenazim and Sephardim, affluent Jews and less-affluent — the entire spectrum of Hatzolah was there to help.

"So the story here," concluded Heshy Jacobs, "is that if Klal Yisrael [Jewry] is unified, we would also be able to see miracles in many other places."

That is what needs to happen on Yom Kippur. If we come to the realization that we're all in this together, then we will be *zocheh* to וְנִסְלַח לְכָל עֲדַת בְּנֵי יִשְׂרָאֵל וְלַגֵּר הַגָּר בְּתוֹכָם כִּי לְכָל הָעָם בִּשְׁגָגָה.

The War on Rote

Have you ever noticed that the president of the United States will often begin his annual address to the joint session of Congress with the words, "The state of the union is robust, vibrant, or strong" — only to go on to describe the various challenges facing the country, some of which make the country seem vulnerable and weak?

Interestingly, the state of Klal Yisrael today can be described in the very same terms.

In certain ways, our generation has risen to higher levels than those preceding ours. We may be more *medakdek* (scrupulous) in mitzvah observance. We have more *shiurim*, with more people learning than perhaps any time in Jewish history. The level of Jewish scholarship is mind-boggling. Perusing a *sefarim* store, you can find recent works on every topic imaginable. A two-volume set caught my eye on a recent visit to a *sefarim* store: הצ׳ק בהלכה, *The Check in Halachah*. A full two volumes just about the halachos governing checks!

Aside from the higher level of education and scholarship, you can now find a Minchah *minyan* in the business district of nearly every major city in the United States, with businessmen taking care not to miss a *minyan*.

On one hand, then, the "union" is robust, vibrant, and strong.

There's only one problem — a problem that leaves us vulnerable and weak: all of this observance often lacks *hartz*. There's no heart and soul invested into it. We "go through the motions," but with little or no passion for Yiddishkeit.

Rabbi Moshe Weinberger pointed out that there can be a marriage in which the duties are split up evenly, and there's perfect harmony in handling the family — but husband and wife do not love each other. It's not much of a marriage, because marriage without love is not a real, deep marriage. Similarly, Yiddishkeit that's lacking in passion, in feeling, in *hartz*, is a deficient Yiddishkeit.

> *Yiddishkeit that's lacking in passion, in feeling, in hartz, is a deficient Yiddishkeit.*

To be fair, this is not a new problem. Already in the times of the Nevi'im, Yeshayah warned the Jewish people of the devastating results of a Judaism lacking vitality:

וַיֹּאמֶר ה' יַעַן כִּי נִגַּשׁ הָעָם הַזֶּה בְּפִיו וּבִשְׂפָתָיו כִּבְּדוּנִי וְלִבּוֹ רִחַק מִמֶּנִּי וַתְּהִי יִרְאָתָם אֹתִי מִצְוַת אֲנָשִׁים מְלֻמָּדָה. לָכֵן הִנְנִי יוֹסִף לְהַפְלִיא אֶת הָעָם הַזֶּה הַפְלֵא וָפֶלֶא וְאָבְדָה חָכְמַת חֲכָמָיו וּבִינַת נְבֹנָיו תִּסְתַּתָּר

The Lord said: Inasmuch as this people has drawn close, with its mouth and with its lips it has honored Me, yet it has distanced its heart from Me — their fear of Me is like rote learning of human commands. Therefore, behold, I will continue to perform more wonders against this people — wonder upon wonder; the wisdom of its wise men will be lost and the understanding of its sages will become concealed (29:13-14).

Although Yeshayah HaNavi was describing the circumstances of his times, it is hard to deny that in our times, too, everything tends to feel like "old hat; same old, same old; day in, day out."

In fact, I would venture to say that this millennia-old problem is particularly exacerbated in our times, because Western society focuses so much on externals. Everyone has to go to the right schools, have the right résumé, wear the right clothes, drive the right car, and live in the right zip code. No one really cares what's behind the résumé or inside the suit; it's all about appearances. Unfortunately, that attitude has permeated our community as well. It's all about the right yeshivos and seminaries, the right neighborhoods, the right *mechutanim*, and the right *shidduch*.

I want to share a letter a Bais Yaakov girl sent to her principal. Before I share it, I will point out that this stinging indictment is one girl's opinion, but I think it is somewhat indicative of what many other children nowadays may be feeling:

> So your parents push you into the right Bais Yaakov. You go to the right camp and seminary. You build your résumé. Then your father buys you some cliché to marry. Then you have a daughter whom you push to the right school, the right camp, the right seminary, so that *she* can marry a cliché.
>
> And then we all die.

This girl is saying that she feels nothing for her Yiddishkeit. She feels like her life is a mechanized charade.

This girl is saying that she feels nothing for her Yiddishkeit. She feels like her life is a mechanized charade.

The problem of children leaving the fold is a complex one, with no one overriding cause. But at least part of the problem is that when children see their parents "going through the motions" in their Yiddishkeit, they don't see any reason to follow suit.

✑ Stuck in Elementary School

As much as this is a serious problem, it is nearly unavoidable.

The Alter of Kelm said that the best thing about our *chinuch* is that we make mitzvos second nature to our children, but the worst thing about our *chinuch* is that mitzvos become second nature.

We try to instill in our children that when they get up, they should say Modeh Ani, wash *netilas yadayim*, make their *berachos* — until it becomes second nature. The problem is that these habits remain no more than habits throughout our lives. More profoundly, says the Alter of Kelm, not only do the mitzvos we learn to perform as children remain the same, but our understanding of Yiddishkeit also remains the same as it was when we were 5, 6, or 7 years old.

Many people's appreciation of the fundamental principles of Yiddishkeit never graduates beyond the elementary-school level. The Alter comments that the reason why few adults get excited by the story of Yetzias Mitzrayim or Kerias Yam Suf is because their conceptualization of these events is stuck on the level of the song "Pharaoh in pajamas in the middle of the night" that they imbibed in their youth. That works perfectly fine when someone is 5 years old, but it's not going to excite us at 55.

A colleague told me that he knows a fellow who went to a frum doctor for a checkup. The doctor asked him to remove his shirt, and was surprised to see that his *tallis katan* hung about halfway down his chest.

"Why are you wearing such a short pair of *tzitzis*?" the doctor asked.

"These are the *tzitzis* my mother gave me," he proudly replied.

And just like he's wearing the same pair of *tzitzis*, he's wearing the same pair of Yetzias Mitzrayim, and the same understanding of Mattan Torah… everything remains the same, without any vigor, without any passion, without growth.

> *Just like he's wearing the same pair of tzitzis, he's wearing the same pair of Yetzias Mitzrayim, and the same understanding of Mattan Torah.*

✑ Who Is Near, and Who Is Distant?

This issue can be summed up by a humorous article I read during the 1990s, written by a man who lives in the Upper West Side of Manhattan and davens in Lincoln Square Synagogue. Each Friday night, the rav would ask him to take home a few fresh *baalei teshuvah* for the Shabbos *seudah*, so they could experience a Shabbos in a Jewish home.

"I'm what sociologists would call, 'The Tired Jewish Businessman,'" he wrote. "My fantasy on a Friday night is to daven as fast as I can, eat as fast as I can, jump under the covers, assume a fetal position, and conk out until Shacharis.

"And these *baalei teshuvah* want to sing *every niggun in the zemiros book!*"

Addressing the *baalei teshuvah* directly, he writes, "You see, it's not that we dislike you. It's that you make us feel uncomfortable. Because after 20, 30, 40 years of saying the same *Shemoneh Esrei* three times a day, when we are with you, we sense that perhaps our *Shemoneh Esreis* have become flat, routine, and mechanical, while yours is vital and exuberant."

Expressed more seriously, Rav Shimshon Pincus once pointed out an incredible Rashi in *Sefer Yeshayah*. The *pasuk* states: שִׁמְעוּ רְחוֹקִים אֲשֶׁר עָשִׂיתִי וּדְעוּ קְרוֹבִים גְּבֻרָתִי, *Hear, O faraway people, what I have done; and you who are close by, recognize My might* (33:13).

We would assume that the *rechokim*, the distant ones, refers to the *baalei teshuvah*, who were far from Hashem, and the *kerovim* are those who have always been close to Hashem — the so-called "FFBs."

Rashi says exactly the opposite. *Kerovim*, says Rashi, refers to the *baalei teshuvah* who have just recently grown close to Hashem for the first time.

The *baalei teshuvah* are not the *rechokim*. Unfortunately, it is often the *baalei teshuvah* who are truly close to Hashem, and those who grew up frum are often the distant ones, because they don't feel any special connection, any passion.

✺§ Trending in Society: Connection

I think that the problem of people who dress, act, and look frum, but feel no connection to Hashem, may explain two trends that have developed over the last few years.

One is the popularity of "Carlebach Minyanim" for Kabbalas Shabbos. For the uninitiated, a Carlebach Minyan sings every section of Kabbalas Shabbos. If an ordinary shul takes 45 minutes for Kabbalas Shabbos and Maariv, a Carlebach Minyan can take upwards of an hour and a half.

I have wondered: Why would someone subject themselves to such a long davening? Aren't they hungry?

Don't get me wrong, I'm a big Carlebach aficionado. I *love* Shlomo Carlebach's *niggunim.* I still recall when he came to Seattle, Washington when I was in sixth grade. And for those of you who still remember records, I took his *Haneshamah Lach* album to his concert for an autograph.

But much as I love Shlomo Carlebach's *niggunim,* I'm not interested in sitting in shul for an hour and a half on Friday night. What draws people to these *minyanim*?

I think the answer is that they want to *feel* something. They want a Yiddishkeit that's alive, that's vibrant.

The other phenomenon, which I find even more mind-boggling, is the annual pilgrimage to Uman for Rosh Hashanah. If you've never heard of it, Uman is a tiny village in the Ukraine. I'm not much of an expert on Ukrainian geography, but one thing I can tell you is that there is no direct flight from JFK to Uman. Nevertheless, people leave their wives and families and travel to a backward, nearly third-world village, living in primitive conditions so they can daven at the grave of Rav Nachman of Breslov on Rosh Hashanah.

So how many people do you think are doing this? A few hundred? A few thousand?

No. *Tens of thousands* of people are doing this each year.

Am I suggesting that we all go to Uman? I think I'm the last person on the planet who would go to Uman for Rosh Hashanah.

I'm overwhelmed just thinking about *thirty thousand* Yidden converging on a tiny village — with just one *mikveh!*

Why do they go?

They go because they want to be fully *alive*. Because they're tired of *mitzvas anashim melumadah*, of going through the motions without feeling anything. At least once a year, they feel that they are davening as a Yid should daven.

> *They're tired of mitzvas anashim melumadah, of going through the motions without feeling anything. At least once a year, they feel that they are davening as a Yid should daven.*

◄§ Torah, Torah, Torah... But Where Is Hashem?

What these people are experiencing is alluded to in the words of the navi Amos. Many of us are familiar with these words because they have been set to several moving *niggunim*: הַנֵּה יָמִים בָּאִים נְאֻם אֲדֹנָי ה' וְהִשְׁלַחְתִּי רָעָב בָּאָרֶץ לֹא רָעָב לַלֶּחֶם וְלֹא צָמָא לַמַּיִם כִּי אִם לִשְׁמֹעַ אֵת דִּבְרֵי ה'. Simply translated, these words read: *Behold, days are coming — the word of the Lord Hashem/Elokim — when I will send a hunger into the land; not a hunger for bread nor a thirst for water, but to hear the words of Hashem* (8:11).

But listen to the way Rav Moshe Valli, a disciple of the Ramchal, elucidates this *pasuk*. He begins by noting that the words לֶחֶם, *bread,* and מַיִם, *water,* are often used as allusions to the Torah. What this *pasuk* is saying, therefore, is that there will come a day when there will be a hunger for spirituality. But that hunger will not be for *lechem* or *mayim*, both of which represent Torah, *because there will be plenty of Torah being learned.* There will be tens of thousands completing cycles of Daf Yomi. There will be myriad *yungeleit* learning full time in *kollelim* throughout the world; in fact, there will be more people in yeshivos than ever before.

No, the hunger will not be for Torah.

What will the hunger and thirst be for?

כִּי אִם לִשְׁמֹעַ אֵת דִּבְרֵי ה' — *but to hear the words of Hashem.*

People will want to really hear about God!

Because with all of the Daf Yomi *shiurim,* with all of the *kollelim,* with all of the *sefarim* being published, where is the Ribbono Shel Olam?

That's the hunger experienced by those streaming to Carlebach Minyanim and to Uman. To hear about Hashem. They want to *feel* a connection to Hashem. And if this phenomenon was true in the times of Rav Moshe Valli, what would he say about our times?

So how do we attempt to solve the problem of apathy toward Yiddishkeit?

◦§ Pick Your Passion

I'd like to offer three methods that can help us rediscover a passion for Yiddishkeit, or maybe to discover it for the first time, for those who have never had it.

A fellow once wrote me an email describing himself — and I am not trying to be humorous — as an "avid ping-pong player."

He explained that for a long time, he was only an average player, but then he moved to L.A. and decided to take his game to a different level. He hired a Chinese coach, and now — by his own account — he is a "fantastic" ping-pong player.

He described how he approaches ping-pong nowadays: how he takes care of his paddle, making sure it never gets too hot or too cold; how he comes early for each class with his coach; how he videotapes each game and then watches the film so he can improve his stroke; how he learned that the slightest movement in his wrist can affect the spin and the speed of the ball. He even wrote about how his wife is sometimes embarrassed by him in public because he'll launch into a lengthy explanation of his ping-pong technique.

One day, he wrote, he asked himself, "What if I could bring the same passion to my learning?"

He decided to start collecting *divrei Torah* from all around the Web and file them in an organized fashion, and also, as soon as Shabbos was over, he took to writing down *divrei Torah* he heard over the course of Shabbos.

"Just like I show up early for my ping-pong lessons," he wrote, "I began to do the same for my learning and davening. And I make sure that I have access to the *daf* no matter where I go.

"I installed Daf Yomi audio at my computer at work, on my iPod, on my laptop at home, and I listen to Daf Yomi in my car as well.

"In short," he concludes, "I love the game of ping-pong. I enjoy it very much. I always look forward to my Tuesday night lesson, so I make sure to prepare accordingly. With that in mind, I bring the joy and passion to my Jewish life as well."

> *"Just like I show up early for my ping-pong lessons," he wrote, "I began to do the same for my learning and davening."*

The first piece of advice I'd like to offer to those feeling that Yiddishkeit has become rote: there are 613 Torah commandments, and myriad more that are *d'rabbanan* (rabbinically ordained). Pick *one* mitzvah, and make it your passion.

And your yardstick with which to measure whether you're being passionate enough about your mitzvah is to compare it to something else you're passionate about. If your other passion is for money, make sure that you treat your mitzvah as passionately as you treat earning a buck. You like football? You're able to watch football for nine hours on a Sunday? Bring that passion to one mitzvah. *ONE* mitzvah.

And that will become your ticket into Olam Haba.

✍ "You're a Size..."

I have a *talmid* who lives in Chile, and he travels to other countries in South America and Central America to do *kiruv*. He related that on a trip to Costa Rica, a fellow walked over to him and said, out of the blue, "You're a size 8."

"Huh?" was about the most sensible response he could muster.

"You're an 8," the fellow repeats.

"An 8 *what*?" my *talmid* asked.

"You're a size 8 pair of *tzitzis*."

It turns out that this man is willing to provide a pair of *tzitzis* to any Jew in Costa Rica who is willing to wear them. He's gotten so good at figuring out *tzitzis* sizes that he can just walk up to you and tell you your size, and he has spent thousands of dollars distributing *tzitzis*.

You want to hear the real shocker?

He's not religious himself. He decided that this is his mitzvah, and this will get him to Olam Haba.

Whether he's right or wrong about this mitzvah getting him into Gan Eden when he doesn't keep the rest of the Torah is not for me to decide, but he's exemplifying what I'm suggesting here: making one mitzvah your life's passion.

Now whether he's right or wrong about this mitzvah getting him into Gan Eden when he doesn't keep the rest of the Torah is not for me to decide, but he's exemplifying what I'm suggesting here: making one mitzvah your life's passion.

⤳ Grab the Moment

Another suggestion I have is a concept we see repeatedly in *Chazal*.

The Gemara in *Avodah Zarah* (10b; 17a; 18a) mentions three different instances in which a decadent or notoriously evil person did something incredibly good, and bought their way into Olam Haba in that one moment. Regarding each instance, relates the Gemara, Rebbi, Rabbeinu HaKadosh, editor of the Mishnayos, cried and said, "There are some who earn their way into the World to Come in one instant, and some who have to work for many years to earn it."

For example: the Gemara (17a) relates that R' Chanina ben Teradyon was sentenced to death by the Roman government for teaching Torah. As we read in the Yom Kippur Mussaf, he was executed by being burned with the Sefer Torah from which he had been caught teaching wrapped around him. The sadistic Romans weren't satisfied with merely watching him burn. They had the executioner wrap his body in wool soaked in water so the fire wouldn't consume his body too quickly; they wanted to watch him suffer.

While watching him die, the executioner suddenly asked, "If I make the fire hotter and remove the wet wool from your body so that you burn quickly, will you take me with you into Olam Haba?"

R' Chanina answered that he would.

"Swear to me," the executioner said.

R' Chanina swore.

The executioner made the fire hotter and removed the wool — and then, suddenly, he too jumped into the fire and died along with R' Chanina. A *bas kol* (Heavenly voice) then rang out, saying: "R' Chanina and the executioner are accepted into Olam Haba."

This was one of the instances in which Rabbeinu HaKadosh cried, says the Gemara, because the executioner had succeeded in securing for himself a place in Olam Haba through that one instantaneous action, rather than toiling on it for years.

Rav Chaim Shmuelevitz finds Rebbi's reaction puzzling. What was he crying about? That he had to work hard for his Olam Haba, and the executioner had it easy? Was he regretting his lifelong work to build up his merits?

He was crying, answers Rav Chaim Shmuelevitz, because he saw what a person can accomplish with *one moment* when an opportunity presents itself. And how many opportune moments do we have in our lives? But we let those moments pass.

Rav Chaim Shmuelevitz then offers his advice for dealing

with the problem of mitzvos becoming humdrum and rote: When an opportunity to do something great presents itself, *don't let it pass*. Take advantage of that moment.

❧ What Was Mordechai's Rush?

Chazal realized how vital it is to take advantage of the moment when opportunity strikes, lest that moment pass.

When Haman passed his decree to kill all the Jews in the world, Mordechai asked Esther to plead with Achashveirosh to annul the decree. Esther replied that if he would gather all the Jews in Shushan and have them fast for three days, she would visit Achashveirosh. Mordechai immediately declared the fast, and we know the rest of the story.

What isn't spelled out clearly in the Megillah is the exact timing of these fast days. Haman passed his decree on the 13th day of Nissan, and Mordechai declared an immediate three-day fast. In effect, then, he ruled that no Jew in Shushan would eat matzah on the first night of Pesach!

The question practically begs to be asked: What was the rush? Haman's decree wasn't going to take effect until Adar of the following year. Why not wait until after Pesach to declare the three-day fast?

Had you been the *gadol hador*, wouldn't you have preferred to have one more *zechus* — the merit of eating matzah on Pesach — and then begin the fast?

> *Mordechai knew that human nature is such that if you don't grab the moment, you will end up doing nothing. When inspiration strikes, you act on it without delay.*

Mordechai HaTzaddik ruled the opposite. He ruled that the fast should start immediately.

Why?

Because Mordechai knew that human nature is such that if you don't grab the moment, you will end up doing nothing. When inspiration strikes, you act on it without delay.

~§ The Infomercial Principle

When I spoke at a *shiur* about the concept of acting immediately on inspiration, a fellow came over to me afterward to share a fascinating example of how the corporate world utilizes this concept to their advantage.

This man produces infomercials for a living. If you have ever noticed, most infomercials will promise a discounted price for those who call within 20 minutes.

Why 20 minutes?

Does your money expire after 20 minutes?

The companies know, this fellow revealed, that anyone who doesn't buy the product immediately after watching the infomercial won't buy it at all.

They don't want to allow you to let that moment pass, so they make it seem as though it's now or never.

We must apply that rule to our Yiddishkeit.

Have you ever been to a funeral, and been inspired by the eulogies? Do you remember thinking as you walked out, "Wow, what a special person. I would want to emulate him."

What happened afterward? In all likelihood, you went right back to work or shopping, and you forgot all about it.

Have you ever read a biography and been inspired to do something great? What did you do afterward? Did you just put in on your night table, shut the lamp, and go to sleep?

Don't let those moments of inspiration pass. Use them to catapult you into immediate action.

A *baal teshuvah* of recent vintage came to introduce himself to me in yeshivah one day. After becoming frum, he decided to move from Owing Mills, Maryland to Baltimore so he could daven with a *minyan* each day of the week.

"I went to the recent *Siyum HaShas*," he related, "and as I sat there, I thought to myself, *This was a waste of time. The dancing and singing is nice, but I don't understand much of what they are saying — and that's even during the English speeches.*

"I was sitting on the 45-yard-line, looking right at you. You said this story of the 70-year-old who moved to Israel, and he decided to learn Shas."

"Then suddenly," he continued, "you got up to speak. I was sitting on the 45-yard-line, looking right at you. You said this story of the 70-year-old who moved to Israel, and he decided to learn *Shas* (see pg. 179).

"You know what I decided then and there? I'm 69 years old. I decided right then that I would retire at 70, and I too would sit and learn and try to finish *Shas*."

☙ When Hashem Talks to You

The *pasuk* in *Parashas Ki Savo* states: אֶת ה׳ הֶאֱמַרְתָּ הַיּוֹם לִהְיוֹת לְךָ לֵאלֹקִים וְלָלֶכֶת בִּדְרָכָיו וְלִשְׁמֹר חֻקָּיו וּמִצְוֹתָיו וּמִשְׁפָּטָיו וְלִשְׁמֹעַ בְּקֹלוֹ, *You have distinguished Hashem today to be a God for you, and to walk in His ways, and to observe His decrees, His commandments, and His statutes, and to hearken to His voice (Devarim 26:17).*

If the Torah already commanded us to walk in Hashem's ways, to observe His decrees, His commandments, and His statutes, what is this *pasuk* instructing us to do when it adds the words: וְלִשְׁמֹעַ בְּקֹלוֹ, *and to hearken to His voice?*

The words וְלִשְׁמֹעַ בְּקֹלוֹ mean that every once in a while, God talks to us. In fact, those were the very words chosen by the *baal teshuvah* from Owing Mills sitting at the 45-yard-line at the *Siyum HaShas*: "God was talking to me."

How can we capture those moments when Hashem talks to us?

Go to a stationary store and buy a little notebook, or make a new folder on your smartphone, and call it the "Book of Hisorerus." Write down every time something inspiring happens to you — and then make that a feature of your Shabbos meal. Let each person say something that inspired them. If everyone knows that they'll have to say something on Shabbos, they'll be more aware of such moments as they happen during the week, and it will build on itself.

More particularly, we can focus on *hashgachah pratis* (Divine Providence), the moments in life when we see Hakadosh Baruch Hu guiding our lives in a very specific manner.

After mentioning this idea at a *shiur* in a certain city, I was walking back to my car when a woman rolled down her window and waved a notebook at me. "Rabbi," she said, "this is my second *hashgachah pratis* notebook."

You know what the upshot of this is going to be? Hashem will become real to you again. Because that, in essence, is our problem — we don't think of Him as real. Once He is real to us, we'll feel more inspired.

Rav Yaakov Kamenetsky would tell a story about when they were once playing *kugelach* (a game similar to jacks) during recess back in Lita, and one boy lost his set of *kugelach*. He made a deal with his friend: he would trade half of his Olam Haba for his friend's *kugelach*.

Rav Yaakov related that their rebbi chastised this boy for having traded something so eternal for something meaningless. But Rav Yaakov himself noticed the good in this story — Olam Haba was *real* to these children. It was a commodity that could be traded.

> *But Rav Yaakov himself noticed the good in this story — Olam Haba was real to these children. It was a commodity that could be traded*

We need to get back to those days, when Olam Haba, and the Ribbono Shel Olam, are real to us. Keeping this notebook will help us rediscover Him, so our *tefillos* will be full of life, as we will feel as though we are truly talking to Hashem.

❧ The One Percenters

My final advice for those who feel alienated from their Yiddishkeit is to start working with unaffiliated Jews.

Nowadays, it's not too hard to find Jews who would like to know more about their heritage; there are several organizations you can turn to for names.

Working with the unaffiliated will help reinvigorate your Yiddishkeit in two ways.

On one hand, you'll be forced to reexamine all that you've learned on a more mature level. When a secular, adult Jew asks you about tefillin, or Shabbos, or matzah, or *lulav*, or anything else that you do out of rote, you'll be forced to learn about it so you can answer his questions. Learning about these concepts as an adult will make them more profound.

But working with unaffiliated Jews will help in another way: it will give you insight into the way the other half — or perhaps the other 99 percent is more accurate — lives. We'll see what a life without Torah is like, and we'll see how lucky we are. Because Torah is like everything else in life — our good health, our parents, our children, our spouses; we tend to take things for granted, not appreciating what we have unless we are forced to see what it's like without them.

We don't appreciate what it means to have healthy legs unless we see someone who has lost one, and Yiddishkeit is much the same.

There's an organization in New Jersey that takes irreligious Jewish students from Rutgers University and brings them to frum families for Shabbos.

Listen to letters they wrote, describing how they look at us and at our lives:

"I enjoyed [Shabbos] so much, because turning off technology allows me to connect with my inner thoughts and feelings, and just be real with the people I'm with. It forced me to relax and not worry about the incoming emails or my future plans, and it allowed me to be in the moment."

Shabbos. What does it mean to us? *Nu*, another Shabbos, and another Shabbos… Do we stop to think about what it does for us? When the Ribbono Shel Olam called Shabbos a *matanah*, a gift, He knew what He was talking about. These students saw that clearly.

Another example: I always wondered what it was like for a girl who grew up in secular society to daven from behind a *mechitzah* for the first time. Here's what a college girl wrote about it. "I enjoyed the separation between the men and women in the service. I found the separation (I forget what it's called) to help me be more introspective. It was very comfortable to sit among women, but to know that we're praying along with the men."

> *"I found the separation (I forget what it's called) to help me be more introspective. It was very comfortable to sit among women, but to know that we're praying along with the men."*

And how about the reaction to frum people's *hachnasas orchim*? "It's amazing how people just open up their homes and offer you massive amounts of food, even if they don't know you."

Then there's their reaction to the prohibition of *lashon hara*. "On Friday night you spoke about *lashon hara*. This had a profound impact on me. Now I really take into consideration what I say. I always knew that speech was important, and that it had impact on people, but I did not realize how much it reflects on me."

Do we tend to think about *lashon hara* as a gift? If you've ever sat on a train and heard coworkers gossiping about their office, with no consideration for other people's feelings, you would start to notice what a gift it is. We have an *issur* called *lashon hara*. Yes, we slip on occasion, but what a *glik*, what a fortune it is to know that we're generally aware of our words.

Finally, you'll be exposed to how secular people react to frum children. Most secular students come from homes with 1.9 children and a dog. What do they think when they go to a frum house and see six, eight, or ten kids in action?

> *Most secular students come from homes with 1.9 children and a dog. What do they think when they go to a frum house and see six, eight, or ten kids in action?*

"The children amazed us. They all gave each other so much attention in such a pleasant way. Eight-year-old Rivky bathed 2-year-old Malka, after which 4-year-old Nachum Meir and 10-year-old Talya dressed her for Shabbos."

These recollections are *our lives*. By inviting non-frum people into our lives, we might start to notice what a gift the Torah is to the one-percenters who keep it.

✥ Daily Reminders

Chazal understood human nature, and they instituted a long set of *berachos* each morning to remind us to be thankful for the gifts that we might otherwise take for granted.

We begin with a *berachah* on something we are quite likely to overlook — the gift of human intelligence: בָּרוּךְ אַתָּה ה׳... אֲשֶׁר נָתַן לַשֶּׂכְוִי בִינָה לְהַבְחִין בֵּין יוֹם וּבֵין לָיְלָה.

When you get up tomorrow morning and you know what day of the week it is, thank Hashem for the basic intelligence He has given you. Not everyone knows what day it is when they rise in the morning. I knew a Yid who was intelligent and sharp, and he used his wisdom to become a *talmid chacham* as well as to build considerable wealth. Tragically, he became senile. Each night he would tell his wife, "Let's make Havdalah."

If you know what day it is, you're already ahead of the game, and you have to thank Hashem for that.

If you can open up your eyes and see, don't take it for granted: פּוֹקֵחַ עִוְרִים.

You are able to swing your legs over the side of the bed and put them on the floor? הַמֵּכִין מִצְעֲדֵי גָבֶר.

But there's another *berachah* we say that's not part of this series: The *berachah* on the opportunities Hashem gave us, specifically as Yidden, as people who have a purpose in life, who know why they get out of bed in the morning. Where's that *berachah*?

,אֲשֶׁר בָּחַר בָּנוּ מִכָּל הָעַמִּים, וְנָתַן לָנוּ אֶת תּוֹרָתוֹ. בָּרוּךְ אַתָּה ה' נוֹתֵן הַתּוֹרָה

"Who chose us from among the nations, and gave us the Torah. Blessed are You, Hashem, Giver of the Torah."

◈§ What a Siddur Means to a Novice

I want to share one last letter — this one from a woman who runs an organization called "Operation Open Curtain." This organization attempts to disseminate Torah and Judaism among the 250,000 Jews who continue to live in Russia more than two decades after the Iron Curtain parted.

Operation Open Curtain operates a summer camp, a Bais Yaakov, a day school, a yeshivah, and a *kollel*. Girls who graduate the Bais Yaakov are invited to the United States, where they can attend seminary and Touro College free of charge to earn a degree.

The letter I received was from a woman who has been running programs in Russia for over twenty years. She wrote that Rav Shmuel Kamenetsky has visited their summer camp many times, and at the end of each visit, the campers were granted an opportunity to receive a *berachah* from him and ask him questions.

"I'm leaving this camp in a week and a half," one girl said. "Here I keep *kashrus* and Shabbos and I dress in skirts, make *berachos*, and try to emulate my counselor. But in 10 days, I'll be home, and none of this is possible. What do I hold onto? What one mitzvah should I commit to doing?"

"You should daven," Rav Shmuel replied. "Daven every day. It doesn't matter when, it doesn't matter what you say. But make sure to connect to Hashem every day."

The letter-writer continues: "At the end of camp, a few of the girls were standing outside my room, asking me for permission to take home a *siddur*, so that they could daven 'as the *tzaddik* said.'

"I wish I could capture some of the excitement I saw on their

"I wish I could capture some of the excitement I saw on their faces when I gave them their siddurim. I wish I could treasure my siddur as much as they treasure theirs."

faces when I gave them their *siddurim*. I wish I could treasure my *siddur* as much as they treasure theirs. We gave them a lot of good prizes at the end of the camp, but nothing excited them as much as having their own *siddur*."

A couple of weeks after the summer camp in Russia ended, this woman traveled to Eretz Yisrael and went to daven at the Kosel HaMaaravi. "It's at night," she writes, "and there are hundreds of people davening. This is my thought: 'They don't know about my campers. They don't realize what they have, and they don't appreciate it.' "

And neither do we.

Combating *mitzvos anashim melumadah* is about learning to appreciate the spiritual bounty that we have. If we come to realize the value of a Torah that gives us direction, that gives us life, then our davening will be different, our mitzvos will be different, and we will be *zocheh* to be written and signed in the Book of Life.

Legacy of Strength

Remember the very first writing assignment you received year after year throughout elementary school and perhaps even high school? In what became a near cliché, each English teacher would walk in on that first day and say, "Write an essay on the topic of: 'What I did during summer vacation.'"

One year, after returning from a stint as the scholar-in-residence at a group tour for frum Jews in Italy, I felt compelled to share an incredible insight into the Jewish people that I had gleaned during preparation for that job and during the actual tour.

My position as scholar-in-residence was not that of a historian who would explain the significance of each site to the group, but to deliver *shiurim* and lectures that were relevant to Jewish life in Italy. I spent approximately four months preparing for the trip, because I had known very little about Italian Jewry before then. What I learned in the course of those four months, and during the trip itself, about the Jews of Italy can help prepare us for the Yomim Nora'im, and, in fact, help us to become better Jews throughout the year.

✑ The Longest-Standing Jewish Community

The Jewish community in Italy dates back many, many centuries. Yehudah HaMaccabi sent the initial group of Jews to Rome in the year 165 BCE, and the Jews of Italy take pride in their status as the longest-standing Jewish community in the world. There are Jewish communities that were in their homelands before 165 BCE, but whereas other communities were established, abandoned, and subsequently reestablished in later times, Italian Jewry has remained in their home country for nearly 2,200 consecutive years.

The Golden Years of Italian Jewry were the 1500-1600s. During that era, for instance, the city of Venice was the hub of *sefarim* publication for the entire world, as we can deduce from the title pages of numerous old *sefarim* that list וניציא as the city of publication.

The Italian Jewish community swelled during the early 1500s due to an event with which we are all familiar. The expulsion from Spain and the subsequent Inquisition, which were originally set into law in 1492, forced Jews to either convert to Christianity or leave all their possessions behind and resettle outside the area controlled by the Spanish Kingdom. Many Jews who chose to leave resettled in Italy.

Many other Jews remained in Spain and converted to Christianity on the outside, but secretively continued to keep as much of the Torah as possible. Such Jews are called *Anusim* (the forced ones) in our literature, as opposed to the term *Marranos*, the Spanish term that means *"pigs."*

In preparation for my trip, I discovered something incredible while investigating the halachic status of these Jews: The fact that they did not seem to pass the *nisayon* (challenge), choosing to convert rather than forfeit their possessions and leave Spain, does not mean that these Jews were lacking in *mesirus nefesh*. On the contrary, their willingness to forgo human comfort and keep halachah under the threat of being burned at the stake if caught speaks of colossal willpower.

There were Jews who did not eat *chametz* (leaven) during the *entire year*, claiming that it disagreed with their stomachs, just so they would have an excuse not to eat *chametz* on Pesach. Imagine going through an entire year without bread, cake, or pasta — in Italy, no less!

There were Jews who performed *bris milah* on themselves — without anesthesia — because they were afraid that the *mohelim* who offered their services were actually Inquisition spies.

> *Imagine going through an entire year without bread, cake, or pasta — in Italy, no less!*

On Rosh Hashanah, some *Anusim* would go out to caves in the mountains, where they could blow shofar without being detected. The Mishnayos in Rosh Hashanah discuss the case of a person who blows shofar into a pit or a cave. I had always wondered why someone would do such a thing, until I read about the efforts of the *Anusim* in Spain.

I remind you that these were the Jews who *did not* pass the test; they converted to Christianity. Nevertheless, they risked their lives each day to live as Jews as much as humanly possible.

✑ Ghetto Life

In Italy, we visited the ghettos in which the Jews who had left Spain were confined. They lived under the most oppressive conditions in those ghettos; 4,000 Jews were crammed into an area of just several acres (approximately the size of five football fields). Privacy was non-existent.

All they had to do to move out of those ghettos was to convert. But they didn't.

We visited the ghetto in Rome, where each Shabbos, after they finished davening, the Jews were forced to walk across the street to a "conversion church," where a priest harangued and harassed them about their insistence on clinging to their faith. The Jews of Rome created a custom of placing candle wax into their ears so they wouldn't hear the vile words of the preachers.

There is another *minhag* that developed in Rome, and it is still kept by the Roman Jewish community until today: there are no *derashos* by rabbanim on Shabbos morning, lest they evoke memories of those horrible sermons they had to listen to back then.

No *derashos* at all. Which to some might seem like a reason to relocate and do as the Roman [Jews] do…

Carved into that conversion church, there is a *pasuk* they stole from Yeshayah HaNavi (65:2). The prophet quotes Hashem as saying: פֵּרַשְׂתִּי יָדַי כָּל הַיּוֹם אֶל עַם סוֹרֵר הַהֹלְכִים הַדֶּרֶךְ לֹא טוֹב אַחַר מַחְשְׁבֹתֵיהֶם, I *stretched out My hands all day to a straying people, who walk the road that is not good, following after their own thoughts.* Imagine having to see that day after day, and having the church preach that they are welcoming you, the "straying" nation.

◆§ Jewish Tenacity: A Canard?

One of the works I read in preparation for my trip was a book about Italian Jewry titled *The Most Tenacious of Minorities* by Sarah Regeur, a Brooklyn College professor of Jewish History.

In truth, however, the title *The Most Tenacious of Minorities* can be applied not only to Italian Jews, but to all Jews. You and I are also among *The Most Tenacious of Minorities*.

Rav Elyah Lopian has an essay about the perception the nations of the world have of the Jewish people, which, as you may know, is less than flattering. The stereotypical Jew is pushy, aggressive, assertive, and money-hungry. Someone told me that during his long career working with non-Jews, he heard these descriptions from his colleagues many times, although each time they would say, "But you're different."

Is their perception of Jews always acting impatiently and trying to get ahead a pure canard, some falsified perception that has been foisted upon the world by anti-Semites? Or is there perhaps some truth to it?

Rav Elyah Lopian writes something that might surprise you: It's true!

We are aggressive and assertive. But those are not negative traits, he adds, they are positive traits.

If you study nature, says Rav Elyah, you'll notice that Hashem gave each creature the tools it needs to survive. Nowadays, science keeps discovering deeper secrets of Creation, and more of these tools are being revealed each year. They have discovered, for instance, that certain trees will emit odors that attract bees, to ensure that they are pollinated well. In the animal world, these tools are even more dramatic. Hashem gave the skunk the ability to ward off would-be attackers with a scent alone. Porcupines can shoot their quills into their enemies, and chameleons can change colors in order to protect themselves.

Is their perception of Jews always acting impatiently and trying to get ahead a pure canard, some falsified perception that has been foisted upon the world by anti-Semites? Or is there perhaps some truth to it?

The rule that holds true for the plant world and the animal world holds true for us as well. Hashem knew that the Jewish people would spend their years in *galus* under the boot of oppressive governments that would try to forcibly convert or eradicate them. He therefore invested us with survival tools. Those tools, says Rav Elyah, are the national traits that set us apart from the other nations.

The *pasuk* describes us, for instance, as an עַם קְשֵׁה עוֹרֶף, a stubborn people.

Is that good, or bad?

It's good, says Rav Elyah. Had we not been stubborn, we would have succumbed to the pressure and converted to other religions centuries ago.

You know what else we are? We are a *chutzpadik* people. We are an audacious and impudent nation.

Is this a *chisaron*, a negative trait? On the contrary, the

Midrash (*Shemos Rabbah* 42:9) states that there are three entities that are impudent, and the most impudent among the nations is Klal Yisrael. The Midrash adds, however, that this is not meant as a pejorative; the impudence is a badge of honor. It's what has enabled us to stand up to the nations of the world and say, "If you don't allow me to learn Torah, *kill me*."

This is what gave Chanania, Mishael, and Azariah the strength to stand up to the Babylonian king Nevuchadnetzar, a man who makes today's despots seem like boy scouts, and tell him that if he would not allow them to serve Hashem, he was no better than a dog. Of course, this came at the price of being thrown into a fire, but they survived as a result of their strength of character, the *chutzpah* they saved for holy purposes.

That spirit carried forth to the Jews of Spain and Italy, to those living under communist rule in Russia or Nazi guards in German concentration camps, among the numerous other oppressive nations we've survived and outlived.

⊷ The Danger of Grit

Nevertheless, the very traits that helped us survive in these oppressive societies — the strength and power, the grit and fortitude — without the Torah through which we are meant to channel them, make us pushy, aggressive, and overbearing. When we are described in those terms by the nations of the world in a derogatory sense, they may not be wrong, because they may be viewing the way those traits are expressed by Jews who are not refined by the Torah.

> *The very traits that helped us survive... without the Torah through which we are meant to channel them, make us pushy, aggressive, and overbearing.*

Hashem imbued Jews with an insatiable thirst, for instance. Without that thirst, you cannot master Torah. If you don't use that thirst to accumulate Torah, however, you may use it for something else, such as accumulating material wealth — thus the stereotype of the money-hungry Jew.

✍ An Atrophied Middah

While for nearly 2,000 years, Jews have had to employ many of our tough *middos* in order to survive, in the last half-century we haven't had to engage them nearly as much. We haven't had to make the choice of "convert or die," and we haven't even had to make the choice of going to work on Shabbos or losing our jobs, as many Jews did in the early 20th century in the United States.

A *middah* is like a muscle; when you don't use it, it atrophies. The relatively cushy existence we've been handed by the Ribbono Shel Olam over the last 50 or 60 years has left the *middah* of *gevurah* that our parents or grandparents had to exercise throughout their lives in disuse.

Today, we once again face challenges that call for *gevurah*, and we have to learn to reawaken the dormant *middah* to pass those challenges.

As an example: After we concluded our trip to Italy, my wife and I visited Eretz Yisrael for four days.

On Shabbos, I davened in a small shul in a Yerushalayim neighborhood. It was *Parashas Eikev*, and the two *gabba'im* approached me and asked if I would be willing to speak.

To be more accurate, one *gabbai* asked me to speak, and the other said: "Six minutes."

I felt like replying, "My warm-up pitches take six minutes."

Given the time limit, I went up and pointed out that in *Parashas Eikev*, the Torah tells the story of Moshe Rabbeinu descending from Har Sinai

> *The two gabba'im approached me and asked if I would be willing to speak. To be more accurate, one gabbai asked me to speak, and the other said: "Six minutes."*

and finding that Klal Yisrael worshiped the *Eigel* (Golden

Calf), and he immediately threw down the *Luchos* (Tablets) and smashed them to smithereens.

Was this action by Moshe Rabbeinu good or bad?

Actually, the case can be made that Moshe Rabbeinu's decision to destroy the *Luchos* was his crowning achievement. How do we know that? Because the last eight *pesukim* in the Torah, which we read on Simchas Torah, are Hashem's *hesped*, His epitaph, for Moshe Rabbeinu. The very last of those *pesukim* is: וּלְכֹל הַיָּד הַחֲזָקָה וּלְכֹל הַמּוֹרָא הַגָּדוֹל אֲשֶׁר עָשָׂה מֹשֶׁה לְעֵינֵי כָּל יִשְׂרָאֵל, *And by all the strong hand and awesome power that Moshe performed before the eyes of all Israel (Devarim* 34:12). Rashi states that each part of this verse refers to one of Moshe Rabbeinu's amazing accomplishments: וּלְכֹל הַיָּד הַחֲזָקָה refers to his bringing the Torah down from the Heavens to the Jewish people, and וּלְכֹל הַמּוֹרָא הַגָּדוֹל alludes to the miracles he performed in the Wilderness. But what was the apex, what was Moshe's greatest achievement? If I asked you to stop reading and write down his finest moment, I doubt many of you would guess the answer.

Rashi says that the very last words in the Torah, the words that describe Moshe's ultimate achievement — אֲשֶׁר עָשָׂה מֹשֶׁה לְעֵינֵי כָּל יִשְׂרָאֵל — refer to Moshe's "heart being uplifted to break the *Luchos* in front of the eyes of the Jewish people."

Rashi adds that Hashem thanked Moshe for that deed, as alluded to in the words אֲשֶׁר שִׁבַּרְתָּ, *that you broke (Shemos* 34:1), which is a contraction of the words יִישַׁר כֹּחֲךָ שֶׁשִּׁבַּרְתָּ, *thank you for breaking [the Luchos].*

Why was breaking the *Luchos* Moshe's crowning glory? Because Moshe Rabbeinu nearly gave his life for those *Luchos.* He didn't eat or drink for 40 days while he was in the Heavens learning the Torah, and he had to battle the heavenly angels to receive them. Human nature is such that when we invest and put all our energy into something, we don't walk away from it so fast.

If we were the ones descending that mountain after 40 days of self-sacrifice, would we have broken those *Luchos*? Or would we have said, "Sorry fellas, you can't have these now. I'm putting them away until you do *teshuvah*." Who would have had the strength to smash something for which they sacrificed so much?

Moshe overcame the natural human tendency to want to preserve one's hard work, and he said, "If it's not right, then I'll just walk away."

That takes incredible *gevurah*.

> *Moshe overcame the natural human tendency to want to preserve one's hard work, and he said, "If it's not right, then I'll just walk away."*

◈§ Walking Away From an Error

Rav Gifter expressed a similar thought regarding the following Gemara: Shimon HaAmsuni (some say it was Nechemia HaAmsuni), a Tanna, posited that each *pasuk* that contains the word אֶת could have been written without that word. He spent many years expounding every occurrence of אֶת in the Torah. To give you an idea of how much work that is, just the first *pasuk* in the Torah has two occurrences: בְּרֵאשִׁית בָּרָא אֱלֹהִים אֵת הַשָּׁמַיִם וְאֵת הָאָרֶץ!

We don't know how he expounded each one of the approximately 4,000 appearances of אֶת in the Torah. But as an example, he deduced from the seemingly extraneous word אֶת in the verse: כַּבֵּד אֶת אָבִיךָ, *honor thy father* (*Shemos* 20:12) that it is a requirement to honor older siblings as well.

Shimon HaAmsuni continued with this approach until he reached the verse: אֶת ה' אֱלֹקֶיךָ תִּירָא, *You shall be in awe of Hashem, your God* (*Devarim* 6:13). Suddenly, he stopped and said, "There can't be another being that we are required to be in awe of alongside Hashem. It must be that my entire thesis was wrong; the word אֶת in the Torah cannot always be expounded."

Eventually, says the Gemara, R' Akiva found a *derashah* for that אֶת as well: אֶת ה' אֱלֹקֶיךָ תִּירָא לְרַבּוֹת תַּלְמִידֵי חֲכָמִים. This verse is teaching us that we are required to be in awe of *talmidei chachamim* as a corollary of our awe of Hashem.

Asks Rav Gifter: What did R' Akiva see that Shimon HaAmsuni, who had spent all those years expounding every verse containing את,did not? Why couldn't Shimon HaAmsuni come to the same conclusion as R' Akiva?

Says Rav Gifter: You know what R' Akiva saw? He saw Shimon HaAmsuni! He saw a man who gave his lifeblood to a thesis, working night and day to expound each את, yet when he found a single occurrence that he couldn't resolve, he was prepared to walk away from it.

> *Says Rav Gifter: You know what R' Akiva saw? He saw Shimon HaAmsuni!*

Imagine a rosh yeshivah who spends his life developing a certain approach to every *machlokes* in the Gemara, and then he reaches one that doesn't work. He's already given *shiur* to decades' worth of *talmidim*, he's published *sefarim* based on his approach — and suddenly he has to retract.

The Gemara says that Shimon HaAmsuni's students actually asked him, "What will happen to all the *derashos* of the word את that you expounded until this point?"

"כְּשֵׁם שֶׁקִּבַּלְתִּי שָׂכָר עַל הַדְּרִישָׁה, *just as I received reward for expounding those words*," he replied, "כָּךְ אֲקַבֵּל שָׂכָר עַל הַפְּרִישָׁה, *so will I receive reward for abandoning (my thesis)*."

When R' Akiva saw a person so committed to the truth that he was willing to admit that his life's work was without merit, he said, "This person is worthy of our awe. אֶת ה׳ אֱלֹקֶיךָ תִּירָא לְרַבּוֹת תַּלְמִידֵי חֲכָמִים."

It's very difficult to say that you're wrong. But that ability is a function of the *middah* of *gevurah*, the strength that is one of the hallmarks of the Jewish people.

ঙ্গ To Beach, or Not to Beach?

The day after I said this impromptu *vort* in that shul, a fellow walked up to me and said that he would like to share something with me.

"I'm from London," he began, "and each year I bring my family to Eretz Yisrael for vacation. One of our popular destinations each year was the beach. Until this year, I was able to avoid mixed swimming, because at the particular beach we frequent, there are several lifeguard stations, most of which have beach chairs in front of them, but one does not. Naturally, the other beach-goers congregate in front of the stations with beach chairs, leaving the one without beach chairs deserted. My family would go to that part of the beach, where we could enjoy the water without the spiritual danger of a mixed beach.

"This year, they added beach chairs in front of that station as well. When I noticed the new arrangement, I wondered what I should do. *There aren't **that** many women around,* I thought to myself. *Maybe we can come back here and swim.*

"Then, I heard your *derashah* about reviewing your own actions and deciding whether what you're doing is right or wrong. When I thought honestly about whether swimming on the now-mixed part of the beach was acceptable, I had to admit to myself that it wasn't — much to the chagrin of my family. My son was at your *derashah* as well, and he said, 'That's not what he meant!' But I know the truth."

This man had to exercise *gevurah* in reaching this decision. It's not the kind of strength that it takes to jump into a fire *al kiddush Hashem*, and perhaps not even the strength that it takes to give up your job in order to avoid desecrating Shabbos. But it's run-of-the-mill, every-day, garden-variety strength that we must all learn to exercise.

That has to become our goal during the Yomim Nora'im. We have to examine the various facets of our lives and ask ourselves honestly: Is this really right? Are the compromises we are making in our lives really acceptable?

Perhaps even things that our par-

> *We have to examine the various facets of our lives and ask ourselves honestly: Is this really right? Are the compromises we are making in our lives really acceptable?*

ents or grandparents did were not up to snuff, and we have to break with that part of our "inheritance."

⊷§ Mimicking Monkeys

Some questions can be tough to ask yourself: "Is my behavior in my workplace, among secular colleagues, acceptable for a frum person? Am I exposed to forms of media that I shouldn't be viewing or reading? Am I dressing appropriately for my station in life?"

These are hard questions to ask. We all hate change. It's hard to depart from behaviors that we have gotten used to. But we have no choice. We may just have to let go of things that may be comfortable and familiar.

Someone told me a fascinating *vort* on our custom to *"klap"* (strike) our fist onto our chests when we recite *Al Cheit*. The reason we strike our chest, specifically, is because the heart is the seat of desire, and those blows to our chest remind us that our sins were the result of weakness in curbing our desires.

But did you ever wonder why we strike with a closed fist? Why not bang with an open hand?

This person explained that in the olden times, if someone wanted to capture a monkey, he would dig a hole in the ground and put in sweet-smelling food. The monkey would smell the food, stick his open hand into the hole and grab hold of it. Since a closed hand is wider, however, when the monkey would try to pull his hand out, it would get stuck.

Fregt zich a kashya oif dem monkey: Open your fist! Let go of the food, and you'll be free!

The answer is that the monkey *can't* leave go. He keeps his fist closed tightly around the food, even if it means that he'll be captured, because he just can't relinquish that coveted food.

We may be more sophisticated than monkeys, but to some extent, the same holds true for us as well. We bang on our chests with a closed fist to remind ourselves of our unwillingness to let go of things that are dragging us down and causing us to sin in the first place.

✒ Move Your Goalposts

Mixed swimming may not be a challenge for most of us, but we all have our own challenges, and the key in life is to keep growing.

In *Michtav MeiEliyahu*, Rav Dessler has a famous section called *Kuntres HaBechirah*, in which he discusses at length the concept of *nekudas habechirah*. Without going into his entire analysis, the basic concept is about moving our own goalposts, and not being satisfied with mediocrity in our *avodas Hashem*.

An example: When I pass a McDonalds, I am not tempted to go inside. Hashem will not give me much *s'char* for not eating a cheeseburger, because I have no temptation to eat one.

Since it's not a challenge for me, it would be foolish of me to spend my life patting myself on the back for not eating at McDonalds. Rather than focus on my heroism in not eating cheeseburgers, I had better move my goalposts to find areas in life in which I *am* challenged, and embrace those challenges.

I know a fellow in the rabbinate who discussed with his congregants the possibility of making *aliyah*. One man explained — in all seriousness — why he would never, *ever* consider moving to Eretz Yisrael: "The bakery in my neighborhood makes the *best* jelly donuts in the world. I am not moving to Eretz Yisrael because I can't get my jelly donuts there."

Silly? Trivial?

Perhaps.

But we all have our own "jelly donuts." We can laugh at other people's foibles, but are we willing to give up the things that *we* find important?

What is your "jelly donut"?

We can laugh at other people's foibles, but are we willing to give up the things that we find important? What is your "jelly donut"?

ঙ্গ Which Goat Are You?

On Yom Kippur, Klal Yisrael would bring two identical goats, one of which was offered as a sacrifice in the Beis HaMikdash, and other was sent out to Azazel, a barren mountain with sharp peaks, and shoved off.

These two goats, writes Rav Samson Raphael Hirsch, represent different people. The goats look identical, but one will end up in the *Kodesh HaKodashim* as a *korban*, and the other will be sent to Azazel. Why? Because one is willing to make a sacrifice for Hashem, and the other isn't. The word עֲזָאזֵל, says Rav Hirsch, is comprised of the words עֵז אָזַל, the strength has left. The goat that goes to Azazel represents a person who isn't willing to employ the *middah* of *gevurah* to stop himself from acting inappropriately; life is too pleasant without the sacrifice. Where does that lead? In the case of the goat, it sends him off a cliff — and it can do the same for the human it represents.

ঙ্গ Parallel Declarations

Our final stop in Rome during that trip to Italy was at the Arch of Titus. Titus was the general who led the invasion of Yerushalayim and eventually destroyed the second Beis HaMikdash. The Arch, which famously depicts chained Jewish slaves carrying the Menorah from the Beis HaMikdash back to Rome, has the caption Judea Capta — Judah has been captured — running under the picture.

There is a well-known story about the Ponevezher Rav visiting that Arch, and I have an addendum to that story.

The Ponevezher Rav visited Rome on one of his fundraising trips for his yeshivah. He arrived in Rome on a rainy night, and he immediately phoned a student and requested that he take him to the Arch of Titus. "Can't this wait until the morning when the weather will be better?" the *talmid* asked.

"No," the Rav replied. "I want to go now."

When he arrived at the Arch, the Ponevezher Rav uttered these memorable words. "*Titus,*" he said, "*mir zeinen dah. Avu bist du?*"

"Titus, we are here. Where are you?"

If there was ever a question suffused with tragedy and yet filled with *gevurah* and hope, it was that question.

> *If there was ever a question suffused with tragedy and yet filled with gevurah and hope, it was that question.*

To understand the full context, you need to know a little bit about the Ponevezher Rav. He escaped Lithuania after losing his family and his yeshivah. When he arrived in Eretz Yisrael, he decided that come what may, he would rebuild both his family and his yeshivah. In the early 1940s, he bought a plot of land in Bnei Brak for a song, because Erwin Rommel *yemach shemo*, the German general, was leading his troops through North Africa at a rapid clip, en route to Eretz Yisrael. He was planning to fight the British in Egypt, and then move on to what was then known as Palestine to wipe out the hundreds of thousands of Jews who lived there at that time.

Someone asked the Ponevezher Rav, "How can you buy land at this time? Don't you realize that Rommel will be here within days?"

"I heard from the Chofetz Chaim," he replied, "that the verse: וּבְהַר צִיּוֹן תִּהְיֶה פְלֵיטָה, *On Mount Zion there will be refuge (Ovadiah 1:17)*, refers not only to the times of the Prophets, but to our times as well."

The Ponevezher Rav's proclamation at the Arch of Titus spoke not only to that horrendous tyrant, but to all those who followed him in attempting to eradicate the Jewish people.

You can still visit the Coliseum, the stadium in Rome funded by the gold and silver plundered from the Beis HaMikdash, and built by 95,000 Jewish slaves. The stadium sat 70,000 people. For the 500 years after it was built, spectators would gather daily to watch gladiators fight each other to the death. Do you know what the "halftime show" was? Under the stadium there were pits where they would keep lions that they would starve beforehand. They would take Jewish prisoners who were weak and infirm, place them in the middle of the Coliseum, and then release the lions. The floor of the Coliseum had to be filled with sand so the blood of those victims wouldn't pool all over the place.

This description doesn't come from our sources — we heard this from the non-Jewish tour guide who took us there. Standing there at the Coliseum, we felt the sudden urge to recite the *tefillah* of *Av HaRachamim* that we say before Mussaf on Shabbos. Particularly moving was the verse: כִּי דֹרֵשׁ דָּמִים אוֹתָם זָכָר לֹא שָׁכַח צַעֲקַת עֲנָוִים, *That the Avenger of blood has remembered them, He has not forgotten the cry of the humble* (*Tehillim* 9:13), because we realize that Hashem would eventually avenge the cries of those martyrs who died at the hands of the Romans.

Now, perhaps, you can understand the Ponevezher Rav's statement with a little more depth. For all the Romans' efforts to torture us, we're still here, and their once-powerful empire is gone. *Titus, mir zeinen dah. Avu bist du?*

> *For all the Romans' efforts to torture us, we're still here, and their once-powerful empire is gone.*

Here's an addendum to that story.

Before we left for Italy, I received a letter from an acquaintance named Sruly Jacob Eckstein. He sent me a copy of a speech he had delivered at the Bais Yaakov in Manchester, England, in which he told the girls the story of his mother, who had recently passed away. She had been a prisoner in the Birkenau concentration camp as a youngster, and her parents were killed in that camp. Some 60 years later, she returned to Birkenau. I quote verbatim from the letter:

> My mother goes into the room and relates so many stories. Then she stamps her feet on the ground and she screams, "Hitler — *avu bist du? Ich bin dah, mit mein kindt. Dus is mein nekamah tzu dir. Ich hub einiklach, du hust gornisht.*

Ich leb mit mein kindt, un du bist toit, a gornisht."

"Hitler — **where are you?** I'm here with my child. This is my revenge. I have grandchildren, and you have nothing. I'm here with my child, and you're dead, a nothing."

"Hitler — where are you? I'm here with my child. This is my revenge. I have grandchildren, and you have nothing."

It's chilling that this woman from Manchester chose the very same words as the Ponevezher Rav. He demanded, "Titus, *avu bist du,*" and she said, "Hitler, *avu bist du?*"

But the story doesn't end here.

Sruly Jacob Eckstein's mother continued on to the crematoria, where her parents were murdered. She wanted her son Sruly to say a *Kaddish* for them, but alas, there were no ten men to make a *minyan.*

Sixty years of pent-up emotion poured out of this woman. "I davened for three things," she sobbed. "That I should live; that I should marry a *ben Torah;* and that all of my children should be *shomer Shabbos.* Hashem answered all of my *tefillos.* Why does He not let me have *Kaddish* said for my parents?"

Lo and behold, related Mr. Eckstein in his letter, out of thin air, nine men suddenly appeared.

"I turned and said to my mother, 'Look Mammie, look! A *minyan.*'"

And now for the most incredible part of the story: Rather than jump at this opportunity, this feisty woman turned to the nine men and said, "Are you *shomer Shabbos*? My parents, who died *al kiddush Hashem,* were so careful with *shemiras Shabbos.* I can't have *Kaddish* said with a *minyan* of people who are not *shomer Shabbos.*"

Let's pause for a moment.

Halachically, was she permitted to have her son say *Kaddish* if some of the participants weren't *shomer Shabbos*? Yes.

Imagine this scene. Here she was, praying so forcefully that she be able to hear a *Kaddish* recited at the site of her parents' deaths, and she received her wish. So what if they're not all *shomer Shabbos*!

But if you think about it, it's not so shocking, because this is what this elderly woman stood for. All her life she kept to her ideals, remaining a *shomeres Shabbos* as her parents and grandparents had been before her, despite all the pain and tragedy she had endured.

The strength that had brought her to that moment wasn't something she was about to give up.

As it turned out, the nine men were all *shomer Shabbos*, and Sruly Jacob Eckstein was able to say *Kaddish* for his grandparents.

The same indomitable spirit that resided in the heart of the Ponevezher Rav also filled the heart of this regular Jewess from Manchester. And the *gevurah* that rested in their hearts rests in our hearts as well. We're Jews. We have *gevurah*, the strength and the fortitude, and we have grit, and *chutzpah*, and tenacity. We're Yidden.

It may feel dim for some of us, but it can be reawakened. And that is what we have to do this time of year. We have to ask ourselves where we are compromising and cutting corners in our obligations as Jews. And then we have to look ourselves in the eye and say, "I am a Jew, and *gevurah* is part of my national heritage. It's my spiritual DNA. I can stand up to my weakness and overcome it."

And then we have to look ourselves in the eye and say, "I am a Jew, and gevurah is part of my national heritage. It's my spiritual DNA. I can stand up to my weakness and overcome it."

And then we can make the tough decisions to change, because that is the legacy of the Jewish people: A Legacy of Strength.

When Hashem Says, "Hineni"

nyone who has davened in a yeshivah during Yomim
Nora'im knows that no matter how hard organizers
rearrange the furniture in the *beis midrash* to accommo-
date the influx of participants, seats are always at a premium.
Yeshivas Ponevezh in Bnei Brak is certainly no exception to the
rule; there too, organizers are hard-pressed to squeeze in all
those who want to join the yeshivah for the davening.

One year, an administrator came up with an idea: To alleviate
the overcrowding in the *beis midrash*, they would partition part
of the *ezras nashim* balcony and seat some *bachurim* upstairs.

When they came to discuss their plan with the Rosh Yeshivah,
Rav Eliezer Menachem Man Shach, he immediately rejected it.

"Which women can come to daven in yeshivah?" he asked,
by way of explanation. "Married women who have been
blessed with children cannot come. Who's in the *ezras nashim*?
Widows who have no one at home, older girls who haven't
found their *shidduch*, or women who haven't yet had children, and are davening for a child. We cannot eliminate these
women's seats *because the tefillos of the entire yeshivah rise to*

> *"We cannot eliminate these women's seats because the tefillos of the entire yeshivah rise to the heavens on the backs of the prayers of these women."*

the heavens on the backs of the prayers of these women."

The assertion that the *tefillos* emanating from a yeshivah *beis midrash* filled with *talmidei chachamim* and even *gedolei hador* can reach the heavens only on the merit of the women crying for salvation is astounding.

I would like to suggest a deeper understanding of what Rav Shach meant.

✧ Ten Corresponds to Ten

Perhaps the single most frightening *haftarah* we read each year is that of Shabbos Chazon, the Shabbos before Tishah B'Av. In this *haftarah*, Yeshayah HaNavi brings Hashem's warning to the Jewish people of his time, telling them that if they don't repent for their sins, they will suffer dire consequences. The worst possible consequence is: וּבְפָרְשְׂכֶם כַּפֵּיכֶם אַעְלִים עֵינַי מִכֶּם גַּם כִּי תַרְבּוּ תְפִלָּה אֵינֶנִּי שֹׁמֵעַ, *When you spread your hands [in prayer], I will hide My eyes from you; even if you were to intensify your prayer, I will not listen* (1:15).

What could be a worse threat to a Jew than that of Hashem ignoring his *tefillos*?

Yeshayah then enumerates ten steps we must take in order to repent so that Hashem will listen to us, the first nine of which are: רַחֲצוּ הִזַּכּוּ הָסִירוּ רֹעַ מַעַלְלֵיכֶם מִנֶּגֶד עֵינָי חִדְלוּ הָרֵעַ. לִמְדוּ הֵיטֵב דִּרְשׁוּ מִשְׁפָּט אַשְּׁרוּ חָמוֹץ שִׁפְטוּ יָתוֹם רִיבוּ אַלְמָנָה, *Wash yourselves, purify yourselves, remove the evil of your deeds from before My eyes, cease doing evil. Learn to do good, seek justice, vindicate the victim, render justice to the orphan, take up the grievance of the widow* (ibid. vv. 16-17).

If we take those nine steps, then Hashem promises to take the tenth with us: לְכוּ נָא וְנִוָּכְחָה יֹאמַר ה' אִם יִהְיוּ חֲטָאֵיכֶם כַּשָּׁנִים כַּשֶּׁלֶג יַלְבִּינוּ אִם יַאְדִּימוּ

בַּתּוֹלָע כַּצֶּמֶר יִהְיוּ, *Come, now, let us reason together, says Hashem.* *If your sins are like scarlet they will become white as snow; if they have become red as crimson, they will become [white] as wool* (v. 18).

Rashi comments, based on a Midrash in *Pesikta*, that the number of *ten* steps wasn't chosen arbitrarily by Yeshayah HaNavi. These ten steps correspond to the Aseres Yemei Teshuvah, the Ten Days of Repentance, with each step corresponding to a specific day. The one I would like to focus on is that of Erev Yom Kippur: רִיבוּ אַלְמָנָה, *take up the grievance of the widow.* Rashi explains that this means we should seek to help a widow with her legal battles, because she often won't be able to fend for herself. A widow will often be filled with a feeling of helplessness, a feeling that she has no standing in the community, and she may lose all hope. It's our responsibility to fend for her.

Interestingly, though, there is another Midrash (*Tanna DeVei Eliyahu*) that states that the Aseres Yemei Teshuvah correspond to the *Aseres HaDibros*.

The correlation between some of the days and their corresponding commandments are obvious. The first of the *Aseres HaDibros*, for instance, is *Anochi Hashem Elokecha* — recognizing God's Presence in this world. This commandment corresponds, appropriately, to the first day of Rosh Hashanah, on which we declare Hashem's sovereignty over the world.

When we talk about Erev Yom Kippur, however, the correlation is far more difficult to understand.

The correlation between the commandment of לֹא תַעֲנֶה בְרֵעֲךָ עֵד שָׁקֶר, *You shall not bear false witness against your fellow* (*Shemos* 20:13) and Erev Yom Kippur is perplexing enough. I might be going out on a limb here, but I don't imagine that a large percentage of readers have ever even imagined going into *beis din* to deliberately testify falsely against another Jew. Why is this commandment pertinent as we get ready for Yom Kippur?

Furthermore, the *Pesikta* teaches that we should be spending our time trying to fend for widows on Erev Yom Kippur, while the *Tanna DeVei Eliyahu* tells us that we should be repenting for testifying falsely. Can these two seemingly disparate goals be reconciled?

✌§ Creative Concern

In order to gain an understanding of how these two concepts are actually one and the same, we must first understand the precept of *rivu almanah* a bit deeper. It seems obvious that this must mean a lot more than merely paying attention to a widow who comes to our door to ask for help. It's hard to imagine that the height of a person's *teshuvah* is reached when he finds it in himself not to ignore the plight of a widow who has sought out his help.

What this actually means — as we've already seen from Rashi — is that we *seek out* the needs of a widow. We don't wait to respond *reactively* when a widow comes to us to ask for help; we think *proactively* about the struggles of those less fortunate than us, and seek to do whatever we can to alleviate their difficulties.

> *We don't wait to respond reactively when a widow comes to us to ask for help; we think proactively about the struggles of those less fortunate than us.*

It is our duty to think of all those who have been buffeted by the vagaries of life, and find creative ways to help them.

You want an example of *rivu almanah*?

Aside from being a Torah genius and a *tzaddik*, the Rosh Yeshivah of Shaar HaTorah in Queens, Rav Zelik Epstein *zt"l*, was a very wise person. He was the "Rosh Yeshivah's Rosh Yeshivah"; when a Rosh Yeshivah was in a quandary that he didn't feel comfortable dealing with on his own, he would go to Rav Zelik.

Let me tell you a story that happened when Rav Zelik was relatively young.

There was a couple, Holocaust survivors, who had moved to

America, and had a few children. The husband never recovered from the horrors of the concentration camps, and tragically, he took his own life. His wife needed someone to lean on — a figurative shoulder to cry on. Someone to support her, to listen to her.

That person was Rav Zelik Epstein.

Unfortunately, one of her children fell deathly ill. Rav Zelik stepped in and arranged all of the medical care, but as fate would have it, the child died — on Erev Yom Kippur, too late in the day for him to be buried before Yom Kippur. Rav Zelik was walking to Kol Nidrei that night, and suddenly he had a frightening thought: what if this would be the proverbial straw that would break the camel's back? What if the mother would be so overwrought on Yom Kippur that she, too, would be tempted to follow her husband's lead?

Rav Zelik decided that rather than daven in shul, he would go to this woman's house and spend Yom Kippur with her. He realized, however, that he was more than an hour away from her house on foot, and she might not hold out until he arrived. He decided that he would take a bus — on Yom Kippur — to ensure that this woman wouldn't become too distressed.

After arriving at this conclusion, Rav Zelik started to wonder whether it was the right thing to do, so he walked to Yeshiva Torah Vodaas, which was then in Williamsburg, to discuss it with his mentor, Rav Yaakov Kamenetsky. By the time he walked into the *beis midrash*, the yeshivah was already in the middle of *birchos K'rias Shema*. He presented his dilemma to Rav Yaakov, who

> *He decided that he would take a bus — on Yom Kippur — to ensure that this woman wouldn't become too distressed.*

nodded his agreement that Rav Zelik should take a bus to this woman's home to spend Yom Kippur with her and her other children. Rav Yaakov then pointed to a shelf near his seat where he had some money for his own bus fare home on Motza'ei Yom Kippur, indicating that Rav Zelik should take it to save the time it would take for him to go back home and get his own money.

Rav Zelik took the bus to this woman's home and spent the rest of Yom Kippur with the grieving family.

I told this story at a *derashah* in Queens, where Rav Zelik lived after he established his yeshivah there, and a fellow came over to me afterward and told me that during the *shivah* for Rav Zelik, one of this woman's children came to be *menachem avel*. "It would have happened," he told Rav Kalman Epstein, Rav Zelik's son and successor as Rosh Yeshivah. "She wouldn't have made it through that Yom Kippur if not for your father."

Rivu almanah. This is what it means. Think about who needs you, and find a way to help.

⋙ Not Just Widows

You might be thinking, "So this is all about taking care of widows? How common is that?"

Think again. The word *almanah* is shorthand for people who are down on their luck, who feel sad, abandoned, and need support.

The Torah commands: כָּל אַלְמָנָה וְיָתוֹם לֹא תְעַנּוּן, *You shall not cause pain to any widow or orphan* (*Shemos* 22:21). Rashi comments on this verse that the same applies to every person; the Torah uses widows and orphans as an example because they will often feel beaten by the blow life has dealt them and take things to heart more than the average person. In that vein, *rivu almanah* can apply to the fellow who is out of a job for half a year, to the person who has a debilitating disease, or families who are coping with a disabled child, or a child at risk, or no child.

> *Rivu almanah can apply to the fellow who is out of a job for half a year, to the person who has a debilitating disease, or families who are coping with a disabled child, or a child at risk, or no child.*

Perhaps Yeshayah HaNavi singles out *rivu almanah* as the *avodah* for the day before Yom Kippur because it requires us to step out of our little box and start to think about others. For most of us, out of sight is out of mind. The *avodah* of *rivu almanah* is to expand our sphere of concern to include those who aren't always on our minds. Instead of being consumed by "me, myself, and I," we begin to seek out those who need us.

Some people feel hesitant to take on the needs of others, because they feel that if they do, they won't take care of their own needs. The truth is quite the opposite. Someone who was battling cancer wrote me a letter, as follows:

> After two years of battling cancer, I have learned a great deal. I have observed how others deal with life-threatening diseases, and realized that the only thing that we have control over is our attitude and what we choose to do with our lives.
>
> When visiting Rav Nosson Tzvi Finkel this past January, I had the privilege of witnessing how he deals with Parkinson's disease. Rav Finkel is outwardly focused. He thinks of others, and does whatever *chessed* he can — whether it's giving *eitzos*, sharing kind words, or just listening to people. He's not a man who lets his disease define who he is. Rather, he is a man on a mission who happens to have a disease. In my humble attempt to follow his example, I have learned that by turning my attention to others, I am less obsessed with my own situation, and find myself uplifted in the process.

"He's not a man who lets his disease define who he is. Rather, he is a man on a mission who happens to have a disease."

That's a profound thought. People with a serious illness can become so consumed with it that nothing else exists. They're so focused on the disease that they become bitter and angry. This man realized from Rav Nosson Tzvi that when you *don't* allow the disease to define you, you can become uplifted in the process.

I was once shopping in Seven Mile Market, a supermarket

in Baltimore that is the source of some of my most fascinating stories — both good and bad — and a woman walked up to me and said, "I *have* to tell you a story."

She told me that there was a man in our community — we'll call him Reuven — who was stricken with a particularly deadly form of cancer. He heard that "Shimon," another member of the community whom he did not know personally, was not only stricken with that form of cancer, but was also struggling financially. Reuven called up a local *chessed* organization and asked them to help arrange for him to be able to help Shimon through this difficult period.

"How much would you like to give?" the representative of the organization asked.

"I'm not just interested in giving," he explained. "I want to become his *brother*. I want to give $60,000 to help defray his expenses.

"We're partners. We're brothers. And I hope that in this *zechus* we'll both have a *refuah sheleimah*."

That's *rivu almanah*. And if it applies to those who are stricken with their own illnesses, how much more should those of us who are blessed with good health be on the lookout for those who are suffering?

Don't worry about abandoning your own needs.

Rivu almanah will make you so much happier than having your every need met.

⌐§ Flipsides of a Coin

Having gained a deeper understanding of the concept of *rivu almanah*, we can now understand how the Midrash stating that the *avodah* of Erev Yom Kippur is about *rivu almanah*, and the *Tanna DeVei Eliyahu's* teaching that it's about not bearing false witness — are really one and the same.

The placement of the prohibition of bearing false witness altogether should strike us as somewhat incongruous. It is surrounded by some of the most heinous crimes — murder, adultery, kidnaping. What is it doing among those terrible sins?

The Tolna Rebbe of Yerushalayim suggests that bearing false witness is considered so serious because it's a crime of premeditated evil. Murder and adultery are indeed wicked, but they can both happen out of passion, in a moment of fury or desire.

To successfully testify falsely in *beis din*, on the other hand, a person must plan long and hard. *Beis din* is required to interrogate witnesses intensively to ensure that each person's testimony corroborates that of his counterparts. If a false witness walks into *beis din* unprepared, his testimony will be torn apart and he will be thrown out in shame. If he is to have any hope of fooling *beis din*, he had better concoct a very clear account, then rehearse it, anticipating any questions *beis din* may ask, and refine it until he is sure that he won't be shaken under interrogation.

For what purpose is he undertaking all of this planning and practice?

To harm another Jew.

This is creative, imaginative, and premeditated evil.

And even if we may not put all that creative energy into testifying falsely, can we honestly say that there is never a time when we place our mental energy and imagination into committing some other sin?

What's the *kapparah* for premeditated sin?

Rivu almanah. Plan and think creatively about how you can do good for another person.

Lo saaneh and *rivu almanah* are two sides of the same coin. We counteract the planning for sin by planning to do good.

> *What's the kapparah for premeditated sin? Rivu almanah. Plan and think creatively about how you can do good for another person.*

Returning to the story with which we began, perhaps Rav Shach felt so strongly that Ponevezh could not commandeer some of the seats set aside for the downtrodden because that is the *antithesis* of our *avodah* as Yom Kippur approaches. Our entire focus should be to look out for the less fortunate members of Klal Yisrael, not to make them feel even worse about their situation.

✑ It's Just a Phone Call

Even if you cannot solve another person's problem — you cannot give them a baby, you cannot give them a job, you cannot get their daughter into seminary or their son into yeshivah, or get them an appropriate *shidduch* — you can think about them and show your concern. You can show them you care. All it takes is as little as a phone call to ask, "How are you doing?"

The Tolna Rebbe related that Rav Shlomo Zalman Auerbach — the *posek hador* in Eretz Yisrael until his passing — once heard about a 15-year-old girl about whom people had spread unfounded, horrible rumors. He wasn't involved in the case, but he heard that this girl was so embarrassed that she told her father not to get her a seat in shul for Rosh Hashanah, because she couldn't imagine being seen in public with those horrible rumors hanging over her head.

On Erev Rosh Hashanah, the phone rings in this girl's house. Rav Shlomo Zalman Auerbach wants to speak to her. "*Mah shlomeich?*" he asks her. "How are you?"

> On Erev Rosh Hashanah, the phone rings in this girl's house. Rav Shlomo Zalman Auerbach wants to speak to her. "Mah shlomeich?" he asks her. "How are you?"

The girl's father visited Rav Shlomo Zalman after Rosh Hashanah and said, "You were *mechayeh meisim* — you brought her back to life. When she got off the phone with you she said, 'Abba, I want a seat in shul.' "

How are you?
Mah shlomcha?
Vus macht ihr?

That's as little as it can take to turn somebody's perspective around.

Now admittedly, even on days when we wake up with a bad case of delusions of grandeur, our phone calls are not likely to have the effect that Rav Shlomo Zalman's did. At the same time, however, none of us is as busy as Rav Shlomo Zalman on Erev Rosh Hashanah.

If he could make the time to make a phone call, so can we.

Phone calls. How simple is that?

I live across from Dr. Yoel Jakobovits, whose mother, Lady Amélie Jakobovits, the wife of the late chief rabbi of England Lord Immanuel Jakobovits, passed away suddenly in May of 2010.

At her *levayah*, a grandson said that his grandmother, popularly known as Lady J, once spent Pesach with his family. On the day before Erev Pesach, Lady J went up to her room at 9 a.m. and did not come down until midnight.

"What were you doing for the last fifteen hours?" her grandson asked curiously.

"Making phone calls," she replied.

It turns out that Lady J was a genius in the art of making phone calls. Droves of people showed up at the *shivah* — many of whom the family had never met before — with the same story: "Your mother would call me each Rosh Chodesh," or "Your mother would call me every Erev Shabbos."

Apparently, a phone call is all it takes to make a person's day, or month, or year.

Apparently, a phone call is all it takes to make a person's day, or month, or year.

✒ Silence vs. Singing: Two Leil Yom Kippur Tales

Leil Yom Kippur is not Leil Tishah B'Av. It's not a sad night. It's a serious, solemn night, but it's not a somber occasion.

One Leil Yom Kippur when I was a *bachur*, I had the honor of escorting my Rosh HaYeshivah, Rav Ruderman *zt"l*, back home after davening. He was already growing old and physically unsteady. We walked home slowly, arm in arm, as was his wont.

Everyone who knew Rav Ruderman can tell you that the Rosh Yeshivah could not go *dalet amos* without saying a *vort*, asking a Torah question, or delving into a *sugya*.

Do you know what the Rosh Yeshivah told me on Leil Yom Kippur, after Kol Nidrei, as we walked home?

Nothing.

Absolutely nothing.

I don't know whether I fully appreciated it then, but I think I now understand why he was silent that night: *He was afraid.* He knew that his very life was on the line, and he was too scared to talk.

In that context, you can appreciate the following story.

Rav Shlomo Zalman Auerbach was once walking home on Leil Yom Kippur, and he passed by a shul and noticed a group of *baalei batim* sitting and singing *niggunim*.

Singing *niggunim*? Was that in the spirit of Yom Kippur?

His astonishment grew when he realized who was sitting with them: The Tchebiner Rav, Rav Dov Berish Weidenfeld *zt"l*. Even living in a generation of Torah geniuses such as the Brisker Rav and Rav Yechezkel Abramsky, the Tchebiner Rav was considered among the greatest of his day. What was he doing there on Leil Yom Kippur, sitting around with a group of *baalei batim* and singing *niggunim*?

> What was the Tchebiner Rav doing there on Leil Yom Kippur, sitting around with a group of baalei batim and singing niggunim?

A few days after Yom Kippur, Rav Shlomo Zalman met the Tchebiner Rav and asked him what had transpired that night.

"These *baalei batim* are Holocaust survivors," replied the Tchebiner Rav, who had lost four of his own children during the war. "They are sad and depressed. You rarely see them smile. They decided to sing the Yom Kippur *niggunim* they knew from back in Galicia. I realized that singing those *niggunim* would transport them, even if only for a few moments, back to happier times in the *alte heim*.

"Is there a greater mitzvah on Yom Kippur than what Yeshayah HaNavi describes as: לְהַחֲיוֹת רוּחַ שְׁפָלִים וּלְהַחֲיוֹת לֵב נִדְכָּאִים, *to revive the spirit of the lowly and to revive the heart of the despondent?*" (Yeshayah 57:15).

Rivu almanah.

❦ Prayer Rather Than Advice

Most people have a specific passage in the Yom Kippur davening that pulls at their heartstrings, and may even bring them to shed a tear. I'm not talking about *U'nesaneh Tokef*, when many people cry. I'm talking about something more personal, specific words that *you* find meaningful.

For me, those words are in the section following the *avodah* of the Kohen Gadol in Mussaf. We recount how the Kohen Gadol would recite a *tefillah* each year as he left the *Kodesh HaKodashim*, in which human feet could tread only on Yom Kippur.

The *tefillah* reads as follows:

יְהִי רָצוֹן מִלְּפָנֶיךָ ה' אֱלֹקֵינוּ וֵאלֹקֵי אֲבוֹתֵינוּ, שֶׁתְּהֵא הַשָּׁנָה הַזֹּאת הַבָּאָה עָלֵינוּ, וְעַל כָּל עַמְּךָ בֵּית יִשְׂרָאֵל, שְׁנַת אוֹצָרְךָ הַטוֹב תִּפְתַּח לָנוּ, שְׁנַת אֹסֶם, שְׁנַת בְּרָכָה ...

May it be Your will, Hashem, our God and the God of our forefathers, that this year that is coming upon us and upon all Your people, the Family of Israel, be a year in which you open Your treasury for us: a year of abundance, a year of blessing...

After asking Hashem for bounty in every way imaginable, the Kohen Gadol concludes with an addendum:

וְעַל אַנְשֵׁי הַשָּׁרוֹן הָיָה אוֹמֵר: יְהִי רָצוֹן מִלְּפָנֶיךָ, ה' אֱלֹקֵינוּ וֵאלֹקֵי אֲבוֹתֵינוּ, שֶׁלֹּא יֵעָשׂוּ בָתֵּיהֶם קִבְרֵיהֶם.

And concerning the inhabitants of the Sharon, he would say: May it be Your will, Hashem, our God and the God of our forefathers, that their houses not become their graves.

The Kohen Gadol's last words as he leaves the *Kodesh HaKodashim* until the following year are a prayer for the people living in the Sharon valley. The earth in the Sharon area was unstable and there were frequent landslides, to the extent that Talmud Yerushalmi relates that they had to rebuild their houses twice every seven years.

To give a modern example of what this means, in 2005, Hurricane Katrina hit New Orleans, just about wiping out the entire city. Five years later, the BP oil spill hit the same area, once again destroying much of the local economy.

That's what it was like to live in the Sharon.

I always wondered: Why did the Kohen Gadol devote this space to the people of the Sharon year after year? Why didn't he just tell them: "MOVE! Why are you staying in a danger zone?"

> *Why did the Kohen Gadol devote this space to the people of the Sharon year after year? Why didn't he just tell them: "MOVE! Why are you staying in a danger zone?"*

But no. The Kohen Gadol realized that his job was not to give advice to these people, who obviously couldn't afford to move to a more stable location. He knew that as the Kohen Gadol, his job was to empathize with their feelings of uncertainty, to wonder along with them whether this winter's rains would destroy their homes once again — and to daven heartfelt *tefillos* that they survive the rains.

That's *rivu almanah*. Empathizing with the downtrodden in society, rather than giving them unhelpful advice on how to live.

✑ Feelings for the Family

The Baltimore community knew a person who specialized in caring not only for those around him, but for all of Klal Yisrael: Rabbi Herman Neuberger who, aside from being the President of Ner Yisrael, also tended to the needs of so many people in unfortunate circumstances.

I personally witnessed just how far Rabbi Neuberger took the concept of *rivu almanah*.

One fine day in the late spring of 1994, a fellow walked into the *beis midrash* in Ner Yisrael and asked, "Where's a rabbi?"

I sit in the first section of the yeshivah, so a *bachur* pointed to me. This fellow walks over to me holding a paper bag, and removes a knife. I'm thinking, "What's he doing with that knife? Does he have a *sh'eilah*?"

Before I could think any further, he stabs me.

This person was mentally deranged, and he woke up with voices in his head that morning instructing him to kill a rabbi.

It turned out to be nothing; the knife just nicked me, and half the boys in my *shiur* tackled him and held him until the police arrived. I went to the emergency room, ran out of patience waiting for someone to see me, and went home.

> *This fellow walks over to me holding a paper bag, and removes a knife. I'm thinking, "What's he doing with that knife? Does he have a sh'eilah?" Before I could think any further, he stabs me.*

The next day, a Friday, this fellow was going to be arraigned. Rabbi Neuberger was very influential in government circles, and I wanted him to make sure that this guy would be thrown into jail so I wouldn't have to worry about him trying to finish the job.

"Where's he being arraigned?" he asked.

I didn't know, so he took out the phone book, made a few quick phone calls, and found out in which courthouse the arraignment was being held. He dashed out of his office and into his car, returning a couple of hours later.

I walked back into his office and asked, "Nu, what happened?"

After telling me that the attacker would be confined temporarily in a mental institution, he slumped into his chair and uttered a comment that I will never forget:

"*S'iz a rachmanus oif zein elteren,*" he said. "It's a pity on his parents."

This was an elderly couple who had already been dealing with their mentally ill son for decades. They didn't know what he was planning to do that day. Why should they suffer?

✑ Married Widows and Widowers

There's another aspect to *rivu almanah* that we must examine — one that might be painful to consider.

Do you have an *almanah* living in your own home?

What does that mean, you may be thinking. *I'm alive and well, how can I have an almanah in my house?*

So let me clarify the question: Does your wife feel like an *almanah*? Does she feel neglected or ignored because you're never there for her? Does your husband feel like a widower? Do your children feel like *yesomim*?

Yesomim? We're alive!

Yes, there are children out there who feel that they are orphans, even though their parents are alive. They may have all the latest technological toys and designer clothes, but they can be, in effect, *yesomim*.

For some people, *rivu almanah* doesn't even require a phone call. You might just be able to fulfill it by looking across the kitchen table and reaching out to the virtual *almanah, alman, yasom,* or *yesomah* sitting there.

And when we start to apply the concept of *rivu almanah* with our own families, we can tap into something even more powerful.

✑ The Ultimate "Hineni"

In the *haftarah* of Yom Kippur morning, we read an astounding pledge from Hashem: אָז תִּקְרָא וַה׳ יַעֲנֶה תְּשַׁוַּע וְיֹאמַר הִנֵּנִי, *Then you will call and Hashem will respond; you will cry out and He will say, "Here I am" (Yeshayah 58:9).*

If you go through the entire *Tanach*, you'll find thirteen appearances of the term הִנֵּנִי, *Here I am*. In twelve of those instances, the word was uttered by a subordinate to a superior — whether it was Avraham, Yaakov, or Moshe saying it to Hashem, or Yosef saying it to Yaakov, or Shmuel saying it to Eili HaKohen. It is indeed appropriate for a subordinate to present himself as being ready to fulfill his superior's wishes.

In only one example is this reversed: in the verse תְּשַׁוַּע וְיֹאמַר הִנֵּנִי.

We will call out, and Hashem will answer, "*Hineni*, I am here to fulfill your wishes."

Can you imagine that? Is there a greater reward than Hashem Himself "standing at our service"?

So what do we have to do to merit this reward?

Based on the context in which this verse appears, the Gemara (*Yevamos* 62b-63a) gives us a very simple method: "*Hamekarev es krovav.*"

> *Can you imagine that? Is there a greater reward than Hashem Himself "standing at our service"?*

This means be kind to your relatives.

Not to the man on the street.

Not to the unfortunate guy out there without a job.

To your own relatives!

Why would we merit Hashem saying "*Hineni*" for being kind to our own *mishpachah*?

The Maharal (*Chiddushei Aggados* to *Yevamos*, ibid.) explains that this is because our relationship with Hashem is described in the Torah as: כִּי מִי גוֹי גָּדוֹל אֲשֶׁר לוֹ אֱלֹקִים קְרֹבִים אֵלָיו, *For which is a great nation that has a God Who is close to it* (Devarim 4:7).

The Ribbono Shel Olam prides Himself on being *karov*, "related" to us. Says the Maharal, Hashem is telling us, "If you want Me to treat you nicely, as one should do for his relatives, let Me see how nicely you treat your own relatives."

If you are kind to your relatives, Hashem will stand ready to fulfill your every wish. But if Hashem sees that you mistreat your relatives, then He won't give you the special treatment of being His relative.

> *If you are kind to your relatives, Hashem will stand ready to fulfill your every wish. But if Hashem sees that you mistreat your relatives, then He won't give you the special treatment of being His relative.*

So you might be wondering whether this is really something that needs to be discussed before the Yomim Nora'im. After all, aren't most people nice to their relatives?

To be honest, I don't have much personal experience with this issue. I learn in a yeshivah, somewhat removed from typical rabbinic horror stories. But those who are involved tell me that it is far more prevalent than one can imagine.

Rabbi Tzvi Schur is a chaplain in a Baltimore hospital, where he often deals with families who have to make end-of-life decisions for their loved ones. He told me that he has met far too many families in which siblings don't talk to each other, or parents don't talk to their children. He had a case in which a woman was on her deathbed, and her son was with her. "Are you going to call your sister to let her know that your mother is dying?" Rabbi Schur asked this man.

"I will *not* call my sister," he replied.

His mother is about to die — isn't it time to bury the hatchet?

I heard a case of a woman who died, and the father sat *shivah* at one end of a room and the children sat at the other end, because they refused to have anything to do with each other.

You hear these stories, and then you hear people ask why, after all the *Tehillim* gatherings for all the sick people in Klal Yisrael, we don't seem to merit Hashem's mercy. Maybe it's because He views how people are treating their own relatives, and He doesn't find us worthy of that mercy.

❧ Family Reunions: An Ancient Custom

The Maharal's brother, whose name was Rav Chaim, wrote a work called *Sefer HaChaim*. He writes something that seems counterintuitive:

> It is appropriate for a person to draw his neighbors and friends close to him. Even if they are wealthy, he should invite them into his house on occasion to honor them. *This is the mitzvah of hachnasas orchim that our Sages discussed* (Mishnah, *Pe'ah* 1:1, a version of which we recite each morning in *Bircas HaTorah*), for it strengthens the love between man and his fellow.
>
> This was customary during earlier generations, when each family had a specific day on which they would make a joyous family banquet, as David said: זֶבַח מִשְׁפָּחָה לָנוּ בָעִיר, *We have a family feast in the city* (I Shmuel 20:29).

It seems incredible, but in the times of *Tanach*, they had a family reunion, to build familial love!

Now, even if this is not going to happen in your family, the least you can do is pick up the phone, and forge peace between siblings, between warring family members.

> *It seems incredible, but in the times of Tanach, they had a family reunion, to build familial love!*

This is what we have to do to merit Hashem saying, "*Hineni* — Here I am, at your service."

I realize that family dynamics are difficult. Sometimes it's easier to love someone you barely know than it is to love your own relatives. Families are complicated. Our negative emotions toward family members may go all the way back to our childhood years, when we felt that our parents treated one or more of our siblings better than they treated us.

But isn't it worthwhile to look past that to have Hashem stand ready to fulfill all of our wishes? To have Him listen when we daven for all the sick people in Klal Yisrael? Perhaps even to finally merit a *geulah sheleimah*, to have Him eradicate all of the pain and suffering that we endure in the *galus*?

Through the merit of treating our relatives nicely, may we all merit to have Hashem treat us as His relative, and declare to us: "*Hineni.*"

Protecting Your Teshuvah Investment

I n today's financially uncertain times, people look for ways to protect their investments. No one wants to lose his hard-earned money in some bad investment.

When we think about the amount of time we spend on *teshuvah* each year, we might expect people to take similar care of protecting that investment. And yet one of the themes that you commonly hear from people during the Aseres Yemei Teshuvah is the problem of recidivism. People tend to feel that even if they put their most earnest efforts into doing *teshuvah*, their invest-ment will only last for a limited time. "Come the end of Succos," a little voice in our head says to us, "you'll slide back into the very same person you were before Rosh Hashanah."

And then that little voice follows up with the most frighten-ing two words: "Why bother?"

Why go through all the trouble of doing *teshuvah* if we know that in a few weeks, we will be in an inexorable backslide to where we were beforehand?

I would like to take a new approach to this problem — one that doesn't initially seem to have any bearing on *teshuvah*: I would like to suggest that we can protect our carefully invested *teshuvah* hours by beginning to keep Shabbos.

Keep Shabbos? You're probably thinking. *I keep Shabbos every week!*

Let me share a story to explain what I mean.

There was a family in Baltimore that got into one car accident after another. After five traffic accidents in the course of two years, this family's insurer wanted to revoke their automobile insurance policy. Their insurance agent, who was also a member of the *frum* community, contacted the insurance company and pointed out that his client was not at fault in four out of five of the accidents. The insurance company replied that the family must have "bad karma," and that was the reason why they had been in so many accidents.

> The insurance company replied that the family must have "bad karma," and that was the reason why they had been in so many accidents.

The insurance agent suggested that the head of the family, who was a fine *talmid chacham*, visit Rav Yaakov Weinberg, Rosh HaYeshivah of Ner Yisrael. Rav Weinberg listened to the details of the accidents, and remarked that the descriptions reminded him of the Torah's capital punishment of *sekilah* (lit., *stoning*). He suggested that perhaps the family was involved in some sort of transgression that would incur the punishment of *sekilah* and that's why they kept getting into such accidents.

What on earth could a *frum* family be doing that would incur *sekilah*?

Rav Weinberg presumed that the only thing he could imagine them doing that would fall into that category was *chillul Shabbos*.

"*Chillul Shabbos*?" the head of the family asked in shock. "In our family?"

"What's your house like on *Erev* Shabbos?" Rav Weinberg asked.

"Well," this man began, "there's a lot of tension, a lot of screaming and yelling."

"What time does your wife light the candles?" Rav Weinberg continued.

"Usually pretty late," the man admitted. "Sometimes only a few minutes before *shekiah* (sundown)."

"*That's* the kind of *chillul Shabbos* I'm referring to," Rav Weinberg explained. "I'm not accusing you of actually transgressing anything that's prohibited, but of being guilty of things that *shmek* (waft) of *chillul Shabbos*.

"From now on," he suggested, "the entire family should try to be ready a full half-hour before Shabbos. No cleaning, no cooking, no showers from half an hour before Shabbos. Be completely ready, and then sit and learn a *sefer* until Shabbos."

The family implemented Rav Weinberg's suggestion, and lo and behold, the accidents stopped.

The insurance agent then returned to the insurance company and said that it wasn't a driving issue, it was a religious issue. The same company that was ready to revoke the policy due to karma was willing to accept the religion card, and they renewed the policy.

This is what I'm referring to when I suggest that we start keeping Shabbos.

> *The same company that was ready to revoke the policy due to karma was willing to accept the religion card, and they renewed the policy.*

I'm not suggesting that anyone is remiss in keeping the basic *halachos*, but I'm referring to keeping Shabbos "for real."

✑ A Contradiction?

Rav Weinberg's explanation that there are two levels of keeping Shabbos also resolves an apparent contradiction between two passages from *Chazal*.

In Talmud Bavli (*Shabbos* 118b), the Gemara states that if Klal Yisrael would keep two Shabbosos *kehilchasan*, they would merit immediate redemption.

Talmud Yerushalmi (*Taanis* 1:1) states that if Klal Yisrael would keep *one* Shabbos *ketiknah*, Mashiach would come immediately.

Which one is it? Do we have to keep two Shabbosos to merit redemption, or is one enough?

If you pay close attention to the words, the difference is obvious. Talmud Bavli states that if people would keep Shabbos *kehilchasah*, according to halachah — i.e., to the letter of the law — they will merit redemption. This is referring to people who are careful not to do any of the 39 *melachos* (prohibited actions) or any of the *d'rabbanans* (rabbinic prohibitions) on Shabbos. If Klal Yisrael keeps Shabbos at that level, they can merit redemption — but only after two Shabbosos.

It is a level to reach for, but it's not the ultimate.

The ultimate level is the one the Yerushalmi refers to: keeping Shabbos *ketiknah*, as it's meant to be kept. If we can keep Shabbos at that level, we need to keep only one Shabbos in order to merit redemption.

Shabbos shouldn't be only about avoiding transgressing the halachos; there has to be a higher level of Shabbos observance that we're trying to attain.

The Chofetz Chaim finds an allusion to these two forms of Shabbos in a *zemer* we sing at the night *seudah*: כָּל מְקַדֵּשׁ שְׁבִיעִי כָּרָאוּי לוֹ, כָּל שׁוֹמֵר שַׁבָּת כַּדָּת מֵחַלְּלוֹ. The second half of this phrase refers to those who keep Shabbos כַּדָּת מֵחַלְּלוֹ, according to its laws, taking care to avoid *chillul Shabbos*. The first half speaks of those who sanctify Shabbos כָּרָאוּי לוֹ, *as is appropriate*.

Because Shabbos shouldn't be only about avoiding transgressing the *halachos*; there has to be a higher level of Shabbos observance that we're trying to attain.

~§ Shabbos and Teshuvah

Now, what is the correlation between Shabbos and *teshuvah*?

A Midrash (*Bereishis Rabbah* 22:13) alludes to a strong connection between the two.

After Kayin killed Hevel, part of his punishment was: נָע וָנָד תִּהְיֶה בָאָרֶץ, *You shall become a vagrant and a wanderer on earth* (*Bereishis* 4:12). When Kayin heard this, he asked Hashem: הֵן גֵּרַשְׁתָּ אֹתִי הַיּוֹם מֵעַל פְּנֵי הָאֲדָמָה וּמִפָּנֶיךָ אֶסָּתֵר וְהָיִיתִי נָע וָנָד בָּאָרֶץ וְהָיָה כָל מֹצְאִי יַהַרְגֵנִי, *"Behold, You have banished me this day from the face of the earth — can I be hidden from Your presence? I must become a vagrant and a wanderer on earth; whoever meets me will kill me!"* (ibid. v. 14).

Hashem replies: לָכֵן כָּל הֹרֵג קַיִן שִׁבְעָתַיִם יֻקָּם וַיָּשֶׂם ה' לְקַיִן אוֹת לְבִלְתִּי הַכּוֹת אֹתוֹ כָּל מֹצְאוֹ, *"Therefore, whoever slays Kayin, before seven generations have passed he will be punished." And Hashem placed a mark upon Kayin, so that none that meet him might kill him* (ibid. v. 15).

The Torah's narrative ends with the words: וַיֵּצֵא קַיִן מִלִּפְנֵי ה' וַיֵּשֶׁב בְּאֶרֶץ נוֹד קִדְמַת עֵדֶן, *Kayin left the presence of Hashem and settled in the land of Nod, east of Eden* (ibid. v. 16).

The Midrash takes note of the odd use of the words וַיֵּצֵא קַיִן in this *pasuk*. "Where was he leaving from?" wonders the Midrash.

The Midrash answers that he was leaving from his "trial" before Hashem joyously because he had received a favorable verdict. The Midrash says that Adam HaRishon asked his son Kayin what his verdict was, and Kayin's answer was: עָשִׂיתִי תְּשׁוּבָה וְנִתְפַּשַׁרְתִּי, *"I did teshuvah, and I reached a compromise."*

Adam HaRishon found this verdict so favorable, in fact, that he clapped his hands to his face and said, "Such is the power of *teshuvah* and I was never aware of it!" He immediately broke out in praise of Hashem, composing the psalm *Mizmor Shir Leyom HaShabbos*.

There are several significant questions regarding this Midrash. First, did Adam HaRishon not know that there was such a thing as *teshuvah*? Wasn't he doing *teshuvah* for the monumental sin of eating from the Eitz HaDaas?

Second, Kayin's description of his verdict — "I did *teshuvah*, and I reached a compromise" — is astounding. Hashem is not a lawyer or a judge with whom you can reach a compromise; His judgments are purely just. What did Kayin mean?

Third, we can understand that Adam HaRishon was excited about Kayin's verdict, but of all the words he could use to praise Hashem for it, why would he compose the psalm *Mizmor Shir Leyom HaShabbos*? What does Kayin's *teshuvah* have to do with Shabbos?

In *Nesivos Shalom*, the Slonimer Rebbe explains this Midrash beautifully.

He writes that when Kayin said, הֵן גֵּרַשְׁתָּ אֹתִי הַיּוֹם מֵעַל פְּנֵי הָאֲדָמָה וּמִפָּנֶיךָ אֶסָּתֵר וְהָיִיתִי נָע וָנָד בָּאָרֶץ וְהָיָה כָל מֹצְאִי יַהַרְגֵנִי, "*Behold, You have banished me this day from the face of the earth — can I be hidden from Your presence? I must become a vagrant and a wanderer on earth; whoever meets me will kill me,*" he wasn't referring only to physical death; he was referring primarily to spiritual death. He told Hashem, "If You are banishing me from before You, and I am forced to wander בָּאָרֶץ — in this physical, tempting, and materialistic world — what will happen to my *neshamah*? How will I survive spiritually? The temptations of this world will destroy me!"

> "If You are banishing me from before You, and I am forced to wander בָּאָרֶץ — in this physical, tempting, and materialistic world — what will happen to my neshamah? How will I survive spiritually? The temptations of this world will destroy me!"

The Ribbono Shel Olam threw Kayin a lifeline, a way to curb his temptations. What is that lifeline? וַיָּשֶׂם ה' לְקַיִן אוֹת לְבִלְתִּי הַכּוֹת אֹתוֹ כָּל מֹצְאוֹ. Hashem gave Kayin an *os*. Do you know what that *os* is? אַךְ אֶת שַׁבְּתֹתַי תִּשְׁמֹרוּ כִּי אוֹת הִוא בֵּינִי וּבֵינֵיכֶם, *However, you must observe My Sabbaths, for it is a sign between Me and you* (*Shemos* 31:13). Shabbos is an *os*, a lifeline for a *neshamah* that would otherwise be lost here on earth.

Six days a week, we are out in a tempting world, an alluring world, but then we have one day each week in which we can rejuvenate and replenish our *neshamah*.

That's the "compromise" Kayin reached. He would have to pay for his sin of killing his brother by wandering through the world six days each week, looking out not only for his physical safety, but also for his spiritual safety. But he would have an *os*, a lifeline, a weekly break during which his soul would find respite.

This is what excited Adam HaRishon so much. He knew the *koach* of *teshuvah*, but he didn't realize the power of Shabbos as part of the *teshuvah* process.

> *This is what excited Adam HaRishon so much. He knew the koach of teshuvah, but he didn't realize the power of Shabbos as part of the teshuvah process.*

We may not realize this, but when we sin, it does something to our souls. If a person has a stroke, *rachmana litzlan*, and the oxygen supply to his brain is cut off, he will generally lose some motor control of his body, because the corresponding cells in his brain have been damaged.

An *aveirah* is the metaphysical equivalent of a stroke. It damages a portion of the *neshamah*. But whereas in the physical world, it can take many months or years of therapy to restore function — *if* it can be restored altogether — in the spiritual world we have a weekly opportunity to repair the damage done to our *neshamos* during a week of wandering.

When Adam HaRishon heard about this opportunity, he spontaneously broke out in praise of Shabbos: *Mizmor Shir Leyom HaShabbos*.

✑ Channeling Kayin

Shabbos can play the very same role in our lives as it did in Kayin's life after his sin.

We, too, live in a mundane, temptation-filled world. In fact, I daresay that Kayin didn't have nearly the same level of distractions as we do in the 21st century. He didn't hear the filth on regular news reports, he didn't have to avoid billboards hanging in the subway, or the worst kind of depravity just one click away.

How do we, in our morally bankrupt society, maintain a closeness to Hashem?

The answer is that every mitzvah protects our souls to some extent, but Hashem gives us one great mitzvah that can do more to rejuvenate our *neshamos* than any other mitzvah: Shabbos. This is why Hashem told Moshe that he has a מַתָּנָה טוֹבָה, *a great gift*, in his storehouse, וְשַׁבָּת שְׁמָה, *it's called Shabbos.* לֵךְ וְהוֹדִיעָם, *Go inform them.* When Hashem instructed Moshe to inform Klal Yisrael about this gift, He wasn't referring merely to the existence of Shabbos, but to the curative and restorative power of Shabbos, the day when we can repair the damage wrought to our *neshamos* during the weekdays.

In fact, the *Zohar* calls Shabbos *Yoma D'Nishmasa*, because it is the day of the soul, not the day of the body.

⇜§ Pining for Hashem

A rav from Forest Hills, New York, who originally served as a rabbi in Irvine, California, a suburb of Los Angeles, told me that one of his congregants was a woman who had converted to Judaism. Each week at *Seudah Shlishis*, they would sing *Yedid Nefesh*, and each week this woman would begin to cry when they reached the words, "*Nafshi cholas ahavasecha* — my soul pines for Your love." No matter which tune they sang to those words, this woman would have tears rolling down her face.

Why was this woman so overwhelmed by these words? I think it's because the very same inborn spirituality that sent her searching for holiness in Eretz Yisrael and eventually led to her conversion also made her pine for Hashem. And each week, as Shabbos came to a close and her soul had to return to the earthiness of this world, she felt a void. Shabbos was a day for her soul, and those tears were a manifestation of her soul crying out as it contemplated having to return to the mundane pursuits of the week. She understood what life is without the holiness of Shabbos.

Rav Soloveitchik would give yearly *teshuvah derashos* that were attended by thousands of followers. One year, he told the following story.

"Not far from where we lived," he related, "there was a Modzitzer *shtiebel*."

You don't have to know much about Chassidus to know that Modzitz is particularly renowned for its music and singing.

"The chassidim would sing repeatedly *bnei heichala dichsifin* and *Mizmor l'Dovid, Hashem ro'i lo echsar*. It occurred to me that they were not singing because they wanted to sing, but because they didn't want Shabbos to leave.

> *It occurred to me that they were not singing because they wanted to sing, but because they didn't want Shabbos to leave.*

"I remember being at that *shtiebel* as a young child, and one of the men who had been singing most enthusiastically came over to me and asked me if I recognized him. I told him I didn't. He then introduced himself as *Yankeleh der tregger*, Yankeleh the porter."

If you've ever seen Roman Vishniac's photographs capturing *shtetl* life, you might remember the image of the *tregger* — an occupation for which one needed only two things: a length of rope and a strong back. Before the days of cars and trucks, when someone needed a heavy load moved from one place to another, he would hire the *tregger* to tie the box or boxes onto his back and move them.

"During the week," Rav Soloveitchik continued, "I knew Yankeleh as a man who walked around in very shabby clothes, dangling his rope. I could not imagine that this individual with such a regal bearing was that same person — that on Shabbos he wore a *kapoteh* and a *shtreimel*.

"That is because his soul wasn't 'Yankeleh the porter'; it was 'Yankeleh the prince.' "

Truth be told, on Shabbos, this simple Jew wasn't the same person. Shabbos is *Yoma D'Nishmasa*, and on Shabbos, Yankeleh's soul shone through.

"After nightfall," Rav Soloveitchik concluded, "I naively asked him, 'When do we daven Maariv?' (a question that a quintessential *Litvak* would ask!).

" 'Do you miss the weekday so much,' Yankeleh replied, 'that you can't wait for Maariv?' "

This is how a simple Jew of yesteryear loved the *Yoma D'Nishmasa*, the *matanah tovah* from Hakadosh Baruch Hu.

ᐁ The Munkaczer's Newsreel

In the olden days, before and after a movie was played at a theater, they would show newsreels, highlighting interesting events that had occurred in exotic places all over the globe.

It might be hard to believe, but in movie theaters in America during the 1930s, they played a newsreel from a wedding — that of the daughter of the Munkaczer Rebbe, the Minchas Elazar. It was a grand event, with white horses pulling the Rebbe's carriage, a huge entourage — a "royal wedding" of sorts that captured the imaginations of Americans attending the movies.

It was a grand event, with white horses pulling the Rebbe's carriage, a huge entourage — a "royal wedding" of sorts that captured the imaginations of Americans attending the movies.

There are two versions about what happened. It's clear that the Munkaczer Rebbe, who was extremely opposed to people taking as much as a still photograph of him, would have been ideologically opposed to having a movie made of him speaking. Nevertheless, he is seen delivering a message to the Jews of America. Some say that he was duped; the people who approached him told him that his voice was being broadcast, without telling him that he was also being filmed.

Another version is that the Munkaczer Rebbe was so concerned about the state of Jewry in America that he agreed to be filmed.

Either way, his message resounds until today. "My dear brothers in America," he beseeched, "keep Shabbos, and things will go well for you. And I don't just mean going to daven and then going to work."

I still remember, growing up as a child, the dozens of Yidden who would come to shul on Shabbos and then get into their cars and head off to work. This phenomenon was almost universal during the 1930s, when the motto was, "If you don't come to work on Saturday, don't bother coming in on Monday." The Munkaczer Rebbe's message was that Shabbos had to be kept fully.

In our times, that message has to be adapted. Because our challenge goes beyond keeping the technical halachos of Shabbos; it's about treating Shabbos as a special gift from Hashem and gaining the greatest spiritual bounty we can from this day.

I'll never be confused with being a chassid. I spent the last half-century in Litvishe yeshivos; I eat *gebrokts* on Pesach; I don *tefillin* on Chol HaMoed as was the custom of my ancestors in Frankfurt, Germany.

But there's at least one area in which I envy chassidim: the manner in which they observe — or perhaps "celebrate" would be a more accurate term — Shabbos. If you want to know what a Shabbos really is, go to New Square. You can show up 10 minutes before candle-lighting, and they'll welcome you like a prince. They will dine you and fete you, and you will experience an authentic Shabbos. Or if you're ever in Eretz Yisrael, I recommend that you visit the Belzer community and see how they celebrate Shabbos.

A rebbi told me that he asked Rav

There's at least one area in which I envy chassidim: the manner in which they observe — or perhaps "celebrate" would be a more accurate term — Shabbos.

Elya Svei whether he should take his class to visit New Square. He was concerned that seeing the chassidim beginning to daven at 10 in the morning might send a negative message that one can daven after the *zman* has passed. Rav Elya answered that it's still worthwhile, as long as they read *Krias Shema* before davening, because they would get to experience genuine *yiras Shamayim*, and they'll see what a Shabbos is supposed to look like.

❧ Enhanced Shabbos

Does this mean that it's an all-or-none proposition? Is all lost for those of us unwilling to become a full-fledged chassid?

The answer is no. You don't have to change everything about the way you live. But I can promise you that the more you invest into your Shabbos experience, the stronger your *neshamah* will become, and the more chance that the *teshuvah* you do now will carry forward through the year. Because you will have a weekly opportunity to return to where you were during your *teshuvah* process, and you'll reaffirm your commitment to get better each week.

This only works, however, if Shabbos is more than just a day to crash. If Shabbos to you is a weekly effort to set a new indoor speed record for the home-from-shul to asleep-in-bed race, then it won't do anything to bolster your *neshamah*.

One of the challenges we have to overcome in order to make Shabbos work for us is the *nisayon* of viewing Shabbos as just another event that happens 52 times a year. Rather, we have to begin to look at it through the eyes of a non-Jew from Topeka, Kansas.

Rav Yaakov Bender, the Rosh Yeshivah of Darchei Torah in Far Rockaway, related a story that occurred to him on an airplane.

[As an aside, I always wonder why some people have all the luck. Rabbi Wein and Rabbi Bender constantly tell stories that occur with their seatmates on planes. I spend hours upon hours traveling each year, and the closest I can come to some of their stories is the time an African American waiting for a train with me in East New Jersey took one look at me and said, "That's some hat you got there." (I had to edit out at least one of the adjectives he chose to describe my headgear).]

Be that as it may, Rabbi Bender had just settled himself on an airplane and pulled out a *Chumash*, when his seatmate, a Roman Catholic from Topeka, Kansas asked, "Do you have that Shabbat, when the lady of the home dressed in her finest stands around the candles with her children standing beside her, then she recites the blessing, and the house is filled with a special glow. When the husband comes home, he blesses the children and sits down to a beautiful table set with silver and crystal, to a sumptuous meal that mom has prepared, and they sing beautiful songs about the Shabbat?

"Do you have that Shabbat?"

Why is a Roman Catholic asking such questions about Shabbos? Because he must have experienced a Shabbos or two at his Orthodox neighbor's home, and he's been blown away by what he saw.

And to think that we have this every week! We just have to learn to break the rote way we treat Shabbos.

The Avnei Nezer writes that this is the message of a *pasuk* in the *haftarah* we read on Yom Kippur morning: אִם תָּשִׁיב מִשַּׁבָּת רַגְלֶךָ (*Yeshayah* 58:13). The superficial meaning of these words are, *If you restrain your foot because it is the Sabbath.* The Avnei Nezer finds a deeper meaning: If you will refrain from making Shabbos רַגְלֶךָ, becoming something done out of הֶרְגֵּל, *rote*, you will then merit Hashem's promise in the next *pasuk*: אָז תִּתְעַנַּג עַל ה' וְהִרְכַּבְתִּיךָ עַל בָּמֳתֵי אָרֶץ וְהַאֲכַלְתִּיךָ נַחֲלַת יַעֲקֹב אָבִיךָ כִּי פִּי ה' דִּבֵּר, *Then you will delight in Hashem, and I will mount you astride the heights of the world; I will provide you the heritage of your forefather Jacob, for the word of Hashem has spoken* (ibid. v. 14).

So this is something worth working on, but how?

✑ Shabbos Strategies

The first thing we can do to make our Shabbosos special is to learn about it. Rav Dessler teaches that studying about any subject is a tried-and-true method of breaking routine. If you delve into the subject of Shabbos, you will find yourself thinking about it and looking forward to it.

Whether you're able to handle the sublime teachings of Rav Shimshon Pincus in *Shabbos Malkesa*, or you need something a little lighter, there are many *sefarim* — even in English — that can help you gain an appreciation of Shabbos. And the specific focus of the book can vary; whether the book you choose discusses the concepts, the halachos, or the philosophies of Shabbos, it will have you more focused on the uniqueness of the day and you will be more attuned to Shabbos.

A second approach is to make practical changes to make our Shabbosos more meaningful.

During the week, many people choose *minyanim* based on which one has the shortest davening. On Shabbos, choose a slower *minyan*. There's no rush. You have nowhere to go. You can even come 15 minutes before davening and say some *Tehillim* until davening starts.

Limit your reading material to things that are Shabbos'dik. We now have a variety of Shabbos-appropriate books and periodicals to chose from. Refrain from speaking about things that are not Shabbos'dik, such as sports or the stock market. No business conversation on Shabbos. The words, *"Nisht oif Shabbos geredt,* **BUT** ..." should not cross our lips.

And maybe you should try attending one of the later *minyanim* for Maariv on Motza'ei Shabbos instead of running to the first and quickest *minyan*.

Finally, and most importantly, *prepare* for Shabbos.

Most *mitzvos* in the Torah require an actual action: you have to *eat* the matzah, you have to *blow* the *shofar*, you have to *don* the *tefillin*.

Shabbos is an exception. You don't have to do *anything*. The Ribbono Shel Olam comes to visit you. He says, "I'm going to come with My holy *Shechinah* and dwell among you, and make you holier.

"There's only one thing I ask from you: I want you to long for Shabbos. Anticipate it. Show Me that you want the gift!"

Perhaps this is why Rashi (*Beitzah* 2b) states that the preparation for Shabbos is in itself a Torah-mandated mitzvah. By preparing, we show that we want Shabbos. And as Rav Shimshon Pincus writes, "The primary *kedushah* of Shabbos rests on those who want it."

> *"There's only one thing I ask from you: I want you to long for Shabbos. Anticipate it. Show Me that you want the gift!"*

Knowing that this is a mitzvah will infuse your Shabbos preparations with much more meaning. Instead of cooking and baking and cleaning just as a matter of routine, think, "I'm preparing for Shabbos."

You're no longer just peeling potatoes and sautéing onions; you're preparing to host Hashem's *Shechinah*.

⤙ The Chatzos Challenge

I once spoke about Shabbos in Highland Park, NJ, and I read an essay, not realizing that the writer of that essay, a woman by the name of Mrs. Azriella Jaffe, was in the audience.

She wrote how she makes a point of being ready for Shabbos every single week before *chatzos* (midday) on Friday. When I start speaking about this to women, their general reaction is to either laugh or to look at me like I'm insane. But after I spoke in

Highland Park, Mrs. Jaffe wrote to me to explain how this came about.

She wrote that one Friday, her daughter remarked, "Oy, tonight is Shabbos. I wish it wasn't Shabbos."

Do you know why she made that comment? Because Friday meant chores. Friday meant chaos. Friday meant a tense mother.

So Mrs. Jaffe accepted upon herself that by *chatzos* on Friday, everything would be ready. *EVERYTHING*!

This means that, in her words, "The food is prepared, the table is set, the candelabra is ready, and when my kids come off the bus from school, instead of coming home to Shabbos chores and to a tense mother trying to cook and clean and make the deadline, they come home to a happy mother, a clean house, the smells of Shabbos in the air, and a free afternoon to relax.

"When my husband comes home from a long day at work, he comes home to serenity, not chaos."

"But to do *chatzos* right," she adds, "you can't start at midnight on Thursday night. You need to prepare for Shabbos every day of the week.

"My children now think that it's normal to make a new batch of *challos* on Motza'ei Shabbos. Or to plan a Shabbos menu on Sunday. They're accustomed to asking me if the chicken cooking in the oven at 7 a.m. on Friday is for Shabbos."

> *"My children now think that it's normal to make a new batch of challos on Motza'ei Shabbos. Or to plan a Shabbos menu on Sunday."*

Listen to the icing on the cake:

"Shabbos is on our minds all week long. When Friday comes around, our house is one of beauty and serenity, and anticipation of Shabbos, rather than the former feeling of, 'Oh no, when is candle lighting?'"

Mrs. Jaffe started a support group with three women, but she now has women all over the world — in England, Eretz Yisrael, and Australia — in her support group.

Once again, this is not an all-or-none deal. Whether a woman wants to be ready at *chatzos*, or maybe just an hour early, or even just to be ready on time rather than late, it's worth planning ahead.

A woman from New York wrote that she set a goal of being ready *five minutes* before the *zman*, accepting upon herself to be ready 23 minutes before *shekiah* rather than the standard 18 minutes.

This already sends the message to Hashem: Shabbos is something I want, something I look forward to.

Men's Preparation

So men may have just read the previous section with a feeling of relief. Although some men do handle some of the shopping or cleaning, in general, the activities we were discussing until this point fall into the women's realm.

Sorry, dear gentlemen, to burst your bubble, but we must also do something to prepare for Shabbos. And to do so, we have to take a page from our own Pesach playbook. Almost every man prepares before Pesach, some even buy a new Haggadah each year, so that they can come to the Seder prepared.

We have to do the very same for Shabbos. We cannot plop ourselves down at the table Friday night unprepared and yet expect to have a meaningful Shabbos. Especially for those who have children at home — you *must* make Shabbos special for them. Whether it means singing with your children if you're a *baal menagen* or telling stories to keep young children interested, you have to make it special for them.

> We cannot plop ourselves down at the table Friday night unprepared and yet expect to have a meaningful Shabbos.

A friend from Silver Spring came to show me a notebook in which he writes down riddles for his kids during the week. Friday night at the meal, they have family time trying to work out the riddles. Another person told me that at the *seudah* in his home, each person has to say a special thing Hashem did for them during the week. They don't have to say a *vort* or read from their *parashah* sheet, which most people don't pay attention to. All they have to say is one episode in which they noticed the Hand of Hashem in their lives.

Bottom line, we have to instill in our children a sense of specialness about Shabbos, which will leave a long-lasting impact on every area of their lives.

◄§ A Shabbos Legacy

Commenting on the *pasuk:* וְשָׁמְרוּ בְנֵי יִשְׂרָאֵל אֶת הַשַּׁבָּת לַעֲשׂוֹת אֶת הַשַּׁבָּת לְדֹרֹתָם בְּרִית עוֹלָם, *The Children of Israel shall observe the Shabbos, to make the Shabbos an eternal covenant for their generations* (*Shemos* 31:16), the Ohr HaChaim notes that the word שמר is occasionally used in the Torah to connote "awaiting," as it is used in the verse, וְאָבִיו שָׁמַר אֶת הַדָּבָר, *But his father awaited the matter* (*Bereishis* 37:11).

Do you know what the reward is for looking forward to Shabbos and awaiting it?

לְדֹרֹתָם בְּרִית עוֹלָם, we will merit that our descendants will always keep Shabbos.

Your Shabbos legacy can be more concrete. Mrs. Miriam Weiss, the daughter of master *mechanech* Rav Binyamin Steinberg, wrote to me that shortly after her father had contracted cancer, he and his sons sang his Shabbos *niggunim* into a tape recorder, so that he could leave his Shabbos *niggunim* as a legacy for his family.

There was a fellow by the name of Mr. Abe Schmell who was *niftar* a few years back. Abe immigrated to America at the age of six, and by the time he was eleven the Great Depression had struck, and he had to go to work. He starting apprenticing in a bakery by washing the baking pans and cleaning, and eventually he learned the trade and opened his own bakery in Baltimore.

At Abe Schmell's *levayah*, his son said that his father did not know much more than how to be *maavir sedra* and maybe learn a few Mishnayos, because he had not had the opportunity to go to *cheder*. He would work 70 hour weeks, and on Thursday nights he would get to the bakery at 2 or 3 o'clock in the morning. By the time he came to the table Friday night, he was bone tired.

But you know what he did at that table? He sang Shabbos *niggunim* with all his heart and soul. This was his Shabbos. No insights into the *parashah*. But a *niggun*!

Do you know where his children are today? They are fine *talmidei chachamim*, *bnei Torah*, and *n'shei chayil*, because he instilled in them the uniqueness of Shabbos.

⊷§ Shabbos as an Anchor

I often remark to my wife that I'm glad that we're out of the child-rearing business. You're never out of the *parenting* business, because you're parents to your children even when they are adults, but I'm glad I'm not *raising* children in today's society. How difficult it must be to raise children in times when they have such terrible temptations — with the click of a button, they can be in places we shudder to think about.

> *I'm glad I'm not raising children in today's society. How difficult it must be to raise children in times when they have such terrible temptations.*

Rav Mattisyahu Salomon points out that Shabbos will make our children greater *maaminim*, and that will keep them closer to Hashem. He bases this concept on the Gemara that states that if a person keeps Shabbos properly, even if he has worshiped idols, he will be forgiven. In his glosses on *Shulchan Aruch*, the Taz wonders what sort of person we are discussing. If this is a person who hasn't done *teshuvah* for his idolatry, why should he be forgiven just because he keeps Shabbos. And if he *has* done *teshuvah*, then what does he accomplish through his

Shabbos observance that he hasn't already through his repentance?

It must be, answers the Taz, that this person must have done *teshuvah*. But what happens to the damage the *aveirah* has done to his *neshamah*? Isn't that indelible?

The answer is Shabbos. A person who keeps Shabbos properly will purify his mind and his *neshamah* that were tainted during the week.

> *A person who keeps Shabbos properly will purify his mind and his neshamah that were tainted during the week.*

Our children, who are exposed to the *shmutz* out there every day of their lives, need Shabbos as an anchor to keep them *frum*.

In Rav Mattisyahu Salomon's words: "The *kedushah* of Shabbos has the power to cleanse the soul. We live in dangerous times. The influence of the outside world is so pervasive, it tugs at the eyes and the hearts and the minds of our children. By making Shabbos special, we give our children a strong foundation of *emunah* that will last throughout their lifetime."

And if you want an example of what Rav Mattisyahu Salomon is talking about, I'll conclude with one more story. It's a Holocaust story — but perhaps one of the most atypical Holocaust stories you'll ever read.

The story appears in a book called *The Lilac Bush*, written by Judith Mandel-Novac. She was born in Hungary, in a little town called Gerla. Born Judith Cohen, she married a man named Mandel, and after he passed away, she remarried a man named Novac.

In *The Lilac Bush*, she describes her upbringing in Hungary, one of seven girls in her family. She recounts the way her family celebrated Shabbos in Gerla. During the week, they would speak Hungarian in the home, but on Shabbos, they spoke only Yiddish. She describes the beautiful and relaxed atmosphere in her home on Shabbos, and how she and her sisters would sing the Shabbos *niggunim*.

In 1944, her idyllic existence came to an abrupt end. The Nazis started deporting Hungarian Jewry to the death camps, where she lost all six of her sisters.

After the war, she joined a group of survivors heading back to Gerla. Sitting on the train, she wondered to herself, *"Why* am I going back? *To what* am I going back?"

She was broken, depressed, and angry.

In their bitterness, this group of survivors decided that when they got off the train, they would head straight to the shul in Gerla and throw rocks at it, to show the One Above just how furious they were.

Judith Mandel-Novac writes that as she was about to throw her first stone at the shul, she had a sudden flashback to Shabbos in her parents' home. She remembered the *niggunim* at the Shabbos table, and the atmosphere in the home, and she thought to herself, *How can I go through the rest of my life without Shabbos?*

She put down the stone, and she remained a *frum* Jew.

This is what Shabbos can do for our children if we make it meaningful and special. It can keep them *frum* for the rest of their lives.

The *sefarim* state that each of the seven days between Rosh Hashanah and Yom Kippur can atone for the corresponding day of the week in the previous year. Shabbos Shuvah, then, has the power to repair the Shabbosos of the previous year, and to reinvigorate our Shabbosos with excitement.

Let's start now.

Let's make our Shabbosos the *Yoma D'Nishmasa*, the day for the *neshamah*, the day when we reconnect with our spiritual side, so that when we return to Aseres Yemei Teshuvah next year, we find ourselves with lasting results from the *teshuvah* we did this year.

SECTION III:

Together
We Learn

Yes, You Can ...
If You Have a Plan

"The Daf."[1]
This learning program has become so ubiquitous that we no longer describe it as Daf Yomi, but merely as "The Daf." It's a proper noun, part of our lexicon, and finds its way into daily conversation: "Did you do The Daf?" or "Where is The Daf holding?"

> *Rav Meir Shapiro, who instituted the concept of learning a daily folio, actually found much deeper significance in the words "The Daf."*

But it's not only shorthand for Daf Yomi. Rav Meir Shapiro, who instituted the concept of learning a

---

1. This essay is adapted from an address delivered at the 12th Daf Yomi Siyum HaShas to an audience of over 90,000 at Metlife Stadium in New Jersey. The Siyum was also broadcast live to tens of thousands of others in cities throughout the United States.

daily folio, actually found much deeper significance in the words "The Daf."

The Gemara (*Yevamos* 121a) relates that Rabban Gamliel was once traveling on a ship, and he saw another ship sinking. He was distraught because he realized that R' Akiva was on that boat. To his astonishment, when he returned ashore, R' Akiva appeared before him and began to learn Torah as though nothing had occurred. "My son," Rabban Gamliel asked, "who pulled you out of the water?"

"I grabbed hold of a *daf* from a boat that washed toward me, and as each wave came my way, I bowed my head [and allowed it to ride over me]."

In this Gemara, the word *daf* clearly means a plank of wood that had detached from a boat, but Rav Meir Shapiro saw a deep correlation between that *daf* and The Daf that we learn. Just as that *daf* saved R' Akiva from the turbulence of the sea, so does The Daf save us from the turbulence of life. As Dovid HaMelech so poignantly said: לוּלֵי תוֹרָתְךָ שַׁעֲשֻׁעָי אָז אָבַדְתִּי בְעָנְיִי, *Had Your Torah not been my preoccupation, then I would have perished in my affliction* (*Tehillim* 119:92).

Torah study in general — and Daf Yomi in particular — is our lifeline in this world.

◄§ A Constant Companion

In fact, "lifeline" is the exact term a fellow used in describing his own relationship with Daf Yomi. This man had a very difficult life. He was orphaned at a young age, had very little money, and had several medical and social issues. In 2005, after the last *Siyum HaShas*, he wrote me as follows:

> I had been out of yeshivah for about two years, and I was barely learning a word. I was not very happy with myself. I would come home each night and stare at my 19-inch "color companion." I realized that this had to stop, so I tried Daf Yomi.

As I sat in Madison Square Garden [at the *Siyum HaShas*] last Tuesday night, I was at the tail-end of a roller-coaster ride. I had not had the greatest *mazel* socially, job-wise, city-wise, and the list goes on. But what I did have was a **lifeline** — a constant companion on the train, at the doctor's office, late at night, early in the morning… a trusted companion who would never let me down, even if everything and everybody else would. All this companion asked of me is that I visited it every day for an hour or so.

When he cried to the Rebbe about how lonely he felt, the Rebbe said, "Az ah Yid hutt a blatt Gemara, iz ehr kein mohl nisht alein."

This fellow echoed the message the Gerrer Rebbe once told a broken Jew whose wife had recently passed away. When he cried to the Rebbe about how lonely he felt, the Rebbe said, "*Az ah Yid hutt a blatt Gemara, iz ehr kein mohl nisht alein* — If a Jew has a *daf* Gemara, he's never alone."

Who wouldn't want a constant, reliable companion?

❧ Life Itself

Limud HaTorah is so much more than just another mitzvah; it is life itself. The words כִּי הֵם חַיֵּינוּ וְאֹרֶךְ יָמֵינוּ, *for they are our life and the length of our days* (Maariv prayer) are literal. The Torah is our life.

In fact, the words כִּי הֵם חַיֵּינוּ answer a question about a story many are familiar with.

The Gemara (*Yevamos* 121a) relates that Hillel HaZakein was extremely poor, so poor, in fact, that he would use half of his daily wages to support his family, and the other half to pay his way into the *beis midrash* to study Torah. One freezing winter day, he didn't earn enough for both. He gave his earnings to his family and headed off to the *beis midrash*, but the guard would not allow him entry since he couldn't pay.

Hillel climbed onto the roof of the *beis midrash* and put his ear to the skylight, so he could hear words of Torah from his rebbeim, Shemaya and Avtalyon. That day was an Erev Shabbos in the middle of Teves, and while Hillel was enraptured by the Torah being discussed in the *beis midrash* below, snow began to fall. On Shabbos morning, Shemaya said to Avtalyon, "Each morning, the sun lights up the *beis midrash*, and today it has remained dark. Perhaps it is an overcast day?" They then looked up and saw the form of a person in the skylight. They ran up to the roof and found Hillel buried in three *amos* (close to six feet!) of snow.

A powerful story, but the Chofetz Chaim points out that the Gemara (*Kesubos* 50a) teaches that a person should not spend more than one-fifth of his assets in order to perform a mitzvah. How was Hillel allowed to spend half of his meager wages to learn Torah?

The Chofetz Chaim finds an answer in the words the Gemara uses to describe Hillel's daily effort to enter the *beis midrash*. It states that he would use those wages to pay to hear דִּבְרֵי אֱלֹקִים חַיִּים מִפִּי שְׁמַעְיָה וְאַבְטַלְיוֹן. One is indeed not allowed to use more than 20 percent of his wages for any mitzvah, but this was more than a mitzvah. This was דִּבְרֵי אֱלֹקִים חַיִּים — this was life itself. For life itself, there are no spending limits.

❧ What a Jew *Needs*

While we may not need to spend one-fifth of our wages to learn Torah, in the recesses of our souls, a Jew realizes that the Torah is life itself.

Rabbi Aaron Paperman was a military chaplain in the U.S. Army during World War II. After the war, he visited the DP camps to try to help the Jews who had suffered so much during the war. In each DP camp he would ask people, "*Vohs darft ihr* — what do you need?" The answers would invariably be something along the lines of, "*Ah pohr shich* — a pair of shoes" or "*Ah pohr hoizen* — a pair of pants."

One Yid, however, a Bobover chassid by the name of Mr. Seiger, had an unusual request. When Rabbi Paperman asked him what he needed, he said, "*Ich darf a Bava Kamma.*"

Rabbi Paperman said, "Yes, but what do you *really need?*"

The response remained the same. "*Ich darf a Bava Kamma.*"

Rabbi Paperman realized that all Mr. Seiger truly needed was a Gemara *Bava Kamma*, and he succeeded in securing one for him.

Mr. Seiger knew with his entire being that along with food and shelter, a Jew *needs* something else. He needs a *Bava Kamma*. כִּי הֵם חַיֵּינוּ, וְאוֹרֶךְ יָמֵינוּ.

◁§ The Real Thing

Aside from recognizing that Torah is life itself, and it alone can save us from the tribulations of the world, I think that there must be another motivation for learning.

When Rav Meir Shapiro first instituted Daf Yomi, the Jews were, by and large, a downtrodden bunch. They spent their days in menial, often backbreaking labor, and when they were finally able to stop at night, Daf Yomi was their escape, their one hour of peace, a brief daily respite from a life of privation.

Daf Yomi was their escape, their one hour of peace, a brief daily respite from a life of privation.

Today, there are so many distractions, so many ways for a person to occupy his time. There is so much vying for our eyes and our imaginations. And yet people rise at 5 a.m. or head to shul at 11 p.m. — for what? To read an ancient text, written in a difficult language more than 1,500 years ago, dealing with arcane, sometimes very technical subjects. And they will do this on trains, planes, and buses. They will do this at weddings waiting for the *chuppah*. They will do this in doctors' offices and on supermarket checkout lines. They, and their wives, and their children, will bend their schedules to make sure that this will happen.

Why?

Perhaps the motivation is that we all realize that Torah is *real*, and that everything else, no matter how dazzling, is *fake*.

The Torah describes *Mattan Torah* as follows: אֶת הַדְּבָרִים הָאֵלֶּה דִּבֶּר ה' אֶל כָּל קְהַלְכֶם בָּהָר מִתּוֹךְ הָאֵשׁ הֶעָנָן וְהָעֲרָפֶל קוֹל גָּדוֹל וְלֹא יָסָף, *These words Hashem spoke to your entire congregation on the mountain, from the midst of the fire, and the thick cloud — a great voice, that never ended (Devarim 5:19).*

If Hashem's voice never ended, why don't we hear it today?

Rav Aharon Kotler explained that Hashem's voice continues to "speak" to the soul of every Jew through the Torah itself. Despite the dazzling world out there, the Torah trumps every other pursuit, because it is Hashem's voice speaking directly to the heart of every Jew.

It is the real thing, and everything else is fake.

⤳ Hearing the Bas Kol

As we sit here celebrating the *siyum* on Daf Yomi, we're also hearing another voice. In *Pirkei Avos* (6:2) we read that each day, a *bas kol* (heavenly voice) rings forth from Har Chorev (Har Sinai, where the Torah was given), and it declares, "Woe to the people, because of [their] insult to the Torah! For whoever does not occupy himself with the Torah is called 'rebuked.' "

> *It might be fleeting, and it might be faint, but if you have had the feeling that you should really learn more, you have heard that bas kol!*

Have you ever heard this daily *bas kol*? You may not think so, but in actuality, you have heard it.

The Baal Shem Tov said that when a Jew suddenly thinks to himself, "*I waste a lot of time, and I don't learn enough Torah; I really should learn more,*" he is hearing that *bas kol*.

It might be fleeting, and it might be

faint, but if you have had the feeling that you should really learn more, *you have heard that bas kol*!

Sometimes, however, we ignore that voice — or worse, we actively squelch it.

How do we take advantage of that *bas kol* rather than lose the inspiration it can provide?

When we hear that clarion call — and that voice emanates today, from this stadium, and reverberates into the soul of each one of us and says: "learn more" — we have to seize the moment and create *a plan* to learn more.

If you've never learned Daf Yomi, let this *bas kol* be your impetus to start for the first time. If you've already been through the cycle, you can go to a weekly *shiur iyun*, an in-depth *shiur* on a topic in the *daf*. Or maybe go to your *shiur* in the morning and then review it at night. Perhaps you can even be so bold as to take tests on the *daf*.

And if you can't learn a *daf* a day, make it an *amud* a day. Or a *daf* of *Mishnah Berurah* a day. Or a few halachos a day. But learn something *each day*!

One way or another, when you hear that *bas kol*, make sure that you turn it into a concrete plan to learn more; otherwise it can just dissipate.

❧ Now THAT'S a Plan!

Devising a plan is the message Rav Nosson Tzvi Finkel, the Rosh Yeshivah of Mir Yerushalayim, shared with R' Nochum Stilerman, a man who spent half a century working in the United States before moving to Eretz Yisrael as he neared 70.

A methodical person by nature, after completing *Maseches Shabbos* in honor of his 70th birthday, R' Nochum drew up a study program that would enable him to learn a *masechta* in *Shas* and *Sefer Tehillim* by his 71st birthday. When he showed his plan to Rav Nosson Tzvi, the Rosh Yeshivah said, "But what about the rest of the Torah? Draw up a plan to finish *kol haTorah kulah*!"

> *When he showed his plan to Rav Nosson Tzvi, the Rosh Yeshivah said, "But what about the rest of the Torah? Draw up a plan to finish kol haTorah kulah!"*

R' Nochum went home and drew up a five-year plan that would enable him to finish another few *masechtos*, all of *Tanach*, and a *mussar sefer*. He brought the detailed printout to Rav Nosson Tzvi, who reviewed it and said, "But you're not finishing *Shas*!"

"Rosh Yeshivah," R' Nochum protested, "to finish *Shas* according to this program I'll need many, many years."

"Go print out a learning program for the whole *Shas*," Rav Nosson Tzvi insisted.

R' Nochum went home and printed out the plan. Some 2,500 pages later, he had a program to present to the Rosh Yeshivah — a program that would take 23½ years to complete!

When Rav Nosson Tzvi saw the two-volume printout, he exclaimed, "Now THAT'S a plan! THAT'S a plan!"

"But Rosh Yeshivah," R' Nochum objected, "I can't do this! I'm already 70, and it would take me until I'm over 93 to finish this — at a pace of 10 hours of learning a day! I hope to live *ad me'ah v'esrim*, but how can I undertake a plan that I can't possibly complete?"

Rav Nosson Tzvi, who had already been afflicted with Parkinson's disease for over twenty years at that point, struggled mightily to stand up. While quivering in his place he said, "And do you think I can do what I'm doing? Look at *me*!"

He then reached under his tablecloth and pulled out his plans for the Mir, which included adding more buildings to the yeshivah, which already had some 7,000 students, to make space for even more *talmidim*. "Do you think I can do this?" he asked R' Nochum. "Of course I can't.

"But you and I have a great advantage," Rav Nosson Tzvi continued. "We both realize that we can't possibly do what we would like to do. Everyone else fools himself into thinking that he *can* do what he wants to do. You and I realize that we are in the hands of the Ribbono Shel Olam, and that the most we can do is try.

"Accept upon yourself to learn according to your plan, and leave the rest to Hashem."

Each and every person must have a plan. And if it seems out of reach, leave it to the Ribbono Shel Olam to help you fulfill it.

> *"You and I realize that we are in the hands of the Ribbono Shel Olam, and that the most we can do is try. Accept upon yourself to learn according to your plan, and leave the rest to Hashem."*

๑ It's Within Your Grasp

Shortly after Rav Nosson Tzvi became Rosh Yeshivah of Mir, he once remarked to the same R' Nochum Stilerman that he thinks the reason he was afflicted with Parkinson's was because he loves learning so much that there's no way he could learn Torah *lishmah* (for its own sake), because it was too enjoyable to be purely motivated.

"Perhaps," said Rav Nosson Tzvi, "I was stricken with this disease as a punishment for not learning Torah *lishmah*."

Twenty years later, when the Rosh Yeshivah's condition had deteriorated to a terrible degree, R' Nochum came across a Gemara in *Talmud Yerushalmi*, and was so excited by what he saw that he hurried to show it to the Rosh Yeshivah.

The *Talmud Yerushalmi* (*Horayos* 3:5) teaches that when Moshe Rabbeinu ascended to the Heavens and learned Torah there for 40 days and nights, he kept forgetting everything Hashem taught him. At the end of the 40 days, he received the entire Torah as a gift.

"Why was this necessary?" asks the *Talmud Yerushalmi*. "*Bishvil lehachzir es hatipshim* — so there will be an answer to the unwise."

"Imagine Moshe Rabbeinu's plight," R' Nochum said to

the Rosh Yeshivah. "He's in Heaven learning from Hashem Himself, and each time he walks away for a moment and says, 'What did I just learn?' he draws a total blank. It must have been so frustrating.

"Why did Hashem do that to him? So that some unwise people who feel that they can't learn because they keep forgetting the material will take heart and say, 'If Moshe Rabbeinu could forget what he learned and still continue studying Torah, so can we.' "

R' Nochum then reminded Rav Nosson Tzvi that twenty years earlier, the Rosh Yeshivah had suggested that his Parkinson's was a punishment for not learning *lishmah*. "Maybe there's a different reason," suggested R' Nochum. "Maybe the Rosh Yeshivah received this illness so that if any of us would say that we can't learn because we aren't feeling up to it, the Rosh Yeshivah would serve as proof that one *can* learn even with a debilitating disease."

Upon hearing R' Nochum Stilerman's interpretation, Rav Nosson Tzvi leaned over and kissed him, and, paraphrasing the Gemara (*Rosh Hashanah* 25a), he exclaimed, "*Akiva nichamtani, Akiva nichamtani* — you have consoled me."

In this generation, we had a Rav Nosson Tzvi Finkel, who grew up as a regular American boy, graduating from Ari Crowne Day School in Chicago, but he went on to become the Rosh Yeshivah of Mir Yerushalayim. We may never become a Rav Nosson Tzvi Finkel, but we can all take one message from his life:

Devise a plan, and reach for great heights. You might just find that what seemed beyond your reach is within your grasp.

So That It's Not Forgotten

Shortly after World War II, a young man walked into Yeshivas Ponevezh in Bnei Brak and asked the Ponevezher Rav whether he could enroll in the yeshivah.

Realizing that this boy must have been a Holocaust survivor, the Ponevezher Rav asked, "What did you learn before the war?"

"I learned *Eilu Treifos*," the boy replied.

Eilu Treifos is a complex *perek* in *Maseches Chullin* that deals with the intricate halachos of which physical abnormalities render an animal *treif*.

"Do you remember anything you learned?" asked the Ponevezher Rav.

"I do," the *bachur* replied, and proceeded to tell him a Gemara from *Eilu Treifos*.

The Ponevezher Rav grabbed this boy by the hand and ran with him through the streets of Bnei Brak to the home of the Chazon Ish. "This boy is a living embodiment of the *pasuk*:

וְהָיָה כִּי תִמְצֶאןָ אֹתוֹ רָעוֹת רַבּוֹת וְצָרוֹת וְעָנְתָה הַשִּׁירָה הַזֹּאת לְפָנָיו לְעֵד כִּי לֹא

תִּשָּׁכַח מִפִּי זַרְעוֹ, *It shall be that when many evils and distresses come upon it, then this song shall speak up before it as a witness, for it will not be forgotten from the mouth of its offspring"* (*Devarim* 31:21), he exclaimed.

For someone to have gone through the horrors of the Holocaust and still remember the Torah he learned before the war is a clear fulfillment of Hashem's promise that the Torah will never be forgotten.

But there's a corollary to that story.

After the Holocaust, there was a gathering in Bnei Brak to discuss what could be done to resurrect Torah in Eretz Yisrael. The Ponevezher Rav addressed the audience, and said, "לֹא תִשָּׁכַח מִפִּי זַרְעוֹ is not only a pledge from Hashem; it's a challenge to us as well. We can't just sit back and say, 'Hashem will take care of Torah. *We* have to take the initiative and make sure that the Torah is not forgotten.'"

> We can't just sit back and say, 'Hashem will take care of Torah. We have to take the initiative and make sure that the Torah is not forgotten.

The Ponevezher Rav was not the first person to feel the responsibility to resuscitate Torah after history's depradations or when the times demanded it.

✑ A Historical Responsibility

The Gemara (*Kesubos* 103b) states that R' Chiya said, "I will ensure that Torah will not be forgotten from Klal Yisrael. I will plant flax, weave nets, and trap deer. I'll feed the meat to orphans, and make parchment out of the hides. Then I'll go to a village in which there are no Torah teachers, and I'll teach Chamishah Chumshei Torah [which I wrote on the parchments] to five children, and I'll teach Shishah Sidrei Mishnah to six children. I'll tell each one to teach his Seder of Mishnayos to his friends."

The Gemara concludes, "This is what Rebbi was referring to when he said, 'How great are Chiya's deeds.'"

Another example:

The Gemara in *Bava Basra* (21a) says something shocking: If not for R' Yehoshua ben Gamla, Torah would have been forgotten from Klal Yisrael. Why? Because until his times, if a boy had a father, his father taught him Torah. If not, he just roamed the streets. R' Yehoshua ben Gamla was the grandfather of the Day School movement. He was the one who decreed that each city must have *melamdim* to teach children — *all* children — Torah.

Reaching back even farther into our history, the *pasuk* says: וְיֹתֵר שֶׁהָיָה קֹהֶלֶת חָכָם עוֹד לִמַּד דַּעַת אֶת הָעָם וְאִזֵּן וְחִקֵּר תִּקֵּן מְשָׁלִים הַרְבֵּה, *And beyond being wise, Koheles also imparted knowledge to the people; he listened, and sought out, and arranged many proverbs* (*Koheles* 12:9).

This means that during the Golden Years of Jewish history — the era when our nation flourished like it never did before and has never done since — people were not able to learn Torah. It had no *oznayim*, it was like a pot without handles, which just couldn't be lifted. What did Shlomo HaMelech do to rectify the situation? He "invented" the *mashal* method, the concept of parables.

And the *pasuk* goes so far as to state that Shlomo's greatest achievement — surpassing his claim to fame as the wisest of men — was his ability to create good parables, so that people who weren't able to learn Torah without them could learn. He helped people "get a handle" on Torah.

⊰ A Challenge for Today

Nowadays, we don't have the challenge of the roshei yeshivah and rebbes who managed to escape the flames of Europe and then rebuild from scratch in other places in the world: Rav Aharon Kotler, Rav Leizer Yudel Finkel in Mir, the Satmar Rebbe, the Belzer Rebbe, to name just a few. Hashem, in His mercy, spared some Torah giants such as Rav Moshe Feinstein, Rav Yaakov Kamenetsky, Rav Ruderman, Rav Hutner, Rav

Soloveitchik, Rav Shraga Feivel Mendlowitz, and a few others who would go on to build Torah — in a personal fulfillment of לֹא תִשָּׁכַח מִפִּי זַרְעוֹ.

Thankfully, in our times, we do not face the herculean task of having to rebuild a Torah world that has been physically devastated. We even have schools in most areas populated by Jewish people. Nevertheless, we have our own challenges, our own obligation to answer the question: What are *we* doing for Jewish continuity?

Today, three sociological factors combine to present us with an unprecedented challenge in terms of disseminating Torah.

↝§ More Sophistication

Phenomenon number one is that in the past sixty years, we have seen an explosion in the number of yeshivah- and Bais Yaakov-educated youth. Fifty years ago, a large percentage of frum people, many of whom were educated in public schools, felt that all they needed was a weekly *shiur* on Shabbos afternoon — *venomar amen*.

Not today's graduates of Torah schools. They want to feel challenged each day.

In the past, we had very rudimentary Torah works available in English. The children and grandchildren of the same people who used the Birnbaum Siddur and Hertz Chumash, which were fine for those generations, want something more sophisticated, more advanced.

↝§ The Handicap of Ignorance

The second phenomenon is the *baal teshuvah* movement, which began as a trickle and became a torrent. We can speculate as to what set off this search for meaning. Some suggest that the *neshamos* of the 1.5 million children who were killed during the

Holocaust are returning in the bodies of people who are born into irreligious families, and they later seek religion on their own, to "continue" their previous mission that was cut short. They are ready to give up everything they've been raised with to find meaning in their lives, because their *neshamos* — *neshamos* that didn't have a chance to live full Jewish lives — beckon to them.

Others see this as a direct result of the miraculous Israeli wars, and especially the Six Day War. Those who lived through those events know that you had to have been blind not to see the Yad Hashem in Israel winning that war, and those miracles led to mass soul-searching.

Whatever the cause is, we now have a torrent of people — whether it's the college students in their 20s, the hedge-fund managers in their 30s, or the cardiologists in their 40s — returning to Judaism.

For those of us who grew up with Torah study in our mother's milk, learning Mishnayos at the age of 8 and starting Gemara at 10 — perhaps even finishing a Seder of Mishnah or a *masechta* in Gemara at our bar mitzvah — it is hard to fathom just how difficult it is to start from the ground at the age of 20, 30, or later.

> *We now have a torrent of people — whether it's the college students in their 20s, the hedge-fund managers in their 30s, or the cardiologists in their 40s — returning to Judaism.*

You have to realize something about *baalei teshuvah*: A *baal teshuvah* who cannot learn is "disabled."

A person who returns to religion but does not know how to learn is akin to a blind person who goes for some miraculous new treatment that cures his blindness. After the surgery, he suddenly has vision for the first time, but it's not perfect. Now he needs glasses to clear up his vision. If the surgeon doesn't send him to an optometrist to prescribe a pair of glasses, he hasn't accomplished much, because the person is still bumping into trees with his blurry vision.

If *baalei teshuvah* can't learn, their vision of Judaism is not clear. We can't just invest efforts into teaching them the rudimentary rules of Yiddishkeit; we must also make Torah study available to them. If we don't, it comes back to haunt them when their children attend Torah schools, and they want to learn with their parents. If a father cannot open a Chumash and learn a Rashi, or a Mishnah, or a piece of Gemara with his son, he's disabled. If a girl comes home with homework and her mother can't help her because she never learned out of a Chumash, it's frustrating.

So just as we have to deal with the yeshivah graduates who need sophisticated Torah works, so do we have to look out for the precious *baalei teshuvah*, who need the tools and the raw materials that will enable them to learn Torah.

⁓ Age + Health = Time for Torah

The third phenomenon is a combination of two developments — an increase in health and wealth — that morphed into a new demographic: the healthy retiree. Nowadays, it's not so uncommon for people to be secure enough financially to retire at the age of 60, even before the official retirement age, and they can then live in good health — sometimes for 20 or 30 years.

The question then becomes: what now? If you're 62 and in good health, and you don't have to step into an office again in your life, what do you do with the next decades of your life?

The question then becomes: what now? If you're 62 and in good health, and you don't have to step into an office again in your life, what do you do with the next decades of your life?

This applies especially in American society, in which retirement is the ultimate goal. So people retire — frequently even taking early retirement — and do... What? Drive your wife crazy by sitting around the house doing nothing? How many times a day can a person: read the newspaper? Go shopping? Play golf?

Now, in American society, most people earn their retirement honestly, because they are *bnei Noach*, and as such, can follow the lead of their ancestor.

The Torah relates that immediately upon emerging from the *teivah*: וַיָּחֶל נֹחַ אִישׁ הָאֲדָמָה וַיִּטַּע כָּרֶם. וַיֵּשְׁתְּ מִן הַיַּיִן וַיִּשְׁכָּר, *Noach, the man of the earth, debased himself and planted a vineyard. He drank of the wine and became drunk (Bereishis 9:20-21).*

Was there anything wrong with Noach planting that vine-yard?

Chazal comment that the word *vayachel* (which derives from the same root as *chullin*, mundane) teaches us that Noach's choice to plant grapes was *chullin* — prosaic, pedestrian.

Rav Simcha Wasserman wondered why the Torah found fault with Noach. This man experiences a veritable apocalypse, and he emerges from the *teivah* to a desolate world. Who *wouldn't* want to drown that bleakness in some wine?

Notice, answers Rav Simchah, that the Torah doesn't say Noach became *wicked* or *evil*. He was *chullin*, pedestrian. Because after emerging from the *teivah*, a person shouldn't just put up his feet and say, "I saved all humanity and the animals as well. I've done enough."

It's time to rebuild, not to retire.

But a *ben Noach* who does retire is following the lead of his ancestor.

Not so for a frum Jew, because we are considered not only descendants of Noach, but of Avraham Avinu.

According to some commentators, the last *nisayon* Avraham Avinu faced was when he had to purchase a burial plot for Sarah, immediately following the tremendous test of *Akeidas Yitzchak*. Now superficially, that act does not seem to compare to *Akeidas Yitzchak*, when he was commanded to sacrifice his only son. After passing that test and being tested yet again with another challenge, however, Avraham could have said: "Haven't I done enough? Don't I deserve to retire?"

But that wasn't his attitude. He went about buying the burial spot without any complaints, clearing yet another hurdle.

In truth, Americans who retire early are making a big mistake — one that Sumner Redstone did not make. Mr. Redstone, the chairman of Viacom who has no dearth of income with his current net worth of a few billion dollars, yet continues to work well into his 90s, said succinctly: "You retire, you die." But retirement is the Great American Dream, and as *bnei Noach*, they've earned it honestly. It is their heritage from their *elter-zeide*. And these are not wicked or evil goals; they are *chullin*, prosaic goals.

> *But retirement is the Great American Dream, and as bnei Noach, they've earned it honestly.*

We proudly trace our roots back to Avraham Avinu, who, at the ripe old age of 137, was still overcoming daunting challenges, without looking to put his feet up. A Jew should not seek to retire. That doesn't mean you should continue your current job indefinitely, but as long as you have your health, and your mind is clear, your question should be, "What next? What can I still accomplish at this stage in life?"

I tell my *talmidim*, who are still young men, "Find your niche in learning, because one day hopefully you will stop working, and if you taught yourself to enjoy learning, you can have a few decades of enjoyment ahead of you. You can finish *Shas* then, or learn *Tanach* — things that you haven't gotten to in your earlier years."

> *"Find your niche in learning, because one day hopefully you will stop working, and if you taught yourself to enjoy learning, you can have a few decades of enjoyment ahead of you."*

It's not enough, though, for the people themselves to want to learn. Once someone has been out of yeshivah for 30 or 40 years, it's not easy to open a Gemara *Menachos* or *Me'ilah*, or a Navi *Yirmiyah* or *Yeshayah*. So this is the final group that we have to think about. What are we doing to make Torah available to the senior population?

←§ Meeting the Challenge

Thankfully, Hashem granted us talented idealists, and the collective ingenuity, creativity, and generosity of Klal Yisrael have combined to provide us with endless opportunities to ensure the continuum of Torah study for these three groups: the yeshivah and Bais Yaakov graduates, the *baalei teshuvah*, and the senior population.

I'm going to list, in no specific order, some of the responses to these challenges that are already in place.

The first response is Jewish publishing. Nowadays, there is no basic Jewish text that hasn't been translated and elucidated: *Shas Bavli* and *Yerushalmi*, *Ramban*, *Chovos HaLevavos*... and the list goes on. There's no longer an excuse of, "It's too hard to decipher the Hebrew or Aramaic." Our generation has followed Shlomo HaMelech's lead and developed its own "handles" for the pot of Torah.

Some will snicker at these handles and say that people shouldn't be relying on these aids. Realize, however, that there were times when *Talmud Bavli* existed without Rashi. The people back then were brilliant enough to figure out the Gemara on their own. But as the generations diminished, that became impossible, so Rashi wrote a commentary to help us understand *Shas*.

Similarly, the *Tur* existed without *Beis Yosef* for some years. In the pre-*Beis Yosef* era, people were able to find the sources for the halachos on their own. Rav Yosef Karo realized that that era had come to an end, so he wrote the *Beis Yosef*.

Those were their *oznayim*, their handles.

Our generation needed someone to translate the *Siddur*, *Tanach*, and *Shas*.

And the plethora of Jewish publications is just breathtaking. The range of what publishers have managed to produce is nothing short of incredible. There is not an area of Jewish scholarship in which you can't find a sophisticated, clear, well-produced translation and elucidation.

Those who are responsible for these publications — whether through the use of their talents or their financial backing — are fulfilling the precept of לֹא תִשָּׁכַח מִפִּי זַרְעוֹ.

Harnessing Technology

Another area in which we've made great strides is in harnessing modern technology to help people learn. It's incredible what's available today — CDs, DVDs, mp3s, teleconferencing — and dedicated people have harnessed all of them for Torah study.

> It's incredible what's available today — CDs, DVDs, mp3s, teleconferencing — and dedicated people have harnessed all of them for Torah study.

The use of technology is yet another example of לֹא תִשָּׁכַח מִפִּי זַרְעוֹ.

Another way to harness technology is through organizations like Partners in Torah, which pairs *chavrusos* from across the world to learn over the phone. People have become frum because someone at the other end of the United States was willing to devote an hour to learn some Torah with them over the phone. When the Ribbono Shel Olam asks you after 120 years, "What did YOU do to fulfill לֹא תִשָּׁכַח מִפִּי זַרְעוֹ?" the minimum you can answer is that you devoted an hour a week of your time to share Torah with another Jew.

Accountability in Learning

One final example of what Klal Yisrael is doing to guarantee that the Torah is not forgotten:

Have you heard of Dirshu? The concept is straightforward: they offer tests on Torah subjects, with a stipend for those who excel on the examinations. The results are astounding. People who were already learning Daf Yomi are now reviewing many times so they can do well on these tests, and they are retaining the material they learned. Dirshu has added tests on *Mishnah Berurah* as well, encouraging Jews from across the globe to study and remember halachah. Their goal of enabling people to become accountable in Torah study is a fulfillment of לֹא תִשָּׁכַח מִפִּי זַרְעוֹ.

⤿ The Torah of Chessed

To summarize this entire essay, the Gemara (*Succah* 49a) notes an interesting turn of phrase in the verse: פִּיהָ פָּתְחָה בְחָכְמָה וְתוֹרַת חֶסֶד עַל לְשׁוֹנָהּ, *She opens her mouth with wisdom, and the Torah of kindness is on her tongue* (*Mishlei* 31:26).

"Is there a form of Torah that is considered *chessed* and another that isn't?" wonders the Gemara.

The Gemara answers that *"Torah lelamdah"* — Torah that is learned with plans to teach it to others — is called Torah of *chessed*, and Torah that is learned without plans to share it with others is Torah that doesn't involve *chessed*.

Not everyone is able to share Torah with others. Even those who can't, however, can often afford to sponsor *shiurim* or other Torah projects so that other Jews can learn.

Jews excel in *chessed*. If someone comes to your door and tells you that he has a large family and he can't afford to put food on his table, you'll help him. If someone approaches you in shul and tells you that he can't afford to clothe his family, you share your *tzedakah* funds generously.

We have to start to think of Torah in the very same light. When a Jew is starving for Torah, we have to be willing to reach into our wallets and feed those starving souls — to ensure that we, too, are doing all we can to guarantee that לֹא תִשָּׁכַח מִפִּי זַרְעוֹ.

> *When a Jew is starving for Torah, we have to be willing to reach into our wallets and feed those starving souls.*

A Detour Off of
Easy Street

O ne of Rashi's most famous comments on the Torah, quoted by nearly every *mashgiach* and *darshan* who speaks about *Parashas Bechukosai*, is actually somewhat perplexing if you read it carefully.

Commenting on the verse: אִם בְּחֻקֹּתַי תֵּלֵכוּ וְאֶת מִצְוֹתַי תִּשְׁמְרוּ וַעֲשִׂיתֶם אֹתָם, *If you will follow My decrees and observe My commandments and perform them* (*Vayikra* 26:3), Rashi says that the first words of the *pasuk*, "If you will follow My decrees," mean that we should be *ameilim baTorah* — we must toil in Torah.

What's perplexing is that Rashi himself writes several times in the Torah that the word חֹק, which is the root of the word בְּחֻקֹּתַי, refers to mitzvos that defy human logic, such as eating prohibited foods or wearing *shaatnez* (mixtures of wool and linen). The purpose for studying Torah does not defy human reason; without learning Torah, how can we possibly know how to live life as Jews? Why, then, is Torah study described as a *chok*?

In his *sefer Sum Derech*, Rav Simcha Zissel Broide, Rosh

Yeshivah of Chevron, writes that Torah study in and of itself is indeed not a *chok*; it's a rational pursuit. What does defy logic, says Rav Simcha Zissel, is the capacity of the Torah to elevate and transform people. No other intellectual pursuit — be it mathematics, physics, literature, or even philosophy — has the power to transform a person. Studying those subjects might make you a more knowledgeable person, and it might even earn you respect from your peers, but it won't make you a better person. Proof positive is from the many experts in those fields who are amoral and immoral. Some of the greatest chemists in the world have used their knowledge to wreak havoc on humanity.

Torah, on the other hand, has the power to change a person for the better. But it's not just any Torah that will change the person; the Chazon Ish writes that only someone who studies Torah with *ameilus* (exertion) will gain the great gifts that Torah brings with it. Simply reading the words of Torah won't change a person; only *"shvitzing"* (lit., *sweating*) for Torah study can elevate and transform a person.

☙ Saying "No" to an Angel

Rav Chaim of Volozhin, the preeminent *talmid* of the Vilna Gaon, writes (in his introduction to *Safra D'Tzniusa*) that his rebbi told him that he had received frequent offers from *malachim* (heavenly angels) to teach him the secrets of Torah without his having to exert himself, and he refused those offers.

> *Imagine toiling to understand a Tosafos, when suddenly a malach shows up at your door offering to explain it to you. Wouldn't you accept?*

Imagine toiling to understand a *Tosafos,* when suddenly a *malach* shows up at your door offering to explain it to you. Wouldn't you accept? The Gaon refused those offers because he wanted to acquire all of his Torah through *ameilus.*

If we find that great *gedolim* like the Chazon Ish or Rav Moshe Feinstein also reached the pinnacle of perfection in *middos* (character traits), it's because of their *ameilus baTorah*.

That, explains Rav Simcha Zissel Broide, is the *chok* of Torah.

✍ Superficial Is Insufficient

The last thing I want to do is denigrate any form of Torah study. Any amount of Torah learning, on any level, at any pace, and in any form is of great value, and should never be belittled. But learning *b'ameilus* — and, if I may add, *chazzering* (reviewing) your learning, which is the father of success in learning — places a Torah learner into a different league.

The Taz (*Orach Chaim* 47:1) notes that the phraseology of the *Birchos HaTorah* we recite each morning is somewhat strange. Why do we say לַעֲסוֹק בְּדִבְרֵי תוֹרָה, to **toil** in the words of Torah, not something more straightforward, such as לִלְמוֹד תוֹרָה, to study Torah?

The connotation of the word *eisek*, answers the Taz, is that it's not enough to simply read the words and turn the pages. You must *toil* to acquire Torah. You have to make a "*gantza eisek*" (roughly: a "big deal") out of Torah study, to quote the yeshivah vernacular.

We recite the *berachah* in that format each morning, says the Taz, to remind ourselves not to be satisfied with superficiality in our learning, but to invest intensive efforts into plumbing the depths of what we are learning.

Rav Elyashiv points out that according to the Taz's explanation of the words לַעֲסוֹק בְּדִבְרֵי תוֹרָה, a Gemara takes on added profundity. The Gemara (*Chagigah* 5b) teaches that there are three types of people that Hakadosh Baruch Hu cries about each day, the first of whom is a person who can be *oseik baTorah* and doesn't.

The simple understanding of the Gemara is that this refers to

> *If you are capable of learning on a high level, with ameilus, and you make do with superficiality, Hakadosh Baruch Hu cries for you.*

a person who is capable of learning, and he doesn't. Rav Elyashiv notes that if you plug the Taz's definition of *oseik* into these words, this Gemara is actually teaching us that if you are capable of learning on a high level, with *ameilus*, and you make do with superficiality, Hakadosh Baruch Hu cries for you as well.

⋙ A Dearth of Depth

The prophet Amos actually foretold of a generation for whom sufficing with superficial learning would be a great *nisayon* (challenge), in the verse: הִנֵּה יָמִים בָּאִים נְאֻם ה' אֱלֹקִים וְהִשְׁלַחְתִּי רָעָב בָּאָרֶץ לֹא רָעָב לַלֶּחֶם וְלֹא צָמָא לַמַּיִם כִּי אִם לִשְׁמֹעַ אֵת דִּבְרֵי ה', *Behold, days are coming — the word of the Lord Hashem/Elokim — when I will send hunger into the land; not a hunger for bread nor a thirst for water, but to hear the words of Hashem* (Amos 8:11).

Read on its own, this verse seems to be talking about good times for Klal Yisrael, an era when people will hunger and thirst for the word of Hashem rather than for food and drink. The Gemara (*Shabbos* 138b) clarifies, however, that this *pasuk* is actually referring to a very bad era for Klal Yisrael. "When the rabbanim arrived in Kerem B'Yavneh (one of their stops in the course of the exile from Eretz Yisrael), they said, 'The Torah will eventually be forgotten by Klal Yisrael, as the *pasuk* says: הִנֵּה יָמִים בָּאִים נְאֻם ה' אֱלֹקִים וְהִשְׁלַחְתִּי רָעָב בָּאָרֶץ לֹא רָעָב לַלֶּחֶם וְלֹא צָמָא לַמַּיִם כִּי אִם לִשְׁמֹעַ אֵת דִּבְרֵי ה'.' "

The Ponevezher Rav explains the derivation by noting that when people are starving or desperately thirsty, they don't wait for delicacies or special beverages; even a morsel of bread or a sip of water can keep them alive. This *pasuk* means, therefore, that there will come a time when there will be such a dearth of Torah, of *dvar Hashem*, that people will literally hunger and thirst for even a drop of it. They'll be happy with a *"breckel,"* a few crumbs of learning.

American Jewry went through such a period during much of the 20th century. As we noted elsewhere (p. 186), in those days, a weekly Talmud *shiur* by the rabbi and a couple of very basic *sefarim* in the home were considered about the most a person needed in order to maintain his connection to Torah. Most of that generation did not have the opportunity to learn in yeshivah for any significant period of time, and through no fault of their own, they didn't have the skills to learn more than they did.

ᵕ§ A Dangerous Temptation

Through Hashem's great *chessed*, that is no longer the case. Jews grew affluent enough in America to be able to send their children to high-level yeshivos, and those children are no longer stuck in the "low gear" of Torah learning.

Today we're capable of learning *b'iyun* and with *chazzarah*, which is also part of the *ameilus baTorah*. Nowadays, some people seek only to cover a lot of ground in learning, which is important, of course, but cannot come at the cost of neglecting *chazzarah*. Rav Chaim of Volozhin writes that when he was 19, he came to the Vilna Gaon and said, "I reviewed *Seder Moed* 14 times, and it's still not clear to me."

"You learned it 14 times and you want it to be clear to you?" the Gaon asked incredulously.

Similarly, I read that a *bachur* visited Rav Chaim Kanievsky and asked him for a *berachah* that he should have a better memory for Torah.

"If you *chazzer* something 40 times and you still don't remember it," replied Rav Chaim, "then you can come back to me, because you truly need a *berachah*. If you haven't

> *If you haven't chazzered 40 times, your memory is not faulty; you simply haven't reviewed it enough times.*

chazzered 40 times, your memory is not faulty; you simply haven't reviewed it enough times."

Perhaps the reason that there's such a *yetzer hara* to continuously learn new material rather than review what we learned is because we can only acquire Torah fully if we *chazzer*. The *yetzer hara* therefore works overtime to convince us not to review. And if you think that you're alone with that *nisayon*, you're mistaken. No less a personage than Dovid HaMelech struggled with that *yetzer hara*, and even composed a *pasuk* in *Tehillim* begging Hashem to help him overcome this temptation: סְעָדֵנִי וְאִוָּשֵׁעָה וְאֶשְׁעָה בְחֻקֶּיךָ תָמִיד, *Sustain me that I may be saved, and I will always be engrossed in Your statutes* (119:117). *Sifri (Parashas Korach)* records Dovid HaMelech's sentiments in writing these words: שֶׁלֹּא אֱהֵא לוֹמֵד תּוֹרָה וְשׁוֹכֵחַ שֶׁלֹּא אֱהֵא לוֹמֵד וְיֵצֶר הָרַע אֵינוֹ מֵנִיחַ לִי לִשְׁנוֹת, *May I not learn Torah and forget, and may I not learn Torah and have the yetzer hara prevent me from reviewing.*

If Dovid HaMelech felt that he had to daven to overcome this very powerful *yetzer hara*, then we can certainly use help in this area as well.

✒ The Song of Torah

I have always marveled about a certain phenomenon that makes my work much harder. Have you ever noticed that when it comes to music, people often adjust to a new song gradually, and are actually quite happy to hear old songs that they are familiar with? If you ever go to a concert, you'll find that the singers tend to sing "oldies," or at least songs that people already know — only rarely singing brand-new compositions.

> *If I as much as start to repeat a vort I've said in the past, people will say, "Oh, I heard that already, tell me something new."*

When it comes to my profession, I can't get away with repeating a single *vort*. If I as much as start to repeat a *vort* I've said in the past, people will say, "Oh, I heard that already, tell me something new."

I'm not sure why the two differ so sharply. Perhaps our brains are hard-wired to enjoy music when we know what the next notes are. Either way, I think that the Torah itself warns us of this phenomenon, stating: וְעַתָּה כִּתְבוּ לָכֶם אֶת הַשִּׁירָה הַזֹּאת, *And now, write for yourselves this song* (*Devarim* 31:19). Torah has to be like a *song* to us. We have to learn to enjoy learning the same material again and again.

Realize, however, that the more you review, the sweeter *chazzarah* becomes. The Gemara (*Eruvin* 54a-b) states that Torah is compared to a fig tree because figs ripen in stages, not all at one time, so as long as you keep picking the fruit, you'll keep finding newly ripened figs. So too, says the Gemara, the more you review your learning, the more "flavor" you'll find in it.

◆§ Make Hashem Proud

One of the most moving statements I have seen about *ameilus baTorah* are the words the Chofetz Chaim wrote to Rav Avraham Elya Kaplan, one of the outstanding *talmidim* of prewar Novardhok and Slabodka, who was named after his own father, a great Torah genius who passed away at a very young age while his wife was expecting. The senior Rav Avraham Elya had been close to the Chofetz Chaim, who expounded the following verse in a letter to the son: וְעַמֵּךְ כֻּלָּם צַדִּיקִים לְעוֹלָם יִירְשׁוּ אֶרֶץ נֵצֶר מַטָּעַי מַעֲשֵׂה יָדַי לְהִתְפָּאֵר, *Your people will all be righteous; they will inherit the land forever; a shoot of My planting, My handiwork, in which to glory* (*Yeshayah* 60:21) .

"There are people who are referred to as 'נֵצֶר מַטָּעַי, *a shoot of My planting*' because all of Klal Yisrael is called the vineyard of Hashem, and a person can become a shoot of that vineyard. There are others, however, who reach the level of מַעֲשֵׂה יָדַי לְהִתְפָּאֵר. Hashem takes pride in them Above, saying, 'Look at the creations of My hand that I have created in My world.' This refers to the people who toil in Torah, upon whom R' Meir said אַשְׁרֵי מִי שֶׁגָּדֵל בַּתּוֹרָה וַעֲמָלוֹ בַּתּוֹרָה, וְעוֹשֶׂה נַחַת רוּחַ לְיוֹצְרוֹ: (*Berachos* 17a), *Praiseworthy is he who grows in Torah and toils in Torah, and brings pleasure to his Creator."*

Can you imagine being among those who bring *nachas* to Hashem? All it requires is extra work to truly understand the Torah you are learning.

⇜ Seeking to Sacrifice

The Chofetz Chaim wrote these words close to 90 years ago, in 5682/1922. The world was radically different back then. *Everything* was hard back then. Most of the basic amenities we are accustomed to nowadays didn't exist: central heating, air-conditioning of any sort, and so on. Even running water was rare, and indoor bathrooms were virtually unheard of. "Work" back then meant menial, often backbreaking labor. The words אָדָם לְעָמָל יוּלָד, *A person was born to toil,* applied in a very literal sense to every area of life.

In those days, it was understood that if you had to *shvitz* to earn a living, if you had to *shvitz* to survive the occasional pogrom, then you also had to *shvitz* to learn a *blatt* Gemara. Difficulty was the norm.

> **In those days, it was understood that if you had to shvitz to earn a living, if you had to shvitz to survive the occasional pogrom, then you also had to shvitz to learn a blatt Gemara. Difficulty was the norm.**

Today, everything is easy. Even Jewish living has become easy. We have every convenience — and even luxury — available nowadays, as evidenced by the advertisements in Jewish periodicals for sushi and wagu beef and every other item you never knew you needed until it became available.

I remember going on vacation with my parents as a child. We had to schlep our own pots and pans! Who schleps cooking utensils to a vacation site nowadays? You have *glatt* kosher available wherever you want to go.

Before Succos, you'll see advertisements for a "non-hassle succah." You can put up this succah in less than three minutes. I remember Rav Ruderman describing to me how his father put up the succah, and it would fall down. He'd put it up again, and it would fall down. That's how it was back then. You *shvitzed*. Life was hard.

Nowadays, as long as you can afford it, everything is easy.

But I would venture to say that the best part of being a Yid in America is that it's easy to be a Yid. And the worst part of being a Yid in America is that it's easy to be a Yid. Because sacrifice engenders commitment. We love our children because we sacrifice for them.

> *The best part of being a Yid in America is that it's easy to be a Yid. And the worst part of being a Yid in America is that it's easy to be a Yid.*

Before davening each morning, we recite *Parashas HaAkeidah* as a prelude to *korbanos*. Perhaps we do so to remind ourselves, as we begin our daily *avodah*, that in order to succeed in serving Hashem, we must sacrifice.

Specifically because leading a Jewish life has become so easy, we must actively seek an area in which to sacrifice for Hashem. This does not mean that you should go to a farm and milk your own cows to make sure it's *cholov Yisrael*. You can get that in your local supermarket with a trustworthy *hechsher*.

There is one area in which we should choose to make it harder on ourselves: Torah. *Lehavdil*, for those of you who are old enough to remember President Kennedy's speech in which he declared the United States's commitment to reach the moon, he said, "We choose to go to the moon not because it's easy; but because it is hard."

As Torah Jews, we have to choose this one area and make it challenging for ourselves, because the more we reject superficial understanding of our learning, the more we'll grow in Torah and as Yidden in general.

The Baraisa in *Avos* (6:4) states: כַּךְ הִיא דַרְכָּה שֶׁל תּוֹרָה פַּת בְּמֶלַח תֹּאכֵל וּמַיִם בִּמְשׂוּרָה תִשְׁתֶּה וְעַל הָאָרֶץ תִּישַׁן וְחַיֵּי צַעַר תִּחְיֶה וּבַתּוֹ רָה עָמֵל. אִם אַתָּה עוֹשֶׂה כֵן אַשְׁרֶיךָ וְטוֹב לָךְ אַשְׁרֶיךָ בָּעוֹלָם הַזֶּה וְטוֹב לָךְ לָעוֹלָם הַבָּא, *This is the way of the Torah: you will eat bread with salt, and drink water in measure, and sleep on the ground, and live a life of difficulty, and you will toil in Torah. If you do so, you will be praiseworthy and it will be good for you; you will be praiseworthy in this world, and it will be good for you in the World to Come.*

Why does the Baraisa have to say אִם אַתָּה עוֹשֶׂה כֵן, *if you do so?* Couldn't it have spelled out the preconditions and the reward without those words?

The answer is that if I tried to sell you something by telling you that you're going to have to work really hard, eating almost nothing and living a hard life, you'll probably say, "Who needs this?" It's not an easy sell.

Says the Baraisa: You can't possibly understand what you'll gain from such a lifestyle by looking at it in a theoretical sense. The only way to understand why you want this is אִם אַתָּה עוֹשֶׂה כֵן, if you actually try it.

In that letter to Rav Avraham Elya Kaplan, the Chofetz Chaim quotes a Midrash in *Tanna DeVei Eliyahu* that states that in Days to Come, Hakadosh Baruch Hu will sit in His *beis midrash* in Yerushalayim, and each *talmid chacham* will sit around him with his face glowing. But not every face will glow with the same intensity; the luminescence of each person's face will depend on the amount of Torah in him.

> **In Days to Come, Hakadosh Baruch Hu will sit in his beis midrash in Yerushalayim, and each talmid chacham will sit around him with his face glowing.**

That's what we can expect in Days to Come, but we don't have to wait until then. אִם אַתָּה ע וֹשֶׂה כֵן, if you just try to toil in your Torah study, אַשְׁרֶיךָ בָּעוֹלָם הַזֶּה, you can merit to enjoy the fruits of your toil in *this world* as well.

SECTION IV:

Together We Teach

Bringing Out the Best in Our Children

I t's a *machlah* that seems to have spread far and wide. What began as a trickle, whispered in hushed conversations — "you heard that So-and-so went off the derech?" — has developed into a full-fledged leak, with many families whom we would never have imagined having *chinuch* issues having to contend with a child who has dropped every vestige of Yiddishkeit.

What can parents nowadays do to stem the tide, and what can those of us who are not in that *parashah* do to help struggling parents?

I would like to share two thoughts on this painful topic.

◄§ Changing Perception

The Gemara (*Yoma* 18a) relates that before Yom Kippur, the elders of Beis Din would review the entire process of the *avodah* of Yom Kippur with the Kohen Gadol, in case he forgot it or in case he never learned it.

The Gemara pounces on that premise. We can understand, posits the Gemara, that a Kohen Gadol could forget the details of the *avodah*. Human beings are forgetful. But how can we suggest that a Kohen Gadol never knew the *avodah* of Yom Kippur. Does it not say that the Kohen Gadol has to be greater than his fellow Kohanim in strength, beauty, wealth — and wisdom?

The Gemara answers that the Kohen Gadol was indeed wiser than his brethren — but only during the first Beis HaMikdash. During the times of the second Beis HaMikdash, the Kohanim Gedolim were political appointees, and some even bought their way into the position. For example, says the Gemara, Marta bas Baysus, an extremely wealthy woman who married a man named Yehoshua ben Gamla, bought the Kehunah Gedolah for her husband.

The Rishonim pose a difficult question on the Gemara's suggestion that Yehoshua ben Gamla became the Kohen Gadol due to a bribe. Wasn't this the very same Yehoshua ben Gamla about whom the Gemara says that if not for him, Torah would have been forgotten from Klal Yisrael (see pg. 185). Would someone who established *chadarim* and day schools in every city in Eretz Yisrael — ensuring that both teenagers and younger children would be able to learn Torah — be guilty of so dastardly a deed as becoming Kohen Gadol by way of a bribe?

The Ritva offers several answers, one of which is that there's a mistake in the text; one of the two citations should read, "R' Yehoshua ben Gamliel."

The Ritva offers another answer: When Yehoshua ben Gamla's wife bought the Kehunah for him, he indeed was not worthy of the position, but he ultimately grew into it.

The Sfas Emes expounds on the Ritva's approach, suggesting that although Yehoshua ben Gamla became Kohen Gadol by virtue of his wife's bribe, the other Kohanim began to treat him with the respect worthy of a Kohen Gadol. They deferred to him as though he truly was the greatest among the Kohanim.

And do you know what happened? Yehoshua ben Gamla became a different person. He became someone worthy of the respect he was receiving — which eventually caused him to establish schools for all those who were wandering the streets without somewhere to learn.

Which leads us to a question. What happened to all the other people of his time? Didn't they notice this truancy crisis, with teenagers out on the streets without anyone teaching them Torah. Why was Yehoshua ben Gamla the first one to actually do something about it?

Perhaps it was because Yehoshua ben Gamla saw himself reflected in those children, in those teenagers who were being ignored by society. Perhaps he concluded that if his life could turn around because he was treated with respect by his fellow Kohanim, then he could replicate that success on a macro level for all of Klal Yisrael.

> *Perhaps it was because Yehoshua ben Gamla saw himself reflected in those children, in those teenagers who were being ignored by society.*

⋘ Great Expectations

Herein lies a great lesson for all *mechanchim* and parents: people — and especially children — will generally rise to the level at which we treat them. If we talk to them and relate to them with respect, as people who can succeed, they will strive to reach that level.

Rabbi Henoch Plotnik of Chicago, who is an alumnus of the Philadelphia Yeshivah, wrote an article in which he recalled an episode with one of the greatest *mechanchim* to step foot in America, Rav Mendel Kaplan. There are myriad biographies out there, but if you're going to read one, I would recommend you read *Reb Mendel*.

Reb Mendel had a *bachur* in his *shiur* whom we would describe nowadays as a "*tut zach.*" This was the guy who ran everything in yeshivah, and had a key to every door — including the door of the soda machine.

One day, this *bachur* was falling asleep during *shiur*. "Go down to the soda machine," Reb Mendel said, "and get two cold cans of Coke. Maybe holding those two cans in your hands will keep you awake."

> "Go down to the soda machine," Reb Mendel said, "and get two cold cans of Coke. Maybe holding those two cans in your hands will keep you awake."

The rest of the class snickered at the thought, but this boy followed Reb Mendel's directive to the last letter. He stood in the back of the room holding those two cans, and he stayed awake through the rest of the *shiur*. "*Du bist an emeser talmid*," Reb Mendel remarked to this boy. By following Reb Mendel's instructions despite the embarrassment, he had proven he was a true *talmid*.

Rabbi Plotnik relates that the moment those words came out of Reb Mendel's mouth was a defining one for this *bachur*. Reb Mendel changed the way this boy thought about himself, and today he heads a successful yeshivah.

Rav Shlomo Freifeld, who was also known as a master *mechanech*, once received a call from a *talmid* whose daughter had been suggested as a *shidduch* for a boy from a very prominent family. "I'm not sure whether we should go into this *shidduch*," he told Rav Shlomo. "This boy is from such a *chashuveh* family, and I'm a *baal teshuvah*."

"It's a good thing you're not sitting in front of me," Reb Shlomo said in his inimitable style, "because I would hit you for saying that."

> "Don't you ever again call yourself a baal teshuvah," added Reb Shlomo firmly.

"Don't you *ever again* call yourself a *baal teshuvah*," added Reb Shlomo firmly.

Rav Freifeld realized that this *talmid* thought of himself as a second-class citizen because of his background, and he wouldn't tolerate that.

Great *mechanchim* treat *talmidim* not as who they are now, but as who they can become. And as parents, we must do the same.

What message do we send our children when we have to chastise them? How do we talk to them? What names do we call them?

The way we view a child can make all the difference in how he sees himself, and can change his life.

✑ He's a Sfas Emes Bachur

The Tolna Rebbe, Rav Yitzchak Menachem Weinberg, tells a story that happened in his youth.

A *bachur* was learning in the Gerrer yeshivah, and he went into a downward spiral that eventually landed him in a secular *kibbutz*, sans any Gerrer *levush* (garb) or even as much as a yarmulka. This boy's father went to the Gerrer Rebbe and said, "This is why I had to survive Auschwitz — so my son could become a *chiloni* (irreligious Jew)?"

> This boy's father went to the Gerrer Rebbe and said, "This is why I had to survive Auschwitz — so my son could become a chiloni (irreligious Jew)?"

Now, you have to be a Rebbe to make this next decision, which I'm neither condoning nor condemning. The Rebbe called in some trusted chassidim, and said, "Go into that *kibbutz* in the middle of the night, and bring him back here."

These fellows sneaked in, wrapped the boy in a blanket, and dragged him out of the *kibbutz*. When they returned, they put him into a "modern" yeshivah, because they figured that there was not a chance in the world that he could succeed in Ger after his freefall.

A few days later, the Rebbe called them in and said, "I want him back in Yeshivah Sfas Emes (the Gerrer yeshivah)." He instructed the then-young Tolna Rebbe, "I want you to take him under your wing. Be *mashpi'a* on him, talk *hashkafah* to him, spend time with him... do whatever it takes to turn him back into a regular chassid."

Sure enough, this *bachur* did a complete turnaround. On the day of the *bachur's* wedding, the Tolna Rebbe accompanied him to the Gerrer Rebbe for a *berachah*. When the duo was about to leave after receiving the blessing, the Rebbe told the Tolna Rebbe, "Wait a minute."

When the *chassan* left the room, the Gerrer Rebbe explained why he had insisted, years before, that this boy be reenrolled in Ger after his brief stint in the *kibbutz*. "I wanted everyone to call him a 'Sfas Emes *bachur*,' because *mah habriyos omrim alav*, what people say about a person, exerts great influence on him."

In truth, this *chinuch* approach dates all the way back to the times of the Mishnah.

The Gemara (*Bava Metzia* 85a) relates that Rabbeinu HaKadosh, editor of the Mishnah, visited the city in which R' Elazar ben R' Shimon (Bar Yochai) had resided. When he inquired whether R' Elazar had any sons, the townspeople answered that he did have a son, but one that the Gemara describes as what we would define nowadays as far beyond the fringe.

What did Rabbeinu HaKadosh do? He took Rav Elazar's son and gave him *semichah*, ordaining him as a rav. He then took him to another Tanna to teach him Torah. Each day, this young man would express a desire to return to his former ways. Each day, his rebbi would reply, "But we've already ordained you as a rav, how can you go back to your old ways?"

It's the same concept. By conferring the title "rebbi" upon this boy, Rabbeinu HaKadosh forced him to change the way he looked at himself, and he eventually lived up to the name bestowed upon him.

◂§ A Trustworthy Friend

The other advice I have pertains to friends.

No, I'm not referring to staying on top of who our children

associate with. While that's certainly important, I'm referring to the friends that *we* keep. Because just as the Torah states that there will never come a time in which there are no impoverished people in Klal Yisrael, in our times, there is almost no block or shul that does not have at least one, if not many, children who are struggling with Yiddishkeit. And this is perhaps *the* most difficult circumstance a parent can face. To make it through such circumstances, what parents need more than anything is just a good friend.

> *In our times, there is almost no block or shul that does not have at least one, if not many, children who are struggling with Yiddishkeit.*

It always struck me as being strange that when Yehudah had his assignation with Tamar (*Parashas Vayeishev*), he sends his payment for services rendered in exchange for the personal collateral he had left with her in the hands of his friend Chirah of Adullam.

Is this something you do through a friend? Couldn't Yehudah have used the ancient version of Fedex or UPS to send this payment anonymously? Wasn't he embarrassed to share with Chirah the circumstances in which he had become indebted to her?

The answer is that Chirah was the first *rei'a*, friend, mentioned in the Torah, and the Torah is alluding to a very important message: a true friend is a person with whom you can share your most embarrassing, ignoble actions — without worrying that it will damage your friendship.

The Rambam (*Avos* 1:6) describes something called a "Chaver Habitachon" — a trustworthy friend — in similar terms:

חבר הבטחון הרי הוא שיהיה לאדם חבר שתבטח נפשו בו, לא ישמר ממנו לא במעשה ולא בדיבור, ויגלה לו כל ענייניו, הנאה מהם והמגונה, מבלי חשש ממנו שישיגהו בכל זה חסרון

A *chaver habitachon* is a friend in whom one entrusts his soul, [and around whom] he is not on guard, not in action and not in speech; [a person to whom] he can reveal all of his issues — both good and bad — without worrying that it will result in any loss.

The Rambam is telling us that a true friend is someone to whom you can reveal your innermost feelings, sharing the most embarrassing details of your life, without worrying that he will lose any respect for you or harm you in any way.

Yehudah's friend Chirah was such a friend, and that's why Yehudah was able to send payment to Tamar through him.

Each one of us needs a friend like that — and we should each therefore strive to be such a friend.

People suffering the ignominy of having a "youth at risk," "child on the fringe," "wayward child" — or whatever other titles we have concocted to label the situation — often have their pain exacerbated because they have no one to share it with. Even a spouse, with whom one is most likely to share their struggles, is not much of a help in these cases, because the spouse is going through the very same struggle and can't be that "shoulder to cry on."

You should be that friend.

If you know that your neighbor, your shul-mate, your employee — or even your employer — is going through this ordeal, be such a friend.

So you're thinking to yourself, "How can I possibly help them?" The answer is that they often don't need your active intervention, they just need a sympathetic ear. Just get the message across that you are there for them, and are willing to listen without judging.

In his commentary to *Iyov*, Rav Schwab writes that when Iyov was suffering so terribly at the hands of the Satan, all he wanted was for his three friends to listen to him without refuting what he was saying. Rav Schwab then adds a personal note, writing that as a rav, there are many times when people come to him to share their problems. "I don't have the answers, but they don't need answers. They just want to open up to me, to have someone to talk to."

> *"I don't have the answers, but they don't need answers. They just want to open up to me, to have someone to talk to."*

Each one of us can be that person who can just listen to a friend without having answers and without judging.

~§ Reading Between the Lines

Reb Mendele Vorker and the Trisker Maggid lived next to each other, and became the closest of friends. At one point, the Trisker Maggid had to move away, to a town that was about an hour's walk from the city in which Reb Mendele lived. They decided that in order to keep up the friendship, they would send letters to each other once a week. Reb Mendele's *gabbai* offered to be the messenger, walking an hour to deliver the letter to the Trisker Maggid and then waiting for him to compose a response to bring back to Reb Mendele.

Each week, when the Trisker Maggid opened the letter from Reb Mendele, he would become teary eyed as he read it, as did Reb Mendele when he read the response from the Trisker Maggid.

After some time in which he carried these letters back and forth, the *gabbai's* curiosity overwhelmed him. *What could possibly be in those letters that they are brought to tears week after week,* he wondered. He decided to open the letter and see for himself.

To his utter shock, the paper he pulled out was… blank. Not one word was written on it!

His shock turned into amazement when he got to the Trisker Maggid, who pulled out the blank paper, looked at it intently, and began to cry as he did each week.

On the way back to Reb Mendele, the *gabbai* opened the letter from the Trisker Maggid.

Blank.

The *gabbai* walked the rest of the way home in a state of confusion and hurt. Reb Mendele immediately sensed that something was amiss. "Is something bothering you?" he asked his *gabbai*.

"I don't understand," the *gabbai* blurted out. "Each week I walk two hours to deliver these letters, and after all this time it turns out that these are just blank papers!?"

"Most people need to express themselves by putting actual words onto a paper," Reb Mendele soothed. "But sometimes you feel so close to someone that the white space between the lines on the paper expresses your thoughts to that person clearly, because they know exactly what you want to say.

"I don't understand," the gabbai blurted out. "Each week I walk two hours to deliver these letters, and after all this time it turns out that these are just blank papers!?"

"That's the relationship I share with the Trisker Maggid," Reb Mendele concluded. "He can discern what my blank lines mean, and I can tell what he wants to express in return."

That's the type of friend we need for ourselves, and in the *zechus* of making ourselves that type of friend for community members suffering from this *tzarah*, may we be *zocheh* to see all of those Yiddishe kinderlach return to our Father in Heaven.

Is a Woman's Place in the Workplace?

T he topic of women in the workplace is one that I first addressed in 1989. I will never forget that speech, because I elicited at least one response to that *derashah* that I've never duplicated in the nearly quarter of a century since: After the speech, a woman came over to me and told me that the woman in front of her said that after hearing my presentation, she felt like vomiting.

So for those of you who are of weak constitution, you might want to have an air-sickness bag on hand before you continue reading.

After the speech, a woman came over to me and told me that the woman in front of her said that after hearing my presentation, she felt like vomiting.

Why did this woman have such a visceral reaction to my speech? Because 25 years ago, this issue was much more emotional than it is today. Back then, it was still a question in people's minds whether women — and more specifically, frum women — should be working outside the home. The tendency back then was to feel strongly one way or another, making this an emotionally fraught topic. As careful and sensitive as I tried to be, I still managed to touch a raw nerve with at least that one woman.

In the last two decades, however, we have witnessed a seachange in this area. Nowadays, it's an accepted norm in many frum circles for women to be out working. All you have to do to establish this trend as fact is to note the number of degrees and graduate programs specifically geared to young frum women. These programs, which provide women with a safe and Torah'dikeh environment in which to pursue their studies, churn out hundreds of professionally trained women each year. Twenty-five years ago, no such programs existed. We are fortunate that our frum communities — whether in the New York metropolitan area or those similar to the Maalot program in smaller cities like my hometown of Baltimore — have grown to the extent that such programs are financially feasible to run.

When my daughter graduated seminary in the early 1990s, there was no Maalot program in Baltimore, and she enrolled in Towson University. I will never forget the culture shock she experienced transitioning from BJJ to Towson. When she came home from the orientation, where she heard warnings about the potential dangers lurking on the Towson campus, she sat down on the couch and cried. The contrast between Yerushalayim and Towson was just too much to bear.

Nevertheless, she forged ahead with her training until she got engaged 1½ years later. After her marriage she moved to Brooklyn, where most of her work at Towson was worthless. She enrolled in Downstate University in New York, which wasn't quite like a frum-run program but was still a whole lot better than Towson, because most of the students in her class were frum girls.

✑ Do Daughters Still Reflect a Home?

So we are definitely in very changed times. Before we can discuss the changes that have taken place in the last 25 years, however, we must discuss what changed in the last 40 — or perhaps even in the last 400 — years. Up until relatively modern times, few women, even secular women, worked out of the home. I'm not saying that there was no such thing as a woman entering the workforce, but those who did work were the exceptions, not the rule.

In frum circles, for several millennia, a Jewish girl was raised in the confines of her parents' home, and went straight from there into her husband's home.

Rav Yaakov Kamenetsky related that back in Europe, it was assumed that a girl was a product of her parents' home. If you were looking into a *shidduch*, you did not make dozens of phone calls — to seminary teachers, to roommates, etc. — to find out about the girl herself. You checked out her parents and the way they ran their home. That was enough, because generally speaking, a girl's parents were the only ones who influenced her in any way.

In fact, says Rav Yaakov, this is how we can understand an otherwise perplexing Gemara (*Succah* 56b) that tells the story of Miriam, a Jewish girl who converted and married a Greek officer. When the Greeks captured the Beis HaMikdash, this girl rushed in, kicked the *Mizbe'ach* (Altar), and called out *"Lokus, lokus* (fox, fox), until when will you consume the money of the Jewish people?"

This Miriam was the daughter of a Kohen who served in the *mishmar* of Bilga, one of the twenty-four families of Kohanim that split the service in the Beis HaMikdash. Each of those *mishmaros* had a place to keep their knives and other implements used in the Beis HaMikdash — a "locker" if you will — but the Gemara states that as a punishment for Miriam's actions, Bilga's locker was closed up.

But if only she misbehaved, wonders the Gemara, why should everyone in her father's *mishmar* suffer?

The Gemara answers: *Shusa d'yenuka b'shuka o da'avuha o d'imei* — the idle chatter of a child in the market comes from either her father or her mother. In other words, Miriam did not decide on her own that the *Mizbe'ach* was overly taxing to the finances of the Jewish people. She must have picked up that attitude from her parents' home.

> *Miriam did not decide on her own that the Mizbe'ach was overly taxing to the finances of the Jewish people. She must have picked up that attitude from her parents' home.*

Rav Yaakov Kamenetsky writes (*Emes LeYaakov* to *Succah* 56b) that this Gemara applies only to a daughter. Had a boy from *Mishmeres Bilga* acted this way, we could have blamed his attitude on something he picked up in *cheder*, in the playground, or in some other venue, because a boy was always a product of a variety of places. But a girl, says Rav Yaakov, was a product only of her home, and that's why the Gemara takes it as a given that Miriam's perception of the *Mizbe'ach* must have come from her parents' home.

✒️ Times Change

The first fact we have to establish, then, is that for much of *history* — not Jewish history, but history in general — women and girls remained in the home, out of the public sphere. Only at the beginning of the 20th century did that begin to change, and even then, the change was gradual.

Through the first half of the 20th century, most women still didn't work outside the home. My mother was born in 1912. Most of her friends did not work; they were involved in the community, but outside of their volunteer work in the shul's ladies auxiliary or raising funds for local schools, they were homemakers in every sense.

The major drift began in the 1960s and the 1970s, with the explosion of the women's liberation movement. That was a tumultuous era in the United States in many ways. Without getting too detailed, the sense of morality in the country began to slip, and social attitudes toward many issues underwent a rapid metamorphosis.

During those years, I discussed the dangers these changes posed for frum Jewry with Rav Yaakov Weinberg, who would later become the Rosh Yeshivah of Ner Yisrael. With his hallmark keen perceptiveness, Rav Weinberg predicted what would happen. "The truly *treifeh* things will not affect us," he foretold. "Issues of morality and immorality, for instance, are clear, and they won't affect us.

"Trends such as women's liberation, however, will affect us, because they're not obviously *treif*. They are subtle and pernicious, and that's why they will succeed in seeping into our society. This is where the real danger lies."

> "Trends such as women's liberation, however, will affect us, because they're not obviously treif. They are subtle and pernicious, and that's why they will succeed in seeping into our society."

Part of the message that the women's lib movement sought to spread was that women are too talented to be "just mothers." It did not take long for this message to gain acceptance in society. Just a few decades later, when asked what their occupation was, mainstream American women were embarrassed to answer "housewife" or "mother," afraid that people might think: *Just a mother? Are you so dimwitted that you can't do more than that?*

✍ Not "Just" a Mother

Unfortunately, this mindset crept into our society as well.

In reality, Torah Jews know that motherhood is one of the greatest pursuits known to mankind. One of the greatest lifetime achievements is to leave behind good, successful, *ehrlicheh* children and grandchildren.

And denigrating motherhood can be perilous.

At one point during the era of the Shoftim, the *Aron HaBris* had been sent into battle and been captured by the Philistines. They kept it for many years, until it was finally returned during the reign of Dovid HaMelech. The Navi (*II Shmuel* 6:14-15) relates that when it was returned, the Jewish people celebrated with great fanfare, with Dovid HaMelech leading the festivities: וְדָוִד מְכַרְכֵּר בְּכָל עֹז לִפְנֵי ה׳... וְדָוִד וְכָל בֵּית יִשְׂרָאֵל מַעֲלִים אֶת אֲרוֹן ה׳ בִּתְרוּעָה וּבְקוֹל שׁוֹפָר, *Dovid danced with all [his] strength before Hashem... Dovid and the entire House of Israel brought up the Ark of Hashem with loud, joyous sound, and the sound of the shofar.*

Not everyone viewed Dovid HaMelech's celebration in a positive light. Specifically, his wife Michal, the daughter of the previous king, Shaul HaMelech, considered it inappropriate for a king to dance like the commoners: וַיָּשָׁב דָּוִד לְבָרֵךְ אֶת בֵּיתוֹ וַתֵּצֵא מִיכַל בַּת שָׁאוּל לִקְרַאת דָּוִד וַתֹּאמֶר מַה נִּכְבַּד הַיּוֹם מֶלֶךְ יִשְׂרָאֵל אֲשֶׁר נִגְלָה הַיּוֹם לְעֵינֵי **אַמְהוֹת** עֲבָדָיו כְּהִגָּלוֹת נִגְלוֹת אַחַד הָרֵקִים, *Dovid returned home to bless his household. Michal daughter of Shaul went out to meet Dovid and said, "How honored was the king of Israel today, who was exposed today in the presence of his servants' maidservants, as one of the boors would be exposed!"* (ibid. v. 20).

Michal used the word אַמְהוֹת, *maidservants*, to describe the womenfolk in front of whom Dovid HaMelech had danced

Dovid HaMelech does not back down from what he did. First he takes issue with her understanding of how a king should or should not act in public, reminding her that Hashem chose his way over that of her father, Shaul:

וַיֹּאמֶר דָּוִד אֶל מִיכַל לִפְנֵי ה׳ אֲשֶׁר בָּחַר בִּי מֵאָבִיךְ וּמִכָּל בֵּיתוֹ לְצַוֹּת אֹתִי

נָגִיד עַל עַם ה' עַל יְשְׂרָאֵל וְשִׂחַקְתִּי לִפְנֵי ה', *Dovid answered Michal, "In the presence of Hashem, Who chose me over your father and over his entire house to appoint me as ruler over the people of Hashem, over Israel – before Hashem I shall rejoice!"* (ibid. v. 21).

He then adds: וּנְקַלֹּתִי עוֹד מִזֹּאת וְהָיִיתִי שָׁפָל בְּעֵינָי וְעִם הָאֲמָהוֹת אֲשֶׁר אָמַרְתְּ עִמָּם אִכָּבֵדָה, *"And I shall behave even more humbly than this, and I shall be lowly in my eyes; and among the maidservants of whom you spoke — among them will I be honored!"* (ibid. v. 22).

Dovid HaMelech tells her never to denigrate Jewish women by calling them maidservants.

This *parashah* in the Navi ends with the *pasuk*: וּלְמִיכַל בַּת שָׁאוּל לֹא הָיָה לָהּ יָלֶד עַד יוֹם מוֹתָהּ, *Michal daughter of Shaul had no child until the day of her death* (ibid. v. 23).

Simply understood, this last verse does not seem to have much to do with those before it; it merely tells us that Michal died in childbirth, and did not merit to raise any children.

Rav Meir Tzvi Bergman, the son-in-law of Rav Shach, suggests that there is a *middah k'neged middah* alluded to in this *pasuk*.

Michal bas Shaul denigrated Jewish mothers, calling them אֲמָהוֹת, and as a consequence, she never merited to be a mother to her own only child.

We must be very careful, then, to treat motherhood with the respect that it deserves. The phrase "just a mother" should not exist in our lexicon.

◆§ The Boomerang Is Too Late

Nevertheless, the reality was that Rav Yaakov Weinberg was absolutely correct. The attitude from the secular world filtered into our own, and mothers who didn't have some sort of high-level occupation felt inferior to those who did. Finally there was a backlash, as there inevitably is after a new movement grows old, and today women once again take pride in saying, "I'm a stay-at-home mom."

By the time that boomerang effect took place, however, other factors came into play, sending women who would have loved to remain at home with their children into the workforce.

Several socioeconomic developments began to affect our society.

First, it became de rigueur for couples to begin married life in *kollel*. What was a rarity 30 years ago is almost a given nowadays. And if *kollel* people of 30 years ago would learn for a year or two after their marriages, today's *yungeleit* can last 3, 5, or 10 or more years in *kollel*. And that is something to be admired.

> *No matter what their plans are for the long term, every couple should invest at least some time at the beginning of their marriage to learning in kollel.*

No matter what their plans are for the long term, every couple should invest at least *some time* at the beginning of their marriage to learning in *kollel*.

But even a pursuit as admirable as *kollel* comes at a price, and that price is that women often have to work in order to support their husbands.

Even when a man leaves *kollel* — or among couples in which the husband does not learn in *kollel* — wives must often work nowadays, because the costs of frum living today are astronomic. As we've discussed elsewhere (see p. 24), the costs of housing, food, tuition, and other basic necessities for a frum family are sky high. Someone told me that a fellow filled out an application for school and listed his annual income at $240,000, yet he still had no choice but to ask for a tuition reduction, because his expenses were so high that he couldn't afford the tuition.

A secular person who earns six-figures can live quite nicely in America: he buys a house in a low-cost suburb, buys himself season tickets to his favorite sports team, and maybe a boat, and he has it made. A frum Jew can spend over six figures just in tuition costs alone!

❦ No Guilt

Today, therefore, it has become a near-necessity for a family to have two salaries to live on. And when something becomes a necessity, we apply to it the maxim expressed in many *sefarim* as: הַהֶכְרֵחַ לֹא יְשֻׁבַּח וְלֹא יְגֻנֶּה, *a necessity is neither praised nor denigrated.* A looser translation might be, "You gotta do what you gotta do."

And so the first thing a woman who must join the workforce should do is to ensure that she is working without guilt.

Okay, that might not be possible.

If you go to work, you will probably have guilt, especially if you are a young mother leaving children at home to be cared for by others. There is nothing that will tear your *kishkes* (roughly: guts) out nearly as much as seeing your baby cry as you leave your house.

In reviewing my notes for the speech I gave on this topic 25 years ago, I found an article — I'm not sure from which publication — that I had clipped and saved. These words, written by a working mother, speak volumes:

> *There is nothing that will tear your kishkes (roughly: guts) out nearly as much as seeing your baby cry as you leave your house.*

"I ease the car out of the driveway," this woman wrote, "and steal a last glance. The faces I see in the window will remain with me: forlorn, sad eyes following me. I speak to myself firmly. *In a few short hours I'll be home. I'll feed the baby, I'll make supper. I'll be home with plenty of time to hear Chani's eager chatter and give Moishe juice in his favorite cup and read them their bedtime special stories.* But why, then, do I feel this jarring pang of guilt?"

So what's the correct approach? If women must work, yet feel guilty for going to work, what should and shouldn't they be doing?

This issue is similar to another problem that we didn't have to contend with 30 years ago, but has become a burning issue in recent years: the internet. Nowadays, despite all its inher-

Is a Woman's Place in the Workplace? / 225

ent dangers, it's nearly impossible for many people to manage without the internet, and so we've been forced to set *gedarim*, boundaries, on how and when to use it.

The same approach should apply to women in the workplace. For better or for worse, the problem seems to be here to stay, at least until Mashiach redeems us, *bimheirah b'yameinu*. We must therefore determine how to go about this in a responsible and reasonable way. I would like to suggest several factors women must weigh when choosing an occupation.

Before I begin, however, I must issue a disclaimer: the following guidelines are for the general population. There are certainly women out there for whom these suggestions will not apply, due to their specific circumstances that are often beyond their control.

If you are one of those exceptions, you must speak to a rav or rosh yeshivah or other wise person to discuss your own *gedarim*.

Having said that, here are my suggestions for the general population.

✑ Less Pay, More Family

The first thing I would suggest is that, if possible, you seek a profession that will allow you to work part time. A full 9-5 job will not leave you much time for your children.

I'll speak from personal experience:

My wife was a Bais Yaakov teacher for most of her 30-plus year career. After our second child was born, she decided to take off from work and be home with the children in those formative years.

I'll be very honest: it was an extremely scary decision to make. I had just started teaching in the yeshivah, and I was not earning six figures annually. In fact, I wasn't even earning five figures. My salary was four figures. *Four figures*! And we were making the choice for my wife not to bring home any income.

Despite our fears, we made a decision that, in retrospect, we're happy we made.

Moving onto the next generation, I have one daughter-in-law who is a Bais Yaakov teacher. Now, teaching in Bais Yaakov is an extremely rewarding profession in every way, except one: the pay. That, in and of itself, could be the subject of its own *derashah*; it's terrible that our Bais Yaakov teachers are being paid so little. I'm not blaming the schools, because they are pressed for funds, but the reality is that a career that could otherwise be perfect for mothers is not going to do much for the family finances. On the other hand,

> *Teaching in Bais Yaakov is an extremely rewarding profession in every way, except one: the pay.*

my daughter-in-law has been able to work for almost her entire married life of close to 15 years, and she has been there for her children much of the time.

This decision, too, was a tough one for this couple, because they had to come to terms with the minimal salary my daughter-in-law brings home, and it doesn't get any easier as the family grows.

My other daughter-in-law has a degree in special education, and she runs a *keriah* program in a *cheder* in Lakewood. Similar to teaching in Bais Yaakov, this job does not require her to work full time. She doesn't have to be there at 8 or 8:30, there's no commute, and she's home by the time her children come off the school bus.

My daughter is an occupational therapist. This is, *bli ayin hara*, a decent paying occupation, and she too is able to choose the number of hours she works.

Now, all three of them could have chosen professions that would require them to work 9-5 — or more — and they would have earned significantly higher salaries. They decided, however, that being there for their families was more important.

To all the young women now choosing their occupations, I highly recommend that you think in terms of jobs that don't require a full-time commitment. Aside from the part-time occupations, there are jobs that will allow you to work from home.

Companies that are willing to outsource to India are usually willing to outsource to Lakewood, New Jersey as well. Even companies that have brick-and-mortar locations often encourage employees to work from home. In some of these jobs, you can have flexibility as to which hours you wish to work. Many women today are able to work after their children go to sleep.

What this comes down to is that there are many careers out there that are financially rewarding, but they come at a cost to frum family life. You have to make a conscious decision: Will I give up money to spend time with my family, or will I give up time with my children during their formative years for more money?

> *You have to make a conscious decision: Will I give up money to spend time with my family, or will I give up time with my children during their formative years for more money?*

I won't make your decision for you, but I will remind you that you will not have little children forever. Even if you consider yourself a person who needs to have some sort of career, your children will eventually grow up. It may take 40 years, but eventually they grow up. If you establish yourself in a profession and continue working in it part time as you raise your children, you can hopefully go back to full-time should you feel the need to do so.

❧ Work Environment

The second factor to bear in mind when choosing an occupation is what sort of work environment this type of work entails. You do not want to work in a place that is hostile to our values as Torah Jews.

If at all possible, the best choice is to work with frum people. To cite my daughter as an example again, when she began working as an OT, the first agency she worked for was a non-sectarian one that placed her in a public school. That was not what you would call a "hostile" environment: most of her coworkers were women, and no one was antagonistic to her. But the kids she worked with ran the gamut of the demographic makeup of Brooklyn today: Hispanic, Indians, Arabs, etc.

After a number of years, she switched agencies, and she was placed in Bobov boys' elementary school. To be sure, when she first stepped through the door, Bobov was nearly as foreign to her as was the public school. This is a girl who grew up without Yiddish spoken in her home, and she had to pick up the chassidishe dialect, to boot. But now she's working with frum young children, and dealing with frum parents, and she has had some very charming moments in the course of her years there. One day, she mentioned to one little boy that something would make her sad. *"Farvus zolzt di zein azoi,"* the boy replied, *"di darfst zugen 'gam zi letoivah'* (Why should you be that way? You should say, 'this, too, is for the good')."

Now, it's quite possible that she would earn more working as an OT in a professional office full-time, but you can't compare the feeling of helping these frum kids to that of someone who spends all day working in a secular office.

It's quite possible that she would earn more working as an OT in a professional office full-time, but you can't compare the feeling of helping these frum kids to that of someone who spends all day working in a secular office.

Like everything else in life, this is a tradeoff. You have to be willing to trade some money for your happiness and your comfort level in the setting in which you will work each day.

⊰ Maintaining the Boundaries

Even someone who works in a frum environment must be careful to maintain the necessary boundaries with their coworkers of the opposite gender. I have a secretary who I have been working with for 25 years. She doesn't call me Yissocher, and I don't call her Helen. I'm Rabbi Frand to her, and she's Mrs. Raskas to me. Is it somewhat awkward? Yes. But it's a necessary and proper formality that maintains the boundaries.

You must make sure not to get too chummy with your coworkers of the opposite gender, even in a frum office. I'm sorry to report that there have been horror stories of frum women who started out very pure, having emerged from the best seminaries, but they quickly absorbed the loose atmosphere of the world out there. Some of these stories have ended in tragedy.

I have a *talmid* who works in one of the most prestigious accounting firms in New York, and he told me that the "*sichas chullin*," the water-cooler chatter between coworkers, is just horrifying, both in the subjects they'll discuss and how they'll discuss them.

Things have gotten so bad, in fact, that I've had *talmidim* who asked me whether they should wear wedding bands to the office. Now, *bnei Torah* do not wear wedding bands. It's just not done. But these *talmidim* explained that in the secular world, if your fingers are bare, that means you're unattached. And a person who is unattached is "fair game."

I had to tell them that it wasn't a bad idea to wear a wedding band. I did add a word of caution to remember to take the wedding band off before walking into shul, lest their shul-mates begin to wonder what happened to them…

That is the world we're living in, and that's why it's generally better to be in a *heimishe* environment.

If you do end up in a secular office, however, I highly recommend that you try to find at least one other frum employee whom you will be embarrassed to face if you were caught acting in a way that's inappropriate for a frum person. That *shomer* or *shomeres* can keep you from falling prey to your own *yetzer hara*.

Does this mean that you have to act like an anti-social creep in the office? No. As I've mentioned elsewhere (p. 30), there's a way to be professionally friendly and not socially friendly. If you can strike that balance, you can make a great *Kiddush Hashem* in the workplace, while maintaining your standards as a frum person.

✑ It's All in the Mindset

Finally, there's an attitude that we have to learn to take toward our work that will no doubt be of tremendous benefit to every working member of Klal Yisrael.

Every action we do in this world can be raised to the level of *l'Sheim Shamayim* (actions performed for the sake of Heaven), including our work. It's quite possible for two people to do the very same job, and one will get immeasurable reward for it in *Olam Haba*, while the other will merely bring home a salary.

> *It's quite possible for two people to do the very same job, and one will get immeasurable reward for it in Olam Haba, while the other will merely bring home a salary.*

An example: two people play clarinet in Jewish bands. Both of them play at weddings nearly every night, both of them get home quite late, and both of them take home a salary. But one might do it only for the money, and the other might go to work each night thinking that he's going to be *mesame'ach chassan v'kallah* — to bring joy to the *chassan* and *kallah*. When these two get to the *Olam HaEmes*, the former will find himself in the "bleachers," while the latter will have "box seats." The first clarinetist isn't doing anything *wrong*. He's just not elevating the work he must do *anyway* into a mitzvah. The second fellow has to show up to work just as much as the first, but he will receive immeasurable reward for the nightly mitzvos of *simchas chassan v'kallah.*

It's all in the mindset.

The same applies to every Jewish person going into the workplace. If you go to work *l'Sheim Shamayim* — to support a husband in *kollel,* or to have the money you need to raise a happy Jewish family of *shomrei Torah u'mitzvos* — your work is for Hashem. And if you work with that mindset, you can expect to be blessed with great *siyata d'Shmaya* to see *banim uvnei vanim oskim baTorah uv'mitzvos.*

Parenting:
It's All About the Relationship

S everal years ago, I received a phone call from a chassid living in Mount Kisco, New York. He said he wanted to consult with me, and he wanted to know when he could drive down to Baltimore for a meeting.

I told him that I honestly didn't think that whatever pearls of wisdom I could share with him would be worth the five- or six-hour drive down.

"But I really want to speak to you," he persisted.

I came up with an idea. "Next time I'm in New York for a *derashah*," I suggested, "you can drive me from the venue to the train station. We'll spend, say, half an hour or 40 minutes together in the car, and you'll save yourself a long trip to Baltimore."

The next time I was in New York, this fellow indeed picked me up in Brooklyn after a *derashah*. I had told him that the lecture I was giving was for *mechanchim*, but he attended anyway, even though he's not a professional *mechanech*.

When I finished, he said, "You know, this lecture applies just as much to parents. Why don't you give it to parents as well?"

So on the advice of this Satmarer chassid, I'm offering these pointers for parents as well as *mechanchim*, and if you don't like it, you can blame that Satmarer chassid…

~§ Trickle-Down Chinuch

Truth be told, there are many similarities in the way *mechanchim* and parents bear influence on their students.

There's a famous *vort* from Rav Yaakov Kamenetsky on the concept of הַשְׁפָּעָה, *influence*. Some commentators suggest that the root of the word is שפע, *abundance*; if you fill yourself up with an abundance of Torah and wisdom, you'll overflow to others, and that's how you influence them.

Rav Yaakov suggested that the root of the word is שִׁיפּוּעַ, *an incline*. The way you influence people, said Rav Yaakov, is similar to the way rain will run off a pitched roof. Everything we do "trickles down" onto them.

> *The way you influence people, said Rav Yaakov, is similar to the way rain will run off a pitched roof. Everything we do "trickles down" onto them.*

What this means is that although formal education — the material we teach our children, whether in the classroom or in the home — is extremely important, that's not how our children will learn *middos* and how to interact with others. They learn that from the way *we* behave, whether in the classroom or the living room. Consciously or subconsciously, our children absorb the way we interact with others in a variety of situations, and that shapes their own way of relating to their peers.

Similarly, we don't teach our children values by lecturing them in the home. We teach them by modeling those values in our regular, everyday lives.

◆§ Show, Don't Preach

Trickle-down *chinuch* has been the *chinuch* method of Jews dating all the way back to the first person to choose to serve as Hashem's representative in this world, Avraham Avinu.

The Torah states, regarding Avraham: כִּי יְדַעְתִּיו לְמַעַן אֲשֶׁר יְצַוֶּה אֶת בָּנָיו וְאֶת בֵּיתוֹ אַחֲרָיו וְשָׁמְרוּ דֶּרֶךְ ה' לַעֲשׂוֹת צְדָקָה וּמִשְׁפָּט, *For I have loved him, because he commands his children and his household after him that they keep the way of Hashem, doing charity and justice (Bereishis* 18:19). Given that Avraham's mandate was to teach his descendants to follow the path of Hashem, one would expect that he would be heard delivering impassioned speeches to his son Yitzchak Avinu.

In reality, however, the Torah records all of about nine words that were exchanged between the two. Contrast that to the conversation Avraham had with that sleazy salesman Efron at the beginning of *Parashas Chayei Sarah*, in which he has a long discussion about purchasing *Me'aras HaMachpelah*. If Avraham was the original master *mechanech*, how is it that we see so little dialogue between him and Yitzchak? And how is it that with so little conversation between father and son, Yitzchak spent the rest of his life trying to protect the legacy of his father?

The answer is that the Torah is teaching us that we do not transmit our values to the next generation by engaging in chit-chat with our children. Avraham Avinu didn't have to preach his values to Yitzchak, because his entire being was one great big lesson in how a person must live. He *showed* Yitzchak how to live properly.

Until this very day, the way to teach our children is not by lecturing about Torah, but by living Torah. The most profound influence we can have on our children is to live the way we would want them to live.

⋖§ Better No Lessons Than the Wrong One

Unfortunately, this is a two-way street. We can have a tremendous positive effect on our children, but on the other hand, if we are sarcastic and biting when speaking to or about other people, then our children will do the same. If a parent can say hurtful things to a child, then so will the child. If a couple constantly

If a couple constantly levels sharp rejoinders at each other, that's how their children will interact with one another.

levels sharp rejoinders at each other, that's how their children will interact with one another. And if parents erupt in anger when things don't go their way, so will the child.

The Chazon Ish had a *minyan* assemble in his home for Minchah each day. One day, a fellow came to daven with that *minyan*, and he brought his young child in tow. The child didn't have patience to sit still, so he moved around the tables, making a lot of noise that disturbed the *mispallelim* in the process — typical behavior for a young child in shul.

The father kept shushing his son and trying to get him to sit still, but to no avail. Finally, he landed several hefty blows on him.

When Minchah concluded, the Chazon Ish summoned this father and said, "Your son apparently learned two things today: First of all, he learned that you shouldn't make noise in shul. He learned this lesson through what we call לִמּוּד, *didactic learning.* You taught it to him by *instructing* him not to make noise.

"The other lesson he learned is that when someone gets upset, it's okay for him to lose control and fly into a rage. He learned this through שִׁמּוּשׁ, through watching the way you act in practice.

"Unfortunately for you, *Chazal* taught us that גָּדוֹל שִׁמּוּשָׁהּ יוֹתֵר מִלְמוּדָהּ, what a person learns through practical lessons has more of an effect that what he learns through didactic learning. Since the second, negative lesson will be the lasting one, you would have done better not to teach him either of the two."

⸙ Always on Stage

One of the reasons parenting is so difficult is because we're always on stage.

In their day jobs, people are used to being on their best behavior, but that's after getting a fair amount of sleep, interacting with other adults, and with the knowledge that at the end of the day — no matter how long that day may be — you get to go home. Even an intern on a 24-hour shift eventually gets to go home and let his hair down.

As a parent, whether you've slept seven hours or seventeen minutes, your kids are still watching you. Everything trickles down off your proverbial roof, and your kids absorb it all.

> *As a parent, whether you've slept seven hours or seventeen minutes, your kids are still watching you.*

The *pasuk* states: הַנִּסְתָּרֹת לַה׳ אֱלֹקֵינוּ וְהַנִּגְלֹת לָנוּ וּלְבָנֵינוּ עַד עוֹלָם לַעֲשׂוֹת אֶת כָּל דִּבְרֵי הַתּוֹרָה הַזֹּאת, *The hidden [sins] are for Hashem, our God, but the revealed [sins] are for us and our children forever, to carry out all the words of this Torah (Devarim* 29:28). Perhaps we can suggest an alternative elucidation: הַנִּסְתָּרֹת, the things that we do in private, such as how much concentration we have during davening and the thoughts that occupy our minds, לַה׳ אֱלֹקֵינוּ, those are things that only Hashem knows about. But הַנִּגְלֹת, the things that are done in the open — how we talk, how we interact with others — לָנוּ וּלְבָנֵינוּ, are known not only to ourselves, but to our children as well. And what they see, they'll imitate. *What's good enough for Daddy and Mommy is good enough for me*, they think to themselves. If we want to be sure that their life objective is לַעֲשׂוֹת אֶת כָּל דִּבְרֵי הַתּוֹרָה הַזֹּאת, to carry out all the words of the Torah, we have to be sure to model that behavior for them.

⊰ Mussar Is Like Radiation

The problem of being on display 24/7 is compounded by the fact that parents cannot simply sit on the sidelines and allow their children to act as they please; they are required to discipline their children, to set them on the Torah path. Even as a rebbi in yeshivah, I don't have that requirement. I teach men ranging between the ages of 20 and 75 (I mean that literally; there are dedicated retirees who attend my *shiur*). I have never had a discipline problem. Rebbeim and teachers who teach younger grades, however, must set their students straight, and they must sometimes do so in public.

Now, there is a halachah that one may not give *tochachah* (rebuke) in public, but the exceptions to that rule are teachers and parents, who have no choice but to speak up when they see their charges acting incorrectly. And sometimes that has to be done either in a classroom or in front of a family.

Nevertheless, parents and teachers must remember that *tochachah* is like radiation; while it is sometimes necessary, it can be extremely dangerous and has devastating side effects. Rav Avraham Pam, one of the greatest *mechanchim* of our generation, wrote that it is more common for *tochachah* to harm the child than it is to have a positive effect. If it is at all possible, he adds, one should try to discipline a child with respect and through pleasant means.

> *Parents and teachers must remember that tochachah is like radiation; while it is sometimes necessary, it can be extremely dangerous and has devastating side effects.*

Either way, Rav Pam concludes, one must be *exceedingly careful* in the way he gives *tochachah*, exercising great patience and acting only with peace of mind.

Let me give you an example of what Rav Pam was referring to when he wrote that one should try to discipline a child with respect and through pleasant means.

The name Rav Aron Lopiansky, whose great Torah wisdom is

coupled with deep insight into Jewish philosophy, is familiar to many people because of his current status as the Rosh Yeshivah of the Yeshivah of Greater Washington. But like all of us, he was once a young child, and he behaved as children sometimes do. His father, R' Benzion Lopiansky, was the *shammes* (caretaker) of the iconic Bialystoker Shul on the Lower East Side of Manhattan. There was a homeless fellow who took up residence in the furnace room of the shul, and he unfortunately became the target of taunts from the young children of the neighborhood, including one very young Aron Lopiansky.

One day, R' Benzion caught Aron and his friends ridiculing this man. Now, R' Lopiansky could have told his son, "That's *disgusting*. That's *terrible*. If I ever catch you doing that again, I'll…" But he chose a different approach. He took Aron aside and said softly, "You see this man? He was once a cute little boy whose mother cuddled him, just like your mother cuddles you. His father probably had high hopes for him, just as I have for you. Now look what has become of him. Isn't it a tragedy? How do you think he feels about himself?

"This is how you have to deal with people," R' Benzion concluded. "Always try to put yourself in their shoes. This way, you'll never do such a thing again."

What a beautiful lesson to impart to a young child: always put yourself into someone else's shoes.

As Rav Pam wrote, you can take the chance of making your point harshly, or you can take it slow and make your point softly. You can act out of anger, or out of wisdom. The choice is yours.

The world now has a catchphrase for this type of moment in life: a "teachable moment." What do you do when you have an opportunity to impart a lesson? If you scream and holler and flail, the lesson might just

If you scream and holler and flail, the lesson might just be that a person can reasonably expect to be taken seriously when he shouts and derides someone. But if you choose to teach a life lesson, you're more likely to have a long-term effect on your child.

be that a person can reasonably expect to be taken seriously when he shouts and derides someone. But if you choose to teach a life lesson, you're more likely to have a long-term effect on your child.

The same holds true for when we want to encourage a child to do something extraordinary.

The Kapycznitzer Rebbe summoned his granddaughter as she was about to begin high school. "Realize that as a popular girl, a bright girl, and a *meyucheses*, the granddaughter of a rebbe, everyone will want to be your friend," he said. "Your job is to befriend all the girls whom no one else wants as a friend."

The Kapycznitzer Rebbe and R' Benzion Lopiansky both took advantage of teachable moments to impart vital life lessons. Teachable moments are few and far between. When you think about it, most of our parenting hours are invested into carpools, attending PTAs, helping children with their homework, reminding them to clean up, and tending to their physical and material needs. Whenever such moments do present themselves, be sure to capitalize on them.

✇ Take It Slow

In order to maximize the effect of your teachable moments, however, you have to think carefully. Or as I tell teachers, "Don't shoot and ask questions later. Think before you shoot."

At one event for teachers, a man came up to me after my lecture and told me that his daughter just started to teach elementary school. One day a child came in with a note that read: *My daughter has a sore throat. Can you please let her suck candies in class today?*

The teacher read this note, and automatically smelled something suspicious, because the note was written in black magic marker, and not one line was straight. *I may be a rookie teacher,* she thought to herself, *but I wasn't born yesterday.* It seemed painfully obvious that this girl wanted to suck candies, so she forged a note from her "parents."

The teacher was about to say, "Don't you ever try to lie to me again," but something stopped her in her tracks. Instead of unleashing a lecture, she said, "Okay, but please be quiet about it, and don't make noise with the wrappers."

Her forbearance bordered on the miraculous. A little while later, the girls were working on some kind of assignment, and the teacher was making her rounds between the desks. Suddenly, this little girl looks up and says, "You know that my father is blind, right? He wrote the note."

Suddenly, this little girl looks up and says, "You know that my father is blind, right? He wrote the note."

The note was written in black magic marker and no line was straight because the little girl's blind father had written it!

Now just think what would have happened had that teacher unloaded on this girl. How devastating would that have been?

And this is true for parents as well. Something goes wrong in the home, and one child looks guilty as sin.

Wait.

Hold off.

You might just be shocked at the true story if you bother to find out what that is.

There was a family that moved from an out-of-town community to the Big Apple. They enrolled their son, whom we'll call Yitzy, in an elementary school in their new neighborhood. A few months into the year, the secular studies teachers were off from work due to a legal holiday, and the school brought in a staff of substitutes to teach in the afternoon hours. Needless to say, this was a recipe for all bedlam breaking loose — and it did. Each lively group of youngsters "treated" their substitute to a rough afternoon, to say the least.

This school had an intercom system, through which the principal could listen in to the goings-on in the classrooms.

He decided at some point to lay down the law in Yitzy's class. He strode into the room purposefully, but all the children had perceived his imminent arrival and quickly sat down before he walked into the room. Only one child wasn't sitting when he walked in: Yitzy, whose out-of-town upbringing had taught him that when a principal walks into the room, you stand up as a sign of respect.

When the principal walked in, you had thirty-odd children sitting nicely, and only one child standing. It seemed obvious who was the culprit, and the principal hollered at Yitzy to go to his office and wait.

Tzaddik v'ra lo. The righteous one was punished.

That day, when Yitzy's mother came to pick him up, she noticed immediately that something was amiss. She asked him what was wrong, but he wouldn't say anything. Finally, while they were still driving he says, "I HATE him."

Slowly but surely, the story trickled out. Yitzy's mother tried to get him to forgive the principal, but Yitzy was having none of it. The next morning, Yitzy refused to go to school. His mother decided that it was not worth forcing the issue, so she went off to a dentist appointment, leaving Yitzy with his older sister.

A few hours into the school day, the phone rings. Yitzy's sister brings it to him. "The principal wants to talk to you," she announces.

"Well, I don't want to talk to *him*!" Yitzy replies.

Yitzy's mother admitted that had she been at home, she wouldn't have forced him to speak on the phone with the principal. But you know how older sisters are — they somehow manage to get what they want from their younger brothers.

When Yitzy got on the phone, the principal says, "Yitzy, I apologize. I made a mistake. I'm sorry.

"Do you know where I am?" he continued. "I'm calling from your classroom, and all of your friends have a message for you.

"Boys," he said, "what do you want to say to Yitzy?"

Thirty voices chimed in, "We want Yitzy, we want Yitzy..."

"Will you please come back to class?" the principal begged.

"I'll come back," Yitzy replied, "but my mother is not home."

"Where do you live?" the principal countered. "I'll be there in ten minutes."

This principal did something that every parent, teacher, and rebbi has to learn to do: he admitted that he was wrong, and apologized.

Perhaps this seems counterintuitive, but when you apologize to a child or student, you don't become smaller in their eyes; you become bigger in their eyes.

> *This principal did something that every parent, teacher, and rebbi has to learn to do: he admitted that he was wrong, and apologized.*

⤳ The Steipler's Apology

When the Steipler Gaon, who was renowned for having written great *chiddushim* on almost every *masechta* in *Shas*, was already very old, he appeared unexpectedly at a bar mitzvah. Everyone stood up and watched in surprise as he took a seat next to the bar mitzvah boy, whispered a few words in his ear, sat there for a few more moments, and then left.

Needless to say, everyone was curious: What did the *gadol hador* have to say to this young boy?

"A few years ago," the bar mitzvah *bachur* said, "I was davening in the same shul as the Steipler Gaon. I was davening out of a *siddur* that was the size of a Gemara, and he thought that I was learning in middle of davening. He came over and said, 'We don't learn during davening — *zman Torah lechud u'zman tefillah lechud* (the time for Torah study is separate and the time for *tefillah* is separate).'

"When he realized that I had actually been davening, he apologized. But since I was not bar mitzvah yet, I wasn't able to issue a proper *mechilah*. The Steipler asked me when I would be bar mitzvah, and he made a mental note to come tonight to ask me *mechilah* as soon as I would be able to forgive him as an adult."

◆§ Don't Kill the Relationship

Perhaps the most important concept to bear in mind when it comes to *chinuch* — whether in the home or in the classroom — is that *chinuch* is all about the relationship. This does not mean that your children or students get away with murder. Undoubtedly, there will be times when you will have to chastise or punish a child or student. You must make sure, however, that you don't ruin your overall relationship with that child in the process of setting him or her straight. Because ultimately, you can only keep your children on the path you have blazed for them if they feel that they have a warm and loving relationship with you that they don't want to lose.

> *Because ultimately, you can only keep your children on the path you have blazed for them if they feel that they have a warm and loving relationship with you that they don't want to lose.*

Rav Yaakov Kamenetsky points out that the only thing that kept Yosef HaTzaddik from falling prey to the temptation of his master's wife was the image of his father appearing to him, and the feeling that, "I can't do this to my father."

We, too, have to build a relationship with our children that will make them feel, "I can't do this to my parents."

And this doesn't apply only to parents. There was a fellow in Baltimore, Harry K. Wolpert, who lived to be over 100. Harry immigrated to the United States in the early 1900s, and eventually became the chairman of the board of Ner Yisrael. He was a special Yid, who had learned in Kaminetz under Rav Baruch Ber before he came to the U.S.

Mr. Wolpert mentioned several times that when he first immigrated, he was tempted many times to be *mechallel Shabbos*, as so many people in his generation did. Back in those days, the bosses would say, "If you don't come in on Saturday, don't come in on Monday." There was no social welfare, no food stamps, nothing to keep a family going if the man of the house wasn't earning a salary. If you didn't work, you starved. Nevertheless, said Mr. Wolpert, he never succumbed to the temptation because, in his words, "I couldn't do it to Rav Baruch Ber."

What's your mental image of Rav Baruch Ber, the *talmid muvhak* of Rav Chaim Soloveitchik? Most men imagine him as the "*shpitz lamdan*," the one who can literally split hairs in developing an approach to a *sugya*. We don't necessarily imagine the very same person being a doting rebbi to his *talmidim*. And yet Harry K. Wolpert remained a *shomer Shabbos* because Rav Baruch Ber had that loving relationship with his *talmidim*, and Harry Wolpert couldn't fathom disappointing his rebbi.

> *Harry K. Wolpert remained a shomer Shabbos because Rav Baruch Ber had that loving relationship with his talmidim, and Harry Wolpert couldn't fathom disappointing his rebbi.*

Relationships. That's what it's all about. And unfortunately, in many families, those relationships have been destroyed because of the way parents treated their children.

Have you ever heard the name "Zero Mostel"? For those of you who have not, I'll just tell you that Zero Mostel is someone who did not give his parents Yiddishe nachas.

How did he get the first name "Zero"? It seems that his father, who was an *ehrliche Yid* living in the Bronx, had a hard time dealing with his handful of a son. He would frequently tell his son: "*Du bist a gornisht* — You are a nothing."

This young Mostel boy said, "If I'm a nothing, I'll call myself Zero." And from self-identifying as a Zero to his shenanigans as an actor was a short trip.

⊰ The Expensive Keyboardist

I'd like to conclude with two stories, one horrific episode that ended well, and one beautiful one to end on a high note.

In *People Speak*, there is a story about a middle-aged man, Avrohom, who had a sideline as a keyboard player at small *simchos*, such as bar mitzvahs and *sheva berachos*. One day, Avrohom received a call from someone requesting that he play at his child's *sheva berachos*. Avrohom immediately recognized the voice. This was his rebbi from elementary school, who had once punished his misbehavior by taking a ruler and rapping him on the knuckles until they swelled up and bled.

The hands that were beaten to pulp should play at this man's simchah? Avrohom thought to himself. Seething with anger, he said, "It will be $2,000."

"Really?" the former rebbi asked in astonishment. "Isn't that a little bit steep for a *sheva berachos*?"

"Take it or leave it," Avrohom answered curtly. The rebbi thanked him and hung up.

A few minutes later, Avrohom's phone rang again. "Okay," the rebbi said. "I hear that you're very good. I'll pay you $2,000."

Shocked at his rebbi's willingness to pay the price, Avrohom had no choice but to show up at the *simchah*. He played well, but kept an angry scowl on his face all night.

A few months later, the rebbi called again. "I'm making a *simchah* again, and I want to know if you can play."

"$2,000," Avrohom retorted.

"No problem," the rebbi replied.

This process repeated itself several times over the span of a few years. Avrohom noticed, however, that with every passing *simchah*, his anger dissipated more and more.

Finally, his rebbi called up and said, "Can you play at my grandson's bar mitzvah?"

To his surprise, this time Avrohom said, "Okay, it will be $1,000."

For the first time, Avrohom played at his rebbi's *simchah* with a smile on his face.

After the bar mitzvah, the rebbi came over to him. "Avremeleh," he said, using the nickname that the keyboard player had back in elementary school, "you played so beautifully."

Avrohom froze, realizing suddenly that his rebbi had known all along who he was. Before he could react, the rebbi began to cry. "All these years," he sobbed, "I felt terrible about what I had done. I don't know what came over me that day. I've been waiting for the opportunity to ask you *mechilah*, but as long as you were asking me for $2,000 to play at a small *simchah*, I knew that you were still fuming at me.

> *Avrohom froze, realizing suddenly that his rebbi had known all along who he was. Before he could react, the rebbi began to cry.*

"When you charged me less this time, and I noticed your demeanor was different, I felt that I could finally ask you for *mechilah*. Will you be *mochel* me?"

Avrohom tearfully accepted the apology.

We read this sort of story and think: "That was in the old days, when teachers hit their students. No one does that today; they would get sued or lose their job."

True, we don't hit with rulers. But we hit even more forcefully with something far more damaging than any ruler: we hit with words. And words can break a person no less than a ruler can damage knuckles.

ᴇᴈ Reaffirming the Trust

Here's a beautiful story. The *menahel* of Mesivta Rabbeinu Chaim Berlin was a brilliant *mechanech* named Rav Chaim Segal *zt"l*. Rav Chaim was widely sought for *chinuch* advice, and this story might explain why.

There was a boy in the mesivta who was the black sheep in his family. His brothers all learned well, but he just didn't take to it. He would sit in class, bored, just looking for a diversion.

One of his classmates, who was from a wealthy family, would drive to yeshivah in his own car each day — a great rarity for high school students in those days. One day, this troublemaker pilfered the car keys out of his classmate's jacket pocket, and took the car for a spin.

This happened a few times, with no one being the wiser. Each time, after completing his joy ride, he would park the car in the very same spot he had taken it from, and the owner never noticed it missing. Until one day, when his parents happened to pass by the mesivta during the day, and they noticed their son's car was not in its usual spot. When they found out that their son had been in class all day and someone had "borrowed" the car, they insisted that the school launch an investigation, and eventually the culprit was caught. The parents wanted him expelled or at least suspended, but Rav Chaim Segal withstood the pressure.

A few days after this boy was caught, Rav Chaim Segal approached him, reached into his pocket, and dug out his own car keys. "I left a *sefer* in my car," he said. "Do you mind going to get it for me?"

Thankfully, this boy had the sense not to take the *menahel's* car for a spin. He returned with the *sefer* several minutes later.

> *Rav Chaim Segal later remarked to a member of the hanhalah that he hadn't "forgotten" the sefer, he had left it there on purpose. "I wanted this boy to know that I still trusted him."*

Rav Chaim Segal later remarked to a member of the *hanhalah* that he hadn't "forgotten" the *sefer*, he had left it there on purpose. "I wanted this boy to know that I still trusted him."

This *bachur* went on to make something of his life, because his *menahel* had proven to him that even after he had erred — grievously — he was still worthy of a relationship built on trust.

On a final note, the *Tanna Devei Eliyahu* (*Eliyahu Rabbah, Parashah* 18) tells the story of a man who would prostrate himself each day and daven that he should see good children.

Because ultimately, you can listen to all the lectures and read every parenting book in print, but to succeed in *chinuch*, you need *siyata d'Shmaya*. And to merit that sort of Divine assistance, you need to ask for it.

May we be *zocheh* to watch our children and all our future generations follow in the Torah path our parents paved for us and we have transmitted to them.

> *You can listen to all the lectures and read every parenting book in print, but to succeed in chinuch, you need siyata d'Shmaya. And to merit that sort of Divine assistance, you need to ask for it.*

This volume is part of
THE ARTSCROLL SERIES®
an ongoing project of
translations, commentaries and expositions on
Scripture, Mishnah, Talmud, Midrash, Halachah,
liturgy, history, the classic Rabbinic writings,
biographies and thought.

For a brochure of current publications
visit your local Hebrew bookseller
or contact the publisher:

Mesorah Publications, ltd

4401 Second Avenue
Brooklyn, New York 11232
(718) 921-9000
www.artscroll.com